ANDALS

HUNS

GOTHS

Caucasus Mnts

rmium

Danube

Balkans

Hadrianopolis ✕

Constantinople

GOTHS

E A S T E R N

Tigris

Asia Minor

PERSIA

Greece

Ephesus

Antioch

Euphrates

E M P I R E

SYRIA
Levant

S E A

Alexandria

EGYPT

Nile

SARATOGA SPRINGS PUBLIC LIBRARY

DONATED BY THE
Ex Libris
Society

THE FALL OF ROME
AND THE END OF CIVILIZATION

THE FALL OF
ROME

AND THE END
OF CIVILIZATION

BRYAN WARD-PERKINS

OXFORD
UNIVERSITY PRESS

OXFORD
UNIVERSITY PRESS

Great Clarendon Street, Oxford OX2 6DP

Oxford University Press is a department of the University of Oxford.
It furthers the University's objective of excellence in research, scholarship,
and education by publishing worldwide in

Oxford New York

Auckland Cape Town Dar es Salaam Hong Kong Karachi
Kuala Lumpur Madrid Melbourne Mexico City Nairobi
New Delhi Shanghai Taipei Toronto

With offices in

Argentina Austria Brazil Chile Czech Republic France Greece
Guatemala Hungary Italy Japan Poland Portugal Singapore
South Korea Switzerland Thailand Turkey Ukraine Vietnam

Oxford is a registered trade mark of Oxford University Press
in the UK and in certain other countries

Published in the United States
by Oxford University Press Inc., New York

© Bryan Ward-Perkins 2005

British Library Cataloguing in Publication Data
Data available

Library of Congress Cataloging in Publication Data
Data available

Typeset by RefineCatch Limited, Bungay, Suffolk
Printed in Great Britain
on acid-free paper by
Biddles Ltd. King's Lynn, Norfolk.

ISBN 0–19–280564–9

1 3 5 7 9 10 8 6 4 2

PREFACE

This book has taken an unconscionable time to write; but, as a result, it has had the benefit of being discussed with a large number of colleagues, and of being tried out in part on many different audiences in Britain and abroad. I thank all these audiences and colleagues, who are too many to name, for their advice and encouragement. I also thank the very many students at Oxford, who, over the years, have helped make my thinking clearer and more direct. The career structure and funding of universities in the UK currently strongly discourages academics and faculties from putting any investment into teaching—there are no career or financial rewards in it. This is a great pity, because, in the Humanities at least, it is the need to engage in dialogue, and to make things logical and clear, that is the primary defence against obscurantism and abstraction.

I owe a particular debt of gratitude to Alison Cooley, Andrew Gillett, Peter Heather, and Chris Wickham, for reading and commenting in detail on parts of the text, and, above all, to Simon Loseby, who has read it all in one draft or another and provided invaluable criticism and encouragement. I have not followed all their various suggestions, and we disagree on certain issues, but there is no doubt that this book would have been much the worse without their contribution.

The first half of this book, on the fall of the western empire, was researched and largely written while I held a Visiting Fellowship at the Humanities Research Centre in Canberra; this was a wonderful experience, teaching me many things and providing the perfect environment in which to write and think.

Katharine Reeve was my editor at OUP, and if this book is at all readable it is very much her doing. To work with a first-class editor has been a painful but deeply rewarding experience. She made me prune many of the subordinate clauses and qualifications that scholars love; and above all forced me to say what I really mean, rather than hint at it through delphic academic utterances. The book also benefited greatly from the very helpful comments of two anonymous readers for OUP, and from the Press' highly professional production team. Working with OUP has been a real pleasure.

My main debt inevitably is to my family, who have put up with this book for much longer than should have been necessary, and above all to Kate, who has been endlessly encouraging, a constructive critic of my prose, and ever-helpful over difficult points.

Finally I would like to record my heartfelt gratitude to my friend Simon Irvine, who always believed I would write this book, and to the three men who, at different stages of my education, taught me a profound respect and love of History, David Birt, Mark Stephenson, and the late Karl Leyser.

Bryan Ward-Perkins

20 January 2005

CONTENTS

1.1 London in ruins, as imagined by Gustave Doré in 1873. A New Zealander, scion of a civilization of the future, is drawing the remains of the long-dead city.

I

DID ROME EVER FALL?

O N AN OCTOBER evening in 1764, after some intoxicating days visiting the remains of ancient Rome, Edward Gibbon 'sat musing amidst the ruins of the Capitol', and resolved to write a history of the city's decline and fall.[1] The grandeur of ancient Rome, and the melancholy of its ruins, had awoken his curiosity and imagination, and had planted the seed for his great historical endeavour. Gibbon's fascination with the dissolution of a world that seemed quite literally set in stone is not surprising—deep within the European psyche lies an anxiety that, if ancient Rome could fall, so too can the proudest of modern civilizations (Fig. 1.1).

In Gibbon's day, and until very recently, few people questioned age-old certainties about the passing of the ancient world—namely, that a high point of human achievement, the civilization of Greece and Rome, was destroyed in the West by hostile invasions during the fifth century. Invaders, whom the Romans called quite simply 'the barbarians' and whom modern scholars have termed more sympathetically 'the Germanic peoples', crossed into the empire over the Rhine and Danube frontiers, beginning a process that was to lead to the dissolution not only of the Roman political structure, but also of the Roman way of life.

The first people to enter the empire in force were Goths, who in 376 crossed the Danube, fleeing from the nomadic Huns who had recently appeared on the Eurasian steppes. Initially the Goths threatened only the eastern half of the Roman empire (rule at the time being divided between two co-emperors, one resident in the western provinces, the other in the East (see front end paper)). Two years later, in 378, they inflicted a bloody defeat on the empire's eastern army at the battle of Hadrianopolis, modern Edirne in Turkey, near the border with Bulgaria. In 401, however, it was the turn of the West to suffer invasion, when a large army of Goths left the Balkans and entered northern Italy. This began a period of great difficulty for the western empire, seriously exacerbated at the very end of 406, when three tribes—the Vandals, Sueves, and Alans—crossed the Rhine into Gaul. Thereafter there were always Germanic armies within the borders of the western empire, gradually acquiring more and more power and terri- tory—the Vandals, for instance, were able to cross the Straits of Gibraltar in 429, and by 439 had captured the capital of Roman Africa.

In 476, seventy five years after the Goths had first entered Italy, the last Roman emperor resident in the West, the young and aptly named Romulus Augustulus (Romulus 'the little emperor'), was deposed and sent into retirement. The West was now ruled by independent Germanic kings (see back end paper). By contrast, the eastern Roman empire (which we often call the 'Byzantine empire') did not fall, despite pressure from the Goths, and later from the Huns. Indeed, in the 530s the eastern emperor Justinian was strong enough to intervene in the Germanic West, capturing the Vandals' African kingdom in 533 and starting a war of conquest of the Ostrogoths' Italian kingdom two years later, in 535. Only in 1453 did the Byzantine empire finally disappear, when its capital and last bastion, Constantinople, fell to the Turkish army of Mehmed 'the Conqueror'.

According to the conventional view of things, the military and political disintegration of Roman power in the West precipitated the end of a civilization. Ancient sophistication died, leaving the western world in the grip of a 'Dark Age' of material and intellectual poverty, out of which it was only slowly to emerge. Gibbon's contemporary, the Scottish historian William Robertson, expressed this view in a particularly forceful manner in 1770, but his words evoke an image of the 'Dark Ages' that has had very wide currency:

> In less than a century after the barbarian nations settled in their new conquests, almost all the effects of the knowledge and civility, which the Romans had spread through Europe, disappeared. Not only the arts of elegance, which minister to luxury, and are supported by it, but many of the useful arts, without which life can scarcely be contemplated as comfortable, were neglected or lost.[2]

In other words, with the fall of the empire, Art, Philosophy, and decent drains all vanished from the West.

ooo

I was born and brought up in Rome, the heart of the empire, surrounded by the same ruins of past greatness that had moved Gibbon, and my father was a classical archaeologist whose main interest was the remarkable technical and architectural achievements of the Romans. The essential outlines of Robertson's view have therefore always come naturally to me. From early youth I have known that the ancient Romans built things on a scale and with a technical expertise that could only be dreamed of for centuries after the fall of the empire. Ancient Rome had eleven aqueducts, bringing water to the city through channels up to 59 miles long (which is roughly the distance from Oxford to London), sometimes on arches 100 feet high; and sixteen of the massive columns that form the portico of the Pantheon are monoliths, each 46 feet high, laboriously extracted from a quarry high up in the eastern desert of Egypt, manhandled down to the Nile, and brought hundreds of miles by water to the empire's capital. It is very difficult not to be impressed by achievements like these, particularly when one finds them replicated, on a smaller and more human scale, throughout the provinces of the empire. Pompeii—with its paved streets, raised pavements, public baths, and regularly spaced water fountains—and the hundreds of others cities of the Roman world that were like it, in their own quiet way make an even deeper impression than the overblown grandeur that was Rome.

Despite my upbringing, I have never much liked the ancient Romans— to me they too often seem self-important and self-satisfied—and I have much more sympathy for the chaotic and difficult world of post-Roman times. On the other hand, it has always seemed self-evident that the Romans were able to do remarkable things, which, after the fall of the empire, could not be done again for many hundreds of years.

Banishing Catastrophe

It has therefore come as a surprise to me to find a much more comfortable vision of the end of empire spreading in recent years through the English-speaking world.[3] The intellectual guru of this movement is a brilliant historian and stylist, Peter Brown, who published in 1971 *The World of Late Antiquity*. In it he defined a new period, 'Late Antiquity', beginning in around AD 200 and lasting right up to the eighth century, characterized, not by the dissolution of half the Roman empire, but by vibrant religious and cultural debate.[4] As Brown himself subsequently wrote, he was able in his book to narrate the history of these centuries 'without invoking an intervening catastrophe and without pausing, for a moment, to pay lip service to the widespread notion of decay'. 'Decay' was banished, and replaced by a 'religious and cultural revolution', beginning under the late empire and continuing long after it.[5] This view has had a remarkable effect, particularly in the United States, where Brown now lives and works. A recent *Guide* to Late Antiquity, published by Harvard University Press, asks us 'to treat the period between around 250 and 800 as a distinctive and quite decisive period of history that stands on its own', rather than as 'the story of the unravelling of a once glorious and "higher" state of civilization'.[6] This is a bold challenge to the conventional view of darkening skies and gathering gloom as the empire dissolved.

The impact of this new thinking has, admittedly, been mixed. In particular, amongst the wider reading public a bleak post-Roman 'Dark Age' seems to be very much alive and well. Bernard Cornwell's historical novels about this period are international best-sellers; the blurb on the back of *The Winter King* sets the grim but heroic scene: 'In the Dark Ages a legendary warrior struggles to unite Britain . . .'. Arthur (for it is he) is a battle-hardened warlord, living in a wooden hall, in a Britain that is manly, sombre, and definitely decaying.[7] At one point the remains of a half-ruined Roman mosaic pavement are further shattered, when dark-age warriors bang their spear ends on the floor to approve the decisions of their leaders.

However, amongst historians the impact of the new Late Antiquity has been marked—particularly on the way that the end of the Roman world is now packaged. There has been a sea change in the language used to describe post-Roman times. Words like 'decline' and 'crisis', which suggest problems at the end of the empire and which were quite usual into the 1970s, have largely disappeared from historians' vocabularies, to be replaced by neutral terms, like 'transition', 'change', and 'transformation'.[8] For instance, a massive European-funded project of research into the period 300–800 chose as its title 'The Transformation of the Roman World'.[9] There is no hint here of 'decline', 'fall', or 'crisis', nor even of any kind of 'end' to the Roman world. 'Transformation' suggests that Rome lived on, though gradually metamorphosed into a different, but not necessarily inferior, form. The image is of a lively organism evolving to meet new circumstances. It is a long way from the traditional view, in which catastrophe destroys the magnificent Roman dinosaur, but leaves a few tiny dark-age mammals alive, to evolve very slowly over the coming centuries into the sophisticated creatures of the Renaissance.

Accommodating the Barbarians

Along a parallel route, leading in essentially the same direction, some historians in recent decades have also questioned the entire premiss that the dissolution of the Roman empire in the West was caused by hostile and violent invasion. Just as 'transformation' has become the buzzword for cultural change in this period, so 'accommodation' is now the fashionable word to explain how peoples from outside the empire came to live within it and rule it.

Here too old certainties are being challenged. According to the traditional account, the West was, quite simply, overrun by hostile 'waves' of Germanic peoples (Fig. 1.2).[10] The long-term effects of these invasions have, admittedly, been presented in very different ways, depending largely on the individual historian's nationality and perspective. For some, particularly in the Latin countries of Europe, the invasions were entirely destructive (Fig. 1.3). For others, however, they brought an infusion of new and freedom-loving Germanic blood into a decadent empire—witness, for instance, the words of the eighteenth-century German philosopher Herder: 'Expiring Rome lay for centuries on her deathbed . . . a deathbed extending over the whole World . . . which could . . . render her no assistance, but that of accelerating her death. Barbarians came to perform this office; northern giants, to whom the enervated Romans appeared dwarfs; they ravaged Rome, and infused new life into expiring Italy.'[11]

But, while there has always been a lively debate about the long-term consequences of the invasions, until recently very few have seriously questioned the violence and disruption of the Germanic takeover of power.[12] Indeed, for some, a good bloodletting was a decidedly purgative experience. In a book written for children, the nineteenth-century English historian Edward Freeman robustly defended the brutality with which his own Anglo-Saxon ancestors had eliminated their rivals the Romano-Britons, the ancestors of the Welsh: 'it has turned out much better in the end that our forefathers did thus kill or drive out nearly all the people whom they found in the land . . . [since otherwise] I cannot think that

6

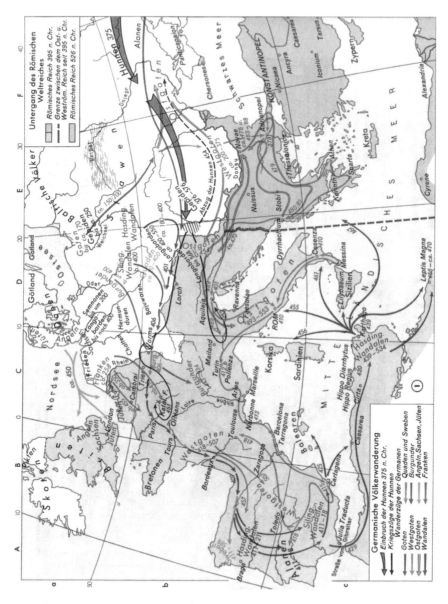

1.2 The 'Wandering of Peoples' (*Völkerwanderung*), which overran the western empire, as shown in an historical atlas.

1.3 'Attila followed by his barbarian hordes tramples on Italy and the Arts'. Detail from Delacroix's painting of 1847 in the library of the Assemblée Nationale, Paris.

we should ever have been so great and free a people as we have been for many ages.'[13] While the children of Victorian England may have enjoyed Freeman's prose, one wonders what was made of it in Wales.

Unsurprisingly, an image of violent and destructive Germanic invasion was very much alive in continental Europe in the years that immediately followed the Second World War.[14] But in the latter half of the twentieth century, as a new and peaceful western Europe became established, views of the invaders gradually softened and became more positive (Fig. 1.4). For instance, book titles like *The Germanic Invasions: The Making of Europe* AD 400–600 (of 1975) did not question the reality of the invasions, but did present them as a positive force in the shaping of modern Europe.[15]

More recently, however, some historians have gone very much further than this, notably the Canadian historian Walter Goffart, who in 1980 launched a challenge to the very idea of fifth-century 'invasions'.[16] He

1.4 The barbarian tamed. Two late-twentieth-century images of Germanic settlers. In one, a warrior-king has removed his helmet, to show that he is a worldly-wise, even kindly, middle-aged man, not a testosterone-driven thug. In the other, the shield has become a fashion accessory.

argued that the Germanic peoples were the beneficiaries of a change in Roman military policy. Instead of continuing the endless struggle to keep them out, the Romans decided to accommodate them into the empire by an ingenious and effective arrangement. The newcomers were granted a proportion of the tax revenues of the Roman state, and the right to settle within the imperial frontiers; in exchange, they ceased their attacks, and diverted their energies into upholding Roman power, of which they were now stakeholders. In effect, they became the Roman defence force: 'The Empire . . . had better things to do than engage in a ceaseless, sterile effort to exclude foreigners for whom it could find useful employment.'[17]

Goffart was very well aware that sometimes Romans and Germanic newcomers were straightforwardly at war, but he argued that 'the fifth century was less momentous for invasions than for the incorporation of barbarian protectors into the fabric of the West'. In a memorable sound bite, he summed up his argument: 'what we call the Fall of the Western Roman empire was an imaginative experiment that got a little out of hand.'[18] Rome did fall, but only because it had voluntarily delegated away its own power, not because it had been successfully invaded.

Like the new and positive 'Late Antiquity', the idea that the Germanic invasions were in fact a peaceful accommodation has had a mixed reception. The world at large has seemingly remained content with a dramatic 'Fall of the Roman empire', played out as a violent and brutal struggle between invaders and invaded (Fig. 1.5). But, amongst historians, the new thinking has definitely had an effect, particularly on the overall packaging of the Germanic settlements. For instance, a recent European volume about the first post-Roman states is entitled *Kingdoms of the Empire: The Integration of Barbarians in Late Antiquity*.[19] There is no hint here of invasion or force, nor even that the Roman empire came to an end; instead there is a strong suggestion that the incomers fitted easily into a continuing and evolving Roman world.

To be fair, Goffart himself acknowledged that his account of peaceful accommodation was not the full story—some of the Germanic incomers had simply seized what they wanted by violence. After all, he stated clearly that the late Roman experiment in buying military support had 'got a little out of hand'. But such nuances seem to have been forgotten in some recent works, which present the theory of peaceful accommodation as a universally applicable model to explain the end of the Roman empire. For instance, two distinguished American historians have recently stated that

1.5 The traditional view of the fall of empire—Romans and barbarians fight it out.

the barbarian settlements occurred 'in a natural, organic, and generally eirenic manner', and take issue with those historians who still 'demonize the barbarians and problematize the barbarian settlements'—in other words, those who still believe in violent and unpleasant invasion.[20] As someone who is convinced that the coming of the Germanic peoples was very unpleasant for the Roman population, and that the long-term effects of the dissolution of the empire were dramatic, I feel obliged to challenge such views.

PART ONE

THE FALL OF ROME

II

THE HORRORS OF WAR

I N 446 LEO, bishop of Rome, wrote to his colleagues in the North
African province of Mauretania Caesariensis. In this letter Leo
grappled with the problem of how the Church should treat nuns
raped by the Vandals some fifteen years earlier, as they passed through
Mauretania on their way to Carthage—'handmaids of God who have
lost the integrity of their honour through the oppression of the barbarians', as he discretely put it. His suggestion was intended to be
humane, though it will seem cruel to a modern reader. He agreed that
these women had not sinned in mind. Nonetheless, he decreed that the
violation of their bodies placed them in a new intermediate status, above
holy widows who had chosen celibacy only late in life, but below
holy virgins who were bodily intact. Leo advised the raped women that
'they will be more praiseworthy in their humility and sense of shame, if
they do not dare to compare themselves to uncontaminated virgins'.[1]
These unfortunate nuns and Bishop Leo would be very surprised, and not
a little shocked, to learn that it is now fashionable to play down
the violence and unpleasantness of the invasions that brought down
the empire in the West.

The Use and the Threat of Force

The Germanic invaders of the western empire seized or extorted through
the threat of force the vast majority of the territories in which they settled,
without any formal agreement on how to share resources with their new
Roman subjects. The impression given by some recent historians that
most Roman territory was formally ceded to them as part of treaty
arrangements is quite simply wrong. Wherever the evidence is moderately

full, as it is from the Mediterranean provinces, conquest or surrender to the threat of force was definitely the norm, not peaceful settlement.

A treaty between the Roman government and the Visigoths, which settled the latter in Aquitaine in 419, features prominently in all recent discussions of 'accommodation'. But those historians who present this settlement as advantageous to Romans and Visigoths alike do not go on to say that the territory granted in 419 was tiny in comparison to what the Visigoths subsequently wrested by actual force, or by the threat of force, from the Roman government and from the Roman provincials. The agreed settlement of 419 was centred on the Garonne valley between Toulouse and Bordeaux. By the end of the century the Visigoths had expanded their power in all directions, conquering or extorting a vastly larger area: all south-west Gaul as far as the Pyrenees; Provence, including the two great cities of Arles and Marseille; Clermont and the Auvergne; and almost the entire Iberian peninsula (Fig. 2.1).[2] From Clermont we have some contemporary evidence of the local response to their expansion. Armed resistance was organized by the city's bishop and aristocracy, and was for a time vigorous and effective. Clermont surrendered to the Visigoths only on the orders of the Roman government in Italy, which hoped thereby to save Provence and the strategically much more important cities of Arles and Marseille. We are told, admittedly by a very partisan source, that at one point during a siege, rather than surrender, the starving inhabitants of Clermont were reduced to eating grass.[3] This is all a very far cry from a peaceful and straightforward 'accommodation' of the Visigoths into the provincial life of Roman Gaul.

The experience of conquest was, of course, very varied across the empire. Some regions were overrun brutally but swiftly. For example, the Vandals' conquest of North Africa, starting in 429 and culminating in the capture of Carthage in 439, was a terrible shock to an area of the empire that had escaped unscathed earlier troubles, and we have already encountered the nuns of Mauretania who were caught up in this violence. But after 439 Africa was spared further Germanic invasion, although it increasingly had its own native problems, from the fierce Berber tribes of the interior.

Other regions, particularly those near the frontiers of the empire, suffered from much more prolonged violence. Northern, eastern, and central Gaul, for instance, were contested in the fifth century between a bewildering number of warring groups: Romans, *Bacaudae*, Britons, Saxons, Franks, Burgundians, Thuringians, Alamans, Alans, and Goths all

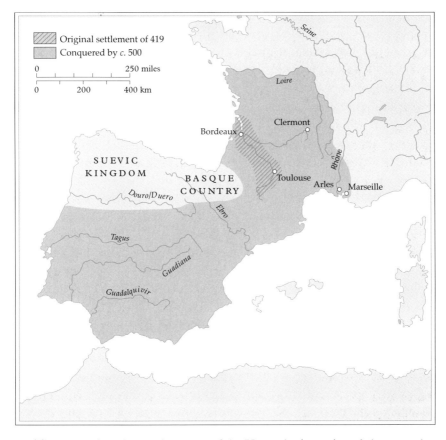

2.1 The original settlement by treaty of the Visigoths (in 419), and the areas they had taken by force by the end of the century.

fought for control of Gaul, sometimes in alliance with each other, but sometimes fragmented into even smaller groupings. This unrest lasted for almost a century after the Germanic crossing of the Rhine during the winter of 406–7. In this part of the Roman world, a degree of internal peace and stability returned only at the end of the fifth century, with the establishment of larger Frankish and Burgundian kingdoms. Similarly, though for a somewhat shorter period—from 409 until the Visigothic conquests of the 470s—control of the Iberian peninsula was fought over by Romans, *Bacaudae*, Alans, Sueves, Goths, and two distinct groups of Vandals. The *Chronicle* written by Hydatius, a bishop based in the north-west of the peninsula, gives a highly abbreviated but none the less depressing account of the repeated raiding and invasion that were the inevitable consequence of this contest for power. Hydatius associated the arrival of the barbarians in Spain with the four scourges prophesied in the Book of Revelations, and claimed that mothers were even driven to kill, cook, and eat their own children. More prosaically, and more reliably, in 460 he himself was seized inside his cathedral church by a band of Sueves who held him prisoner for three months.[4]

Even those few regions that eventually passed relatively peacefully into Germanic control had all previously experienced invasion and devastatation. For instance, the territory in Aquitaine that was ceded to the Visigoths in the settlement of 419 had already suffered raids and devastation between 407 and 409, and in 413 large parts of it had again been ravaged, this time by the Visigoths themselves, the future 'peaceful' settlers of the region.[5] A similar story can be told of Italy and of the city of Rome. During the middle years of the fifth century Italy slipped slowly and quietly into Germanic hands, culminating in a coup and brief civil war in 476, which deposed the last resident western emperor, sent him into retirement, and established an independent kingdom. If this were the whole story of Italy's late antique contact with the Germanic peoples, it would indeed have been a remarkably peaceful transition. However, between 401 and 412 the Goths had marched, at one time or another, the length and breadth of the peninsula, while in 405–6 another invading army had troubled the north and centre. The widespread damage caused by these incursions is shown by the extensive tax relief that the imperial government was forced to grant in 413, the year after the Goths had left the peninsula. This was a time when the emperor desperately needed more, rather than less, money, not only to fight the invaders, but also to resist a string of pretenders to the throne. Yet it was decreed in 413 that, for a five-year period, all the provinces of central and southern Italy were to be excused four-fifths of their tax burden in order to restore them to well-being. Furthermore, the damage that the Goths had inflicted appears to have been long-lasting. In 418, six years after the Goths had left Italy for good, several provinces were still struggling to pay even this substantially reduced rate of taxation, and had to be granted an extended and increased remission.[6]

The city of Rome was a powerful bargaining counter in negotiations with the western emperor, and it was repeatedly besieged by the Goths, before being captured and sacked over a three-day period in August 410.

We are told that during one siege the inhabitants were forced progressively 'to reduce their rations and to eat only half the previous daily allowance, and later, when the scarcity continued, only a third'. 'When there was no means of relief, and their food was exhausted, plague not unexpectedly succeeded famine. Corpses lay everywhere . . .' The eventual fall of the city, according to another account, occurred because a rich lady 'felt pity for the Romans who were being killed off by starvation and who were already turning to cannibalism', and so opened the gates to the enemy.[7]

Nor was the departure of the Goths for Gaul in 412 the end of the woes of Rome and Italy. In 439 the Vandals seized the port and fleet at Carthage, on the North African coast opposite Sicily, and began a period of sea-raiding and conquest in the Mediterranean. Sicily, up to this date immune from trouble, was particularly badly affected, but Vandal raids also reached much further afield. In 455 a Vandal fleet captured Rome itself, and, over a fourteen-day period, subjected it to a second, much more systematic, sack, eventually sailing back to Carthage with its ships laden with booty and captives. Amongst the prisoners were the widow and two daughters of the late emperor of the West, Valentinian III. These imperial women, being very valuable, were certainly treated with care; but other captives had a far harder time—we are told that the then bishop of Carthage sold his church's plate in order to buy prisoners and prevent families from being broken up, when husbands, wives, and children were sold separately into slavery.[8]

Living through Invasion

A remarkable text, the *Life* of a late-fifth-century saint, provides a vivid account of what it was like to live in a province under repeated attack. Severinus was born in the East, but chose for his ministry a western frontier province, Noricum Ripense, on the south bank of the Danube, now within modern Austria and Bavaria (Fig. 2.2). He arrived in Noricum shortly after 453, and remained there for almost thirty years, until his own death. Like the accounts of other saints' lives, that of Severinus does not provide a coherent and full record of political and military events during his lifetime; rather it is a collection of vignettes, centred around his miracles. However, because Severinus served a provincial population under attack, the *Life* provides plenty of circumstantial detail on relations

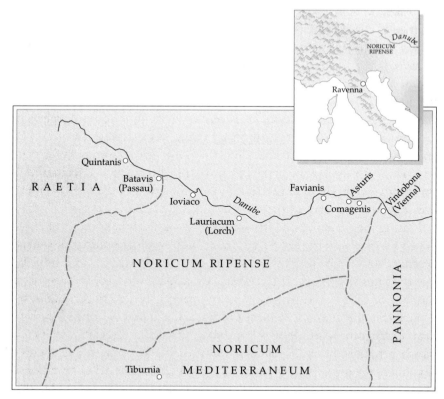

2.2 The upper Danube in the time of Severinus of Noricum.

between Roman provincials and the Germanic invaders. It is also fortunate that the author of the *Life*, Eugippius, who shared many of Severinus'
experiences in Noricum, was a good raconteur.[9]

By the time Severinus arrived, Noricum had already experienced nearly
fifty years of insecurity and warfare, including a short-lived revolt against
imperial rule by the Noricans themselves.[10] It would seem that during
these decades Roman administration, and any control over the province
from the imperial court in Italy, had already disappeared. There is no
mention in the *Life* of a Roman governor of Noricum, nor of an imperial
military commander, and the neighbouring provinces, of Raetia and
Pannonia, seem already to have fallen almost completely into Germanic
hands. Eugippius indeed describes the Roman defences of the Danube as
a thing of the past: 'Throughout the time that the Roman empire existed,

the soldiery of many towns was maintained at public expense for the defence of the frontier. When this practice fell into abeyance, both these troops and the frontier disappeared.' He goes on to tell a wonderfully evocative story of how the last vestige of imperial military power in the region finally came to an end. Apparently, despite the general collapse of the Roman defensive system, one imperial garrison, that of the city of Batavis, was still in existence in Severinus' time. But the only way the soldiers could receive their pay was by sending some of their number south and over the Alps into Italy to collect it. On the very last occasion that this was done, the emissaries 'were killed during the journey by barbarians'; their bodies were later found washed up on the banks of the river. No more imperial pay ever reached Batavis.[11]

During Severinus' time, the defence of the region seems to have depended, not on imperial organization, nor even on a united provincial defence, but on the initiative of individual cities. Furthermore, local control does not seem to have extended far beyond the walled settlements; a number of different Germanic peoples were active, raiding or fighting, deep within the province—above all Rugi and Alamans, but also Thuringians, Ostrogoths, and Herules—and the *Life* records several incidents in which people were either killed or captured in the Norican countryside. Two men, for instance, were seized in broad daylight within two miles of the city of Favianis, having left the safety of the walls to gather in the fruit harvest.[12]

In the years that he spent in Noricum, Severinus was able to help the provincials in their dealings with the invaders in a number of different ways. On one occasion, it was his miraculous foretelling of events that saved the city of Lauriacum from a surprise attack; but for the most part his aid seems to have been more mundane. In particular, he was able to win the respect of successive kings of the Rugi and Alamans, despite the fact that the latter were still pagan, and to intervene with them on his flock's behalf. When an Alaman king came to visit Severinus in Batavis, the latter was able to negotiate the release of around seventy captives.[13] However, the *Life* makes it clear that, over the course of Severinus' stay, what power and independence still remained to the Noricans gradually ebbed away. The city of Tiburnia escaped capture only by buying off its besiegers; while Asturis, Ioviaco, and Batavis all fell to assault. Ioviaco, we are told, was captured by Herules, who 'made a surprise attack, sacked the town, led many into captivity', and hanged a priest who had been foolish enough to ignore Severinus' warnings to abandon the settlement; and at Batavis, when the city fell to Thuringians, those still in the town (having ignored similar saintly warnings) were either killed or led into captivity.[14]

The inhabitants of Quintanis, in the face of danger, abandoned their city for Batavis, and then withdrawn further (along with many of the inhabitants of Batavis) to Lauriacum. The inhabitants of Lauriacum, the last independent city-dwellers of Noricum, were at last helped by Severinus to negotiate their own surrender to the Rugian king, and were re-settled in towns that were already his tributaries.[15] Even before the death of the saint in about 482, all Noricum Ripense was in Germanic hands.

Despite these sorry events, there was some scope for negotiation and for peaceful coexistence. We have already met Severinus negotiating, with varying degrees of success, with leaders of the Rugi and Alamans. According to Eugippius, who of course would want to put as good a gloss on this outcome as possible, the inhabitants of Lauriacum, on surrendering with Severinus' help, left their city, and, 'after being placed peacefully in other settlements, lived with the Rugi on friendly terms'.[16] Even without the help of a saint, townspeople were able to come to agreements with the invaders: before Severinus' arrival, the city of Comagenis had already entered into a treaty arrangement with a group of barbarians, who provided the town with a garrison. This looks at first glance like a mutually advantageous accommodation: the Germanic soldiers simply replaced the absent Roman army, and protected Comagenis. However, since the townsmen then required a miracle from Severinus in order to drive this garrison out, it is clear what kind of 'protection' was being provided.[17] This was an accommodation made in a context of violence, and between parties in a very unequal and tense power relationship.

ooo

The *Life of Severinus* makes it clear that the process of invasion was highly unpleasant for the people who had to live through it, although it is difficult to specify quite how unpleasant—partly because intervening periods of peace are not recorded, and partly because it is always impossible to quantify horror, however vividly described. In other regions of the West, this problem is gravely exacerbated by the lack of good narrative sources covering the fifth century. We are often dependent, at best, on bald chronicle entries almost entirely shorn of detail. The following extract, from the *Chronicle* of Hydatius, describing events in the Iberian peninsula during the year 459, gives an idea of the kind of evidence we have. This, it should be noted, in comparison to most chronicles, is unusually full and detailed:

> Theoderic [king of the Visigoths] sends a section of his army to Baetica under his commander Sunieric; Cyrila is recalled to Gaul. Nevertheless, the Sueves under Maldras pillage parts of Lusitania; others under Rechimund, parts of Gallaecia.
>
> On their way to Baetica, the Herules attack with great cruelty several places along the coast of the district of Lucus.
>
> Maldras [the Sueve] killed his brother, and the same enemy attacks the fort of Portus Cale.
>
> With the killing of several who were nobly-born, an evil hostility arises between the Sueves and the Gallaecians.[18]

This was written by a man in the thick of many of these events; but, besides accepting that a great deal of unpleasant military activity is going on, it is very hard to know what to deduce from such a laconic account. What exactly happened when an 'evil hostility' arose between the Sueves and the Gallaecians?

For more detail, we are often dependent on moralizing tracts, written with a clear purpose in mind, in which accounts of atrocities have been tailored to fit the overall argument. Very occasionally, we have good reason to suspect that their authors have deliberately underplayed the unpleasantness of events. The Christian apologist Orosius, for instance, wrote a *History against the Pagans* in 417–18, in which he set himself the unenviable task of proving that, despite the disasters of the early fifth century, the pagan past had actually been worse than the troubled Christian present. In describing the Gothic sack of Rome in 410, Orosius did not wholly deny its unpleasantness (which he attributed to the wrath of God on Rome's sinful inhabitants). But he also dwelt at length on the respect shown by the Goths for the Christian shrines and saints of the city; and he claimed that the events of 410 were not as bad as two disasters that had occurred during pagan times—the sack of Rome by the Gauls in 390 BC, and the burning and despoiling of the city under the Nero.[19]

Many years later, in the mid-sixth century, the historian and apologist of the Goths, Jordanes, also tackled the topic of the Gothic sack of Rome—an event that created very obvious problems for the implausible central thesis of his work, that Goths and Romans were by nature allies and friends. Jordanes' solution, although hardly satisfactory, was to pass very swiftly over the sack, making the best of it that he could with the help of Orosius: 'On entering Rome at last, on the orders of Alaric they [the Goths] only looted it, and did not, as barbarian peoples normally do, set it on fire; and they allowed almost no damage to be inflicted on the shrines of the saints. They [then] left Rome . . .'. This very brief account (only two lines of printed Latin) can be contrasted with the 171 lines that Jordanes dedicated to an alliance of Goths and Romans, which defeated Attila and the Huns in 451.[20]

However, such toned-down descriptions of atrocities are rare; it is much more common to find violent events presented with very obvious added highlights. Here, for instance, is the sixth-century British historian Gildas, describing the consequences of the revolt and invasions of the Anglo-Saxons: 'All the major towns were laid low by the repeated battering of enemy rams; laid low, too, all the inhabitants—church leaders, priests and people alike, as the sword glinted all around and the flames crackled . . . There was no burial to be had except in the ruins of houses or the bellies of beasts and birds . . .'. While here, in graphic detail, Victor of Vita, the chronicler of Vandal religious intolerance, tells of the horrors that occurred after the Vandals crossed into Africa over the Straits of Gibraltar in 429: 'in their barbaric frenzy they even snatched children from their mothers' breasts and dashed the guiltless infants to the ground. They held others by the feet, upside down, and cut them in two . . .'.[21]

Both Gildas and Victor of Vita were writing at some distance in time from the events they described. But apocalyptic descriptions of the violence of invasion can also be found in the writings of contemporaries. The account of the passage of the Vandals provided by Possidius, who lived through these events, is not, for instance, very different in tone from that given by Victor of Vita: 'Everywhere throughout the regions of Mauretania . . . they [the Vandals] gave vent to their rage by every kind of atrocity and cruelty, devastating everything they possibly could by pillage, murder, various tortures, fires, and other indescribable evil deeds. No sex or age was spared, not even God's priests and ministers . . .'.

It is indeed in a poem contemporary to the events, that we find the most highly coloured description of the invasion of Gaul in the years 407–9:

> Some lay as food for dogs; for many, a burning roof
> Both took their soul, and cremated their corpse.
> Through villages and villas, through countryside and market-place,

Through all regions, on all roads, in this place and that,
There was Death, Misery, Destruction, Burning, and Mourning.
The whole of Gaul smoked on a single funeral pyre.[22]

Of course these descriptions are exaggerated for rhetorical effect: not everyone in Britain was buried in the ruins of a burnt house or in the belly of a beast; the whole of Gaul did not smoke in a single funeral pyre, however striking the image; and Victor of Vita's account of heartless baby-killers is surely an attempt to cast the Vandals in the role of 'new Herods'. But such accounts did not emerge from nowhere. The experience of all wars is that armies, unless under very tight discipline, commit atrocities—and no one would suggest that the Germanic armies were under strict control. The truth, perhaps, is that the experience of invasion was terrible; though not as terrible as the experience of civilian populations in some medieval and modern conflicts, in which ideological difference encouraged cold-blooded and systematic brutality, over and above the 'normal' horrors of war. Fortunately for the Romans, invading Germanic peoples did not despise them, and had entered the empire in the hope of enjoying the fruits of Roman material comfort—but, equally, the invaders were not angels who have simply been badly maligned (or 'problematized', to use modern jargon) by prejudiced Roman observers.

All too rarely can we give substance and support to literary accounts, through the survival of a more prosaic document focused on the painful consequences of a particular episode. We have already encountered Leo's letter to the bishops of Mauretania dealing with the impact of Vandal rape, which shows that the highly coloured accounts of Vandal brutality offered by Victor of Vita and Possidius were not entirely invented. In 458 Leo had to write a similar letter to the bishop of the north Italian city of Aquileia, which six years earlier had been captured and sacked by Attila's Huns—an event that was blamed by later writers as the cause of the town's ruin.[23] In the absence of good archaeological evidence, it is currently impossible to say exactly how destructive this sack really was, but Leo's letter provides a remarkable insight into some of the human misery that it caused. As with the Mauretanian nuns, Leo was asked his advice over a moral conundrum. In 452 the Huns had taken many men off into slavery; some of these had managed to regain their freedom, and were now returning home. Unfortunately, in several cases they had come back to find that their wives, despairing of ever seeing them again, had remarried. Leo, of course, ordered that these wives put aside their second husbands. But, appreciating the circumstances, he commanded that neither the bigamous wives nor their second husbands should be blamed for what had happened, as long as all returned willingly to the previous state of affairs. He does not tell us what should happen to any children of these second unions.[24]

Barbarian Bitterness?

It may be a mistake to assume that the invaders were innocent of all hatred, and at worst only boisterously bad. The Romans were traditionally highly dismissive of 'barbarians', and despite increasing and ever-closer contacts during the later fourth and fifth centuries (including marriage alliances between the imperial family and the Germanic royal houses), some very offensive Roman attitudes survived for a very long time. It is easy to find in the Latin literature of the age the sentiment that barbarians were uncouth and beneath consideration, or indeed that the best barbarian was a dead barbarian.[25] In 393 the Roman aristocrat Symmachus brought a group of Saxon prisoners to Rome, intending that they publicly slaughter each other in gladiatorial games held to honour his son. However, before they were exhibited, twenty-nine of them committed suicide by the only means available to them—by strangling each other with their bare hands. For us, their terrible death represents a courageous act of defiance. But Symmachus viewed their suicide as the action of a 'group of men viler than Spartacus', which had been sent to test him. With the self-satisfaction of which only Roman aristocrats were capable, he compared his own philosophical response to the event to the calm of Socrates when faced with adversity.[26]

In the same year, 393, thousands of Goths died fighting in northern Italy for the emperor Theodosius, at the battle of the River Frigidus, thereby gaining him victory over the usurper Eugenius. Early in the fifth century, the Christian apologist Orosius had no qualms in celebrating this as a double triumph for Theodosius—not only over Eugenius, but also over his own Gothic soldiers: 'To have lost these was surely a gain, and their defeat a victory.' A little later, in around 440, the moralist Salvian praised the barbarians for being better in their behaviour than the Romans. At first sight this seems to represent a marked change in Roman attitudes. But Salvian's praise was intended to shock his fellow Romans into contrition: 'I know that to most people it will seem intolerable that I say we are worse than the barbarians.' Salvian's true feelings towards barbarians are revealed in a passage where he writes of Romans driven by oppression to join them—despite sharing neither their religious beliefs, nor their language, 'nor indeed . . . the stench that barbarian bodies and clothes give off'.[27]

These dismissive and hostile sentiments were not kept quietly under wraps, for discussion only amongst Romans. The monuments of the empire were covered in representations of barbarians being brutally killed (Fig. 2.3); and one of the commonest designs of copper coin of the fourth century shows Rome's view of the correct ordering of things—a barbarian being speared to death by a victorious Roman soldier (Fig. 2.4). The invaders must have been fully aware of these Roman sentiments towards them, and it is unlikely that they were wholly unaffected by them. Indeed we are told that Attila, on seeing a painting in Milan of enthroned Roman emperors with slaughtered Huns under their feet, had a new and more accurate scene depicted, with himself 'upon a throne and the Roman emperors heaving sacks upon their shoulders and pouring out gold before his feet'.[28]

On the rare occasions the Romans of the late empire defeated an invading force in battle, they treated it, as they had always done, in a high-handed and comprehensive way, ensuring that it would never operate again as an independent unit. In 406 an invading Germanic force was trapped and defeated at Fiesole, near Florence. Some of the troops that surrendered were drafted into the Roman army; but its leader was at once executed, and many of his followers sold into slavery. One source, which was admittedly keen to emphasize the scale of the Roman victory, reports that 'the number of Gothic captives was so great, that whole herds of men were sold together, each for a single gold coin, as if they were the cheapest of cattle'.[29]

Sometimes there was very immediate cause for bitterness on the part of the Germanic armies. In 408 Stilicho, a general in Roman service, born of a Roman mother and Vandal father, fell from power and was killed. Stilicho was an able warrior who had gained the trust of the emperor Theodosius (379–95), marrying his niece, Serena, and acquiring a position at the very heart of the Roman establishment. He became effective ruler of the West on behalf of Theodosius' son, the young emperor Honorius (who married Stilicho's daughter); he held the consulship (the

2.3 The right way to treat hostile barbarians, as shown on the column of Marcus
Aurelius in Rome (built at the end of the second century AD). Above, captured males
are being beheaded, apparently by fellow prisoners acting under duress; below, a
woman and child are being led into slavery—while behind them another woman
prisoner is stabbed in the chest by a Roman soldier.

2.4 'The Return of Good Times' (*Fel. Temp. Reparatio*), as imagined on a fourth-century coin: a Roman soldier spears a diminutive barbarian horseman.

most prestigious office in the empire) on two occasions; and he was given the exceptional honour by the Roman Senate of a silver-gilt statue in the Forum. Stilicho's life and career show that the Roman state was well able to use and honour men of 'barbarian' descent; but events at his death reveal that his origins had not been forgotten, and that relations between the Romans and their Germanic soldiery were not entirely pragmatic and straightforward.

When news of Stilicho's death spread, a murderous pogrom was launched in the cities of northern Italy against the defenceless wives and children of Germanic soldiers serving in the Roman army. Unsurprisingly, on hearing of this atrocity, the husbands immediately deserted the Roman army and joined the invading Goths. Later in the same year, as the Goths were camped outside Rome, they were joined by more recruits with no cause to love the Romans, a host of slaves who had escaped from the city.[30] Many of these slaves and most of the soldiers who had lost their families in 408 were probably still in the Gothic army when it finally entered Rome in August 410. The subsequent sack of the city was probably not an entirely gentle affair.

The Roman Reaction to Invasion

Unsurprisingly, the defeats and disasters of the first half of the fifth century shocked the Roman world. This reaction can be charted most fully in the perplexed response of Christian writers to some obvious and awkward questions. Why had God, so soon after the suppression of the public pagan cults (in 391), unleashed the scourge of the barbarians on a Christian empire; and why did the horrors of invasion afflict the just as harshly as they did the unjust? The scale of the literary response to these difficult questions, the tragic realities that lay behind it, and the ingenious nature of some of the answers that were produced, are all worth examining in detail. They show very clearly that the fifth century was a time of real crisis, rather than one of accommodation and peaceful adjustment.[31]

It was an early drama in the West, the capture of the city of Rome itself in 410, that created the greatest shock waves within the Roman world. In military terms, and in terms of lost resources, this event was of very little consequence, and it certainly did not spell the immediate end of west Roman power. But Rome, although it had seldom been visited by emperors during the fourth century, remained in the hearts and minds of Romans *the* City: all freeborn men of the empire were its citizens. Not for eight centuries, since the Gauls had sacked Rome in 390 BC, had Rome been captured by barbarians; and on that occasion the pagan gods, and the honking of some sacred geese, had saved the city's last bastion, the Capitol, from falling to a surprise attack.

The initial response to the news of Rome's fall was one of stunned surprise. It is typified by Jerome, who was living in Palestine at the time, and who recorded his reaction in the prefaces to his commentaries on *Ezekiel*. Jerome, understandably, saw the City as the head of the Roman body politic, and his first response was to expect the empire to die with it:

> The brightest light of the whole world is extinguished; indeed the head has been cut from the Roman empire. To put it more truthfully, the whole world has died with one City.
>
> Who would have believed that Rome, which was built up from victories over the whole world, would fall; so that it would be both the mother and the tomb to all peoples.[32]

Rome's fall, however, did not bring down the empire (indeed its impact on eastern provinces like Palestine was minimal). The longer-term Christian response to the disaster therefore had to be more subtle and sustained than Jerome's initial shock, particularly because the pagans now, not unreasonably, attributed Roman failure to the abandonment by the State of the empire's traditional gods, who for centuries had provided so much security and success. The most sophisticated, radical, and influential answer to this problem was that offered by Augustine, who in 413 (initially in direct response to the sack of Rome) began his monumental *City of God*.[33] Here he successfully sidestepped the entire problem of the failure of the Christian empire by arguing that all human affairs are flawed, and that a true Christian is really a citizen of Heaven. Abandoning centuries of Roman pride in their divinely ordained state (including Christian pride during the fourth century), Augustine argued that, in the grand perspective of Eternity, a minor event like the sack of Rome paled into insignificance.

No other author remotely matched the depth and sophistication of Augustine's solution, but many others grappled with the problem. The Spanish priest Orosius in his *History against the Pagans*, like Augustine, specifically refuted pagan claims that Christianity had brought about Rome's decline. His solution, however, was very different, since he wrote in a brief period of renewed optimism, at the end of the second decade of the fifth century. Orosius looked forward to better times, hoping that some of the invaders themselves would be the restorers of Rome's position and renown. In a rather dreary game of literary tit-for-tat, he matched every disaster of Christian times with an even worse catastrophe from the pagan past (see above, p. 21).[34]

Orosius' optimism soon proved misguided, and Christian apologists generally had to bat on a very sticky wicket, starting from the premise that secular affairs were indeed desperate. Most resorted to what rapidly became Christian platitudes in the face of disaster. The author of the *Poem on the Providence of God*, composed in Gaul in about 416, exhorted Christians to consider whether these troubles had been brought about by their own sins, and encouraged them to realize that earthly happiness and earthly treasures are but dust and ashes, and nothing to the rewards that await us in Heaven (lines 903–9):

> This man groans for his lost silver and gold,
> Another is racked by the thought of his stolen goods
> And of his jewellery now divided amongst Gothic brides.

> This man mourns for his stolen flock, burnt houses, and drunk wine,
> And for his wretched children and ill-omened servants.
> But the wise man, the servant of Christ, loses none of these things,
> Which he despises; he has already placed his treasure in Heaven.[35]

The poem is such a powerful evocation of looting and destruction that one wonders whether anyone would have found consolation in it.

In a similar vein and also in early fifth-century Gaul, Orientius of Auch confronted the difficult reality that good Christian men and women were suffering unmerited and violent deaths. Not unreasonably, he blamed mankind for turning God's gifts, such as fire and iron, to warlike and destructive ends. He also cheerfully reminded his readers that we are all dying anyway, and that it matters little whether our end comes to us immediately and violently, or creeps up on us unseen:

> Every hour draws us a little closer to our death:
> At the very time we are speaking, we are slowly dying.[36]

A little later, in the 440s, Salvian, a priest from the region of Marseille, addressed the central and difficult questions, 'Why has God allowed us to become weaker and more miserable than all the tribal peoples? Why has he allowed us to be defeated by the barbarians, and subjected to the rule of our enemies?' Salvian's solution was to attribute the disasters of his age to the wickedness of his contemporaries, which had brought divine judgement down upon their own heads. In this he was on ground firmly established by the Old Testament, to explain the fluctuating fortunes of the Children of Israel. Salvian, however, gave this very traditional interpretation an interesting, but not entirely convincing, twist. Rather than depict the barbarians as mindless instruments of God, faceless scourges like the Assyrians or Philistines of old, he argued that their success was also due to their own virtue: 'We enjoy immodest behaviour; the Goths detest it. We avoid purity; they love it. Fornication is considered by them a crime and a danger; we honour it.'[37] This was an ingenious attempt to argue for the fall of the West as doubly just: the wicked (Romans) are punished; and the virtuous (Germanic invaders) are rewarded.

ooo

By the mid-fifth century, authors in the West had no doubt that Roman affairs were in a parlous state. Salvian had this to say, albeit within the highly rhetorical context of a call to repentance:

Where now is the ancient wealth and dignity of the Romans? The Romans of old were most powerful; now we are without strength. They were feared; now it is we who are fearful. The barbarian peoples paid them tribute; now we are the tributaries of the barbarians. Our enemies make us pay for the very light of day, and our right to life has to be bought. Oh what miseries are ours! To what a state we have descended! We even have to thank the barbarians for the right to buy ourselves off them! What could be more humiliating and miserable!

A few years later, the so-called Chronicler of 452 summed up the situation in Gaul in very similar terms, bemoaning the spread of both the barbarians and the heretical brand of Christianity to which they adhered: 'The Roman state has been reduced to a miserable condition by these troubles, since not one province exists without barbarian settlers; and throughout the world the unspeakable heresy of the Arians, that has become so embedded amongst the barbarian peoples, displaces the name of the Catholic church.'[38]

It has rightly been observed that the deposition in 476 of the last emperor resident in Italy, Romulus Augustulus, caused remarkably little stir: the great historian of Antiquity, Momigliano, called it the 'noiseless fall of an empire'.[39] But the principal reason why this event passed almost unnoticed was because contemporaries knew that the western empire, and with it autonomous Roman power, had already disappeared in all but name. Jerome, in writing the empire's epitaph in 410, was decidedly premature; but it is hard to dispute the gloomy picture from the 440s and 450s of Salvian and of the Chronicler. These men were well aware of the disasters that had engulfed the West; and they would have been astonished by the modern mirage of an accommodating and peaceful fifth century.

Für den Niedergang des Römerreiches sind bisher die folgenden 210 im Register nachgewiesenen Faktoren herangezogen worden:

Aberglaube, Absolutismus, Ackersklaverei, Agrarfrage, Akedia, Anarchie, Antigermanismus, Apathie, Arbeitskräftemangel, Arbeitsteilung, Aristokratie, Askese, Ausbeutung, negative Auslese, Ausrottung der Besten, Autoritätsverlust, Badewesen, Bankrott, Barbarisierung, Vernichtung des Bauernstandes, Berufsarmee, Berufsbindung, Besitzunterschiede, Bevölkerungsdruck, Bleivergiftung, Blutvergiftung, Blutzersetzung, Bodenerosion, Bodenerschöpfung, Versiegen der Bodenschätze, Bodensperre, Bolschewisation, Bürgerkrieg, Bürgerrechtsverleihung, Bürokratie, Byzantinismus, capillarité sociale, Charakterlosigkeit, Christentum, Convenienzheiraten, Degeneration des Intellekts, Demoralisierung, Despotismus, Dezentralisation, Disziplinlosigkeit des Heeres, Duckmäuserei, soziale Egalisierung, Egoismus, Energieschwund, Entartung, Entgötterung, Entnervung, Entnordung, Entpolitisierung, Entrechtung, Entromanisierung, Entvölkerung, Entvolkung, Entwaldung, Erdbeben, Erstarrung, unzureichendes Erziehungswesen, Etatismus, Expansion, Faulheit, Feinschmeckerei, Feudalisierung, Fiskalismus, Frauenemanzipation, Freiheit im Übermaß, Freilassungen von Sklaven, Friedensromantik, Frühreife, Führungsschwäche, Geldgier, Geldknappheit, Geldwirtschaft, Genußsucht, Germanenangriffe, Gicht, Gladiatorenwesen, Glaubenskämpfe, Gleichberechtigung, Goldabfluß, Gräzisierung, Großgrundbesitz, Halbbildung, Verlagerung der Handelswege, Hauptstadtwechsel, Hedonismus, Homosexualität, Hunnensturm, Hybris, Hyperthermia, moralischer Idealismus, Imperialismus, Impotenz, Individualismus, Indoktrination, Inflation, Instinktverlust, Integrationsschwäche, Intellektualismus, Irrationalismus, Irreligiosität, Kapitalismus, Ka-

stenwesen, Ketzerei, Kinderlosigkeit, Klimaverschlechterung, Kommunismus, Konservatismus, Korruption, Kosmopolitismus, Kulturneurose, Lebensangst, Lebensüberdruß, Legitimitätskrise, Lethargie, Luxus, fehlende Männerwürde, Malaria, moralischer Materialismus, Militarismus, Ruin des Mittelstandes, Mysterienreligionen, Nationalismus der Unterworfenen, Nichternst, kulturelle Nivellierung, Orientalisierung, panem et circenses, Parasitismus, Partikularismus, Patrozinienbewegung, Pauperismus, Pazifismus, Plutokratie, Polytheismus, Proletarisierung, Prostitution, Psychosen, Quecksilberschäden, Rassendiskriminierung, Rassenentartung, Rassenselbstmord, Rationalismus, Regenmangel, Reichsteilung, Angriffe der Reiternomaden, Rekrutenmangel, Rentnergesinnung, Resignation, Rhetorik, naturwissenschaftliche Rückständigkeit, Ruhmsucht, Seelenbarbarei, Selbstgefälligkeit, Semitisierung, Seuchen, Sexualität, Sinnlichkeit, Sittenverfall, Sklaverei, Slawenangriffe, Söldnerwesen, Schamlosigkeit, Schlemmerei, Schollenbindung, Staatsegoismus, Staatssozialismus, Staatsverdrossenheit, Niedergang der Städte, Stagnation, Steuerdruck, Stoizismus, Streß, Strukturschwäche, Terrorismus, fehlende Thronfolgeordnung, Totalitarismus, Traurigkeit, Treibhauskultur, Überalterung, Überfeinerung, Überfremdung, Übergröße, Überkultur, Überzivilisation, Umweltzerstörung, Unglückskette, unnütze Esser, Unterentwicklung, Verarmung, Verbastardung, Verkrankung, Vermassung, Verödung, Verpöbelung, Verrat, Verstädterung, unkluge Vorfeldpolitik, Wehrdienstverweigerung, Wehrlosmachung, Weltflucht, Weltherrschaft, Willenslähmung, Wohlstand, Zentralismus, Zölibat, Zweifrontenkrieg.

3.1 A list of 210 reasons, from A to Z, that have been suggested, at one time or another, to explain the decline and fall of the Roman empire.

III

THE ROAD TO DEFEAT

'ANARCHY, ANTI-GERMANISM, APATHY ... Bankruptcy, Barbar-ization, Bathing ...'—a German scholar recently produced a remarkable and fascinating list of the 210 explanations of the fall of the Roman empire that have been proposed over the centuries (Fig. 3.1).[1] In German they sound even better, and certainly more portentous: *Hunnensturm, Hybris, Hyperthermia, moralischer Idealismus, Imperialismus, Impotenz.* (For those who are intrigued, *Hyperthermia*, brought about by too many visits to overheated baths, could cause *Impotenz.*)

There is therefore good reason not to enter the centuries-old debate over why Rome fell, particularly if one wants to cover the topic in one chapter. However, it would be both cowardly and unsatisfactory to write a book arguing that Rome really did fall without saying something on the subject of how and why this happened. Those who believe that the empire fell to invasion have to be able to show that this disaster was possible.[2]

An Empire at Risk

The Roman empire had always been in some danger, and had in fact almost fallen once before, during the third century, when both East and West came very close to collapse. In this period, a powerful cocktail of failure against foreign foes, internal civil wars, and fiscal crisis nearly destroyed the empire. In the fifty years between 235 and 284, the Romans suffered repeated defeats at the hands of Persian and Germanic invaders, the secession of several of its provinces, a financial crisis that reduced the silver content of the coinage to almost nothing, and civil wars that reduced the average length of an emperor's reign to under three years. One unfortunate emperor, Valerian, spent the final years of his life as a captive at the Persian court, forced to stoop and serve as a mounting block whenever the Persian king wished to go riding—and his afterlife as a flayed skin, set up as a perpetual record of his humiliation. In the event, the Roman empire was pulled together again by a series of tough military emperors; but it was a very close-run thing.[3] Since near-disaster had occurred once before, we should not be surprised that the delicate balance between success and failure happened to tip against the western empire on a second occasion, during the fifth century—though this time it was with fatal results.

Roman military dominance over the Germanic peoples was considerable, but never absolute and unshakeable. The Romans had always enjoyed a number of important advantages: they had well-built and imposing fortifications (Fig. 3.2); factory-made weapons that were both standardized and of a high quality (Fig. 3.3); an impressive infrastructure of roads and harbours; the logistical organization necessary to supply their army, whether at base or on campaign; and a tradition of training that ensured disciplined and coordinated action in battle, even in the face of adversity. Furthermore, Roman mastery of the sea, at least in the Mediterranean, was unchallenged and a vital aspect of supply. It was these sophistications, rather than weight of numbers, that created and defended the empire, and the Romans were well aware of this fact. Vegetius, the author of a military treatise dating from the late fourth or the first half of the fifth century, opened his work with a chapter entitled 'The Romans Conquered All Peoples Only through their Military Training', in which he stressed that, without training, the Roman army would have achieved nothing: 'What could small Roman forces achieve against hordes of Gauls? What could the short Roman soldier dare to do against the tall German?'[4]

These advantages were still considerable in the fourth century. In particular, the Germanic peoples remained innocents at sea (with the important exception of the Anglo-Saxons in the north), and notorious for their inability to mount successful siege warfare. One Gothic leader is said to have advised his followers to concentrate on looting the undefended countryside, observing wryly that 'he was at peace with walls'.[5] Consequently, small bands of Romans were able to hold out behind fortifications, even against vastly superior numbers, and the empire could maintain its presence in an area even after the surrounding countryside had been

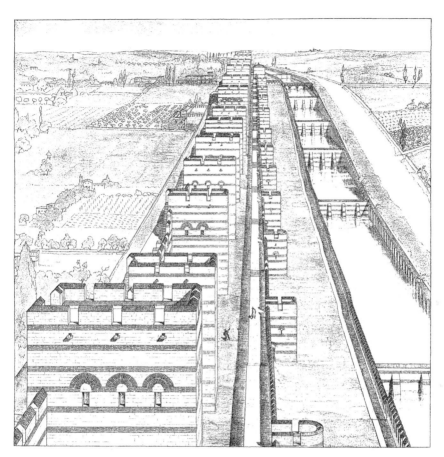

3.2 The greatest defensive work of all Antiquity: the land-walls of Constantinople. The first line of defence is a moat, which needed cross-dams and piped water, since it passes over a ridge; behind it runs a low wall; behind that a somewhat higher wall with towers; and, finally, a third wall reinforced with massive towers large enough to carry ballistas and other stone-throwing artillery. Until 1204, when the western 'Crusaders' took the city, Constantinople successfully resisted all the many attempts to capture it.

completely overrun. For instance, in 378, despite a terrible defeat in the field, Roman forces were still able to hold the nearest town, and, most importantly of all, were able to protect the imperial city, Constantinople.[6]

In open battle, the advantage was lessened, but a Roman army could still be expected to triumph over a substantially larger Germanic force. In

3.3 Standardized military equipment—decorated shields, spears, helmets, axes, cuirasses, greaves, scabbards, and swords—the product of state manufactories under the control of the 'Magister Officiorum'. (From an illustrated list of the officials of the early fifth-century empire.)

357 the emperor Julian defeated a force of Alamans who had crossed the Rhine into Roman territory near modern Strasbourg. Our source for the battle, Ammianus Marcellinus, tells us that 13,000 Roman troops faced 35,000 barbarians. These figures are unlikely to be accurate; but they probably reflect a genuine and considerable numerical superiority on the part of the Alamans. The detailed account of the battle makes it clear that the Romans achieved their victory because of their defensive armour, their close formation behind a wall of shields, and their ability both to stand their ground and to rally when broken. Ammianus' summary description of the two armies is similar to that of many earlier observers when discussing the difference between the Romans and the barbarians in war: '[In this battle] in some ways equal met equal. The Alamans were physically stronger and swifter; our soldiers, through long training, more ready to obey orders. The enemy were fierce and impetuous; our men quiet and cautious. Our men put their trust in their minds; while the barbarians trusted in their huge bodies.'[7] At Strasbourg, at least according to Ammianus, discipline, tactics, and equipment triumphed over mere brawn.

However, even at the best of times, the edge that the Romans enjoyed over their enemies, through their superior equipment and organization, was never remotely comparable, say, to that of Europeans in the nineteenth century using rifles and the Gatling and Maxim guns against peoples armed mainly with spears. Consequently, although normally the Romans defeated barbarians when they met them in battle, they could and did occasionally suffer disasters. Even at the height of the empire's success, in AD 9, three whole legions under the command of Quinctilius Varus, along with a host of auxiliaries, were trapped and slaughtered by tribesmen in north Germany. Some 20,000 men died: six years later, when a Roman army visited the area, it found whitening bones lying all over the site, skulls fastened as trophies to tree trunks, and altars where captured Roman officers had been sacrificed to the Germans' gods. The detritus of this disaster has also been discovered by modern archaeologists, in a remarkable scatter of coins, military equipment, and personal possessions, which were lost in a battle that stretched over more than 15 kilometres, as the retreating Roman army fought desperately and in vain to escape its attackers.[8]

During the fourth century, disaster on a similar scale occurred during the 378 campaign against the Goths in the Balkans. The emperor Valens and the eastern field army faced a large Gothic force near the city of

Hadrianopolis (which gave its name to the subsequent battle). The emperor decided to engage the Goths alone, rather than await the arrival of further troops on their way from the West. The resulting battle was a catastrophe for the Romans: two-thirds of their force is said to have been killed; the emperor himself died in the chaotic aftermath, and his body was never recovered. The historian Ammianus Marcellinus tells us that not for some 600 years, since Hannibal's bloody victory over the Republic at Cannae, had the Romans suffered such a terrible defeat.[9]

The battle of Hadrianopolis shows that, with bad luck or bad management on the Roman side, the Germanic invaders could defeat even very large Roman armies. The prelude to the campaign confirms that the Romans were well aware of this fact and conscious of the need to gather together the greatest possible number of soldiers before confronting an enemy in open battle. Valens faced the Goths in the field only after he had made peace with Persia, allowing him to transfer troops from the eastern frontier to the Balkans, and after he had summoned additional help from his western colleague (although, as we have seen, he then chose to fight the battle before these troops had arrived). Even such a specially assembled force could be annihilated, as the battle of Hadrianopolis showed all too clearly.

A further indication of the delicate balance between Roman and Germanic might was the common practice of swelling imperial forces, when preparing for a major campaign, with troops hired from the Germanic and Hunnic tribes living beyond the frontiers. We do not know the precise economic and military calculations behind this use of tribal mercenaries, because our sources do not provide us with logistical information; but there are good reasons to believe that the practice made sound strategic and financial sense. The soldiers came already trained in belligerence from early youth (if in a rather ill-disciplined and unsophisticated way); they almost certainly cost less in pay than a Roman soldier (because the standard of living beyond the frontiers was lower than that within the empire); they could be sent home after each campaign, rather than being kept on in peacetime; they did not have to be pensioned off when too old to fight; and they were entirely expendable—indeed, as one observer noted, the death of barbarians in Roman service thinned out potential future enemies of the empire.[10] Furthermore, the historical record shows that these foreign troops were almost invariably loyal. Indeed, anyone who assumes that tribal mercenaries in an army are always a 'bad thing' should look at the proud history of the Gurkha regiments in the British army, which have been recruited from the hill tribes of Nepal (beyond the frontiers of direct British rule) from 1815 to the present day, for many of the same reasons that the Romans engaged the services of Germanic and Hunnic warriors from beyond their own borders.[11]

When the emperor Theodosius moved against the western usurper Magnus Maximus in 388, his army contained so many troops from the traditional enemies of the empire that a court panegyrist made a special virtue of the fact: 'A matter worthy of record! There marched under Roman commanders and banners the onetime enemies of Rome; they followed the standards which they had once opposed; and their soldiers filled the cities of Pannonia, which they had only recently emptied by their hostile plundering.' And when the western government faced an invasion of Italy in 405–6, it hired a force of Huns and Alans from beyond the frontiers, and also took the quite exceptional step of recruiting from amongst the empire's slaves, offering money and freedom in return for their service in war.[12] If special forces like these had to be recruited to fight major civil wars and to confront substantial invasions, then the empire was always in some danger.

The needs of an important campaign could even put normal frontier defences at risk. To tackle the Gothic invasion of Italy in 401–2, the western general Stilicho withdrew troops from all the frontiers under his command—from the north of Britain, from the Rhine, and from the upper Danube. The panegyrist Claudian, celebrating Stilicho's subsequent success against the Goths, expressed his wonder that no one had dared to take advantage of this emptying of the frontiers: 'Will posterity believe it? Germany, once so fierce that its tribes could scarcely be contained by the full might of the emperors of old, is now led so placidly by Stilicho's reins, that it neither attempts to tread the soil denuded of its frontier troops, nor crosses the river, too frightened to approach an undefended bank.'[13] Unfortunately for the Romans (and for Claudian's reputation as a purveyor of empty flattery), this cheerful situation did not persist. Four years later, in the winter of 406, many of the Rhineland troops were almost certainly again in Italy (withdrawn in order to defeat the invasion of the peninsula of 405–6, and to prepare for a campaign against the East). This time the tribes across the Rhine were not so coy; on the last day of the year, groups of Vandals, Alans, and Sueves crossed the river and began a devastating invasion of Gaul. The empire simply did not have enough troops to maintain its frontier defences up to full strength while fighting major campaigns elsewhere.

The story of the loss of the West is not a story of great set-piece battles, like Hadrianopolis, heroically lost by the Romans in the field. The other great battle of our period, the Catalaunian Fields of 451, was in fact a Roman victory, with Visigothic help. The West was lost mainly through failure to engage the invading forces successfully and to drive them back. This caution in the face of the enemy, and the ultimate failure to drive him out, are best explained by the severe problems that there were in putting together armies large enough to feel confident of victory. Avoiding battle led to a slow attrition of the Roman position, but engaging the enemy on a large scale would have risked immediate disaster on the throw of a single dice.

Did Rome Decline before it Fell?

Did the invaders push at the doors of a tottering edifice, or did they burst into a venerable but still solid structure? Because the rise and fall of great powers have always been of interest, this issue has been endlessly debated. Famously, Edward Gibbon, inspired by the secularist thinking of the Enlightenment, blamed Rome's fall in part on the fourth-century triumph of Christianity and the spread of monasticism: 'a large portion of public and private wealth was consecrated to the specious demands of charity and devotion; and the soldiers pay was lavished on the useless multitudes of both sexes, who could only plead the merits of abstinence and chastity.'[14] Although, as we have seen, some 209 other causes of decline have, at one time or another, been suggested, none, I suspect, has ever been presented with such dry wit and elegance.

Explanations for Rome's demise have come and gone, often clearly in response to changes in the broader intellectual fashions of society. Sometimes indeed an older theory has been revived, after centuries of absence. For instance, Gibbon's ideas about the damaging effects of Christianity were fiercely contested at the time; then fell into abeyance. In the nineteenth and early twentieth centuries, the fall of Rome tended to be explained in terms of the grand theories of racial degeneration or class conflict that were then current. But in 1964 the pernicious influence of the Church was given a new lease of life by the then doyen of late Roman studies, A. H. M. Jones. Under the wonderful heading 'Idle Mouths', Jones lambasted the economically unproductive citizens of the late empire—aristocrats, civil servants, and churchmen: 'the Christian church imposed a new class of idle mouths on the resources of the empire . . . a large number lived on the alms of the peasantry, and as time went on more and more monasteries acquired landed endowments which enabled their inmates to devote themselves entirely to their spiritual duties.' These are Gibbon's 'specious demands of charity and devotion' expressed in measured twentieth-century prose.

ooo

In my opinion, the key internal element in Rome's success or failure was the economic well-being of its taxpayers. This was because the empire relied for its security on a professional army, which in turn relied on adequate funding. The fourth-century Roman army contained perhaps as many as 600,000 soldiers, all of whom had to be salaried, equipped, and supplied. The number of troops under arms, and the levels of military training and equipment that could be lavished on them, were all determined by the amount of cash that was available. As in a modern state, the contribution in tax of tens of millions of unarmed subjects financed an elite defence corps of full-time fighters. Consequently, again as in a modern state, the strength of the army was closely linked to the well-being of the underlying tax base. Indeed, in Roman times this relationship was a great deal closer than it is today. Military expenditure was by far the largest item in the imperial budget, and there were no other massive departments of state, such as 'Health' or 'Education', whose spending could be cut when necessary in order to protect 'Defence'; nor did the credit mechanisms exist in Antiquity that would have allowed the empire to borrow substantial sums of money in an emergency. Military capability relied on immediate access to taxable wealth.[15]

Until fairly recently it was believed that the entire economy of the empire was in severe decline during the third and fourth centuries, with a falling population and much land going out of use: two things that would undoubtedly have weakened Rome's tax base, and hence its military capability, long before the period of invasions. However, archaeological work in the decades following the Second World War has increasingly cast serious doubt over this interpretation. In most of the eastern Mediterranean, and in parts of the West, excavations and surveys have found conclusive evidence of flourishing economies under the late empire, with abundant and widespread rural and urban prosperity.

Admittedly, in the West, which is where we need to focus, the picture is more varied and less straightforward than that for the eastern Mediterranean: some provinces, including much of central Italy and parts of Gaul, seem to have been in decline during the third and fourth centuries, from a high point of early imperial well-being; but others, including most of North Africa, were apparently doing very well right up to the time of the invasions.[16] Although this may seem a rather weak conclusion, I think, on balance, the jury should remain out on the important question of whether the overall economy of the western empire, and hence its military strength, was in decline *before* it was hit by the problems of the early fifth century. A hung jury, however, suggests that any decline was not overwhelming; and, in common with most historians, I believe the empire was still very powerful at the end of the fourth century. Unfortunately, a series of disasters was soon to change things.

Spiralling Problems in the Fifth-Century West

The relatively benign conditions of the fourth-century West rapidly disappeared in the first decade of the fifth century, as a consequence of invasion. Italy suffered from the presence of large hostile armies in 401–2 (Alaric and the Goths), in 405–6 (Radagaisus), and again from 408 to 412 (Alaric, for the second time); Gaul was devastated in the years 407–9 by the Vandals, Alans, and Sueves; and the Iberian peninsula by the same peoples, from 409. The only regions of the western empire that had not been profoundly affected by violence by 410 were Africa and the islands of the Mediterranean (their turn, at the hands of the Vandals, came rather later). As a result, the tax base of the western empire was very seriously diminished at the precise moment that extra funds were urgently required; the four-fifths tax relief that the imperial government was forced to grant to the provinces of central and southern Italy in 413 gives a clear indication of the scale of the loss.[17]

In April 406 the western government urgently needed more soldiers in order to oppose the incursion into Italy of Germanic tribesmen led by Radagaisus, and it issued a call for new recruits. Each was offered a bounty of ten gold *solidi* on joining up, but the payment of seven of these was delayed until 'things have been brought to a conclusion'—in other words, because the money was not immediately available. At the same time, a highly unusual but even cheaper option was attempted—the levying of slaves, who were to be paid with a mere two *solidi* and with their freedom, the latter presumably at the cost of their owners.[18] Radagaisus' incursion was successfully crushed, but it was immediately followed by a disastrous sequence of events: the crossing of the Rhine by Vandals, Sueves, and Alans at the very end of 406; the usurpation of Constantine III in 407, taking with him the resources of Britain and much of Gaul; and the Goths' return to Italy in 408. 'Things' in the West were never satisfactorily 'brought to a conclusion', and the recruits of 406 may never have received their seven owed *solidi*.

Historians dispute when exactly the military strength of the western army declined. In my opinion, the chaos of the first decade of the fifth century will have caused a sudden and dramatic fall in imperial tax revenues, and hence in military spending and capability. Some of the lost territories were temporarily recovered in the second decade of the century; but much (the whole of Britain and a large part of Gaul and Spain) was never regained, and even reconquered provinces took many years to get back to full fiscal health—as we have seen, the tax remission granted to the provinces of Italy in 413 had to be renewed in 418, even though Italy had been spared any incursions during these intervening years. Furthermore the imperial recovery was only short-lived; in 429 it was brought definitively to an end by the successful crossing of the Vandals into Africa, and the devastation of the western empire's last remaining secure tax base. By 444, when Valentinian III instituted a new sales tax, matters had certainly reached a parlous state. In the preamble to this law, the emperor acknowledged the urgent need to boost the strength of the army through extra spending, but lamented the current position, where 'neither for newly recruited troops, nor for the old army, can sufficient supplies be raised from the exhausted taxpayers, to provide food and clothing'.[19]

ooo

Invasions were not the only problem faced by the western empire; it was also badly affected during parts of the fifth century by civil war and social unrest. During the very important years between 407 and 413, the emperor Honorius (resident in Italy) was challenged, often concurrently, by a bewildering array of usurpers: a puppet-emperor supported by the

Goths (Attalus); two usurpers in Gaul (Constantine III and Jovinus); one in Spain (Maximus); and one in Africa (Heraclian). With the benefit of hindsight, we know that what the empire required during these years was a concerted and united effort against the Goths (then marching through much of Italy and southern Gaul, and sacking Rome itself in 410), and against the Vandals, Sueves, and Alans (who entered Gaul at the very end of 406 and Spain in 409). What it got instead were civil wars, which were often prioritized over the struggle with the barbarians. As one contemporary source wryly noted: 'This emperor [Honorius], while he never had any success against external enemies, had great good fortune in destroying usurpers.'[20]

It is not difficult to show how these civil wars damaged Roman attempts to control the Germanic incursions. In 407 Constantine III entered Gaul as an imperial claimant from Britain. As a result of this coup, the emperor Honorius, when faced with the Goths' second invasion of Italy in 408, was unable to call on the armies of the North. Despite obtaining military assistance from his eastern colleague, and from a large band of Hunnic mercenaries, Honorius and his generals never felt strong enough to engage the Goths in open battle during their four years in Italy; and no attempt was made to avenge the humiliation of the 410 sack of Rome.[21] The military position in Italy had clearly worsened from the time of Alaric's first incursion into Italy, in 401–2; then, with the aid of troops from north of the Alps, the Goths had been restricted to northern Italy, successfully defeated in battle twice, and eventually driven back into the Balkans.

In Gaul, during these same difficult years, Honorius' rival Constantine III had some success against the Vandals, Alans, and Sueves; but his position was always under threat from Honorius in Italy (who eventually succeeded in getting him killed in 411). He also faced challenges elsewhere: first, when relatives of Honorius waged war against him in the Iberian peninsula; and subsequently, when he himself faced a usurpation, again from a power base in Spain. In the meantime, both Constantine III and Honorius (to the extent that his writ ran at all in these regions) faced provincial revolts in both Britain and Armorica (north-western Gaul), aimed apparently at shaking off imperial power altogether. Needless to say, the invaders were able to take full advantage of this highly confused and unsatisfactory situation. One source explicitly tells us that Constantine III's preoccupation with rivals in Spain allowed the Germanic invaders a free hand in Gaul.[22]

Some civil strife went deeper than usurpation aimed at replacing the rule of one emperor with that of another. Areas of fifth-century Gaul and Spain were troubled by people named in contemporary sources as *Bacaudae*. Unfortunately these sources are, without exception, so laconic that scholars have been able to differ widely in their understanding of who exactly these people were, and what they wanted. They used to be seen, when Marxism was in vogue, as oppressed peasants and slaves in revolt—a sign that the imperial system was rotten through and through. Currently they tend to be viewed as local self-help groups from much higher up the social scale, struggling to defend themselves and their interests in difficult times. Probably they were a bit of both. There is certainly good evidence to suggest that dissatisfaction amongst the lower classes played a significant part in these revolts. One of their two recorded leaders was a doctor, an unlikely commander of an aristocratic group; and a number of contemporary sources associated the *Bacaudae* with slaves and oppressed peasants—one text that has no obvious axe to grind says of a particular revolt: 'almost all the slaves of Gaul joined the conspiracy of the *Bacaudae*'. Whatever their social origins, the *Bacaudae* certainly added a further twist to the political and military confusion of Gaul and Spain in the first half of the fifth century.[23]

ooo

There was, of course, a close connection between failure 'abroad' and the usurpations and rebellions 'at home'. It is not a coincidence that Honorius faced so many usurpers in the years following the Vandal, Alan, and Sueve crossing of the Rhine at the end of 406. His failure adequately to defend the empire dealt a devastating blow to the prestige of his regime, and encouraged those who wanted strong rule and successful defence against the invaders to seek them elsewhere—for instance, from Constantine III, whose power base was north of the Alps, and who would therefore keep the northern armies in Gaul, rather than withdraw them to Italy to fight the Goths. Honorius' preoccupation with Alaric in Italy also allowed usurpation to flourish, since it delayed the mounting of a strong imperial response to any outbreak of rebellion. As in other periods of history, failure against foreign enemies and civil war were very closely linked, indeed fed off each other.

Wider social unrest, such as that of the *Bacaudae*, was also almost certainly fanned by weakness in the imperial regime—as well as contributing further to it. The activity of the *Bacaudae* is documented in Gaul in the period between about 407 and 448, which, as we have seen, was a time of considerable military and political instability. This instability could have encouraged local leaders to opt out of central government control (particularly if the taxes they were paying bought no immediate local protection), and it may also have allowed simmering discontent amongst the oppressed to take an open and active form. Evidence from elsewhere in the empire does indeed suggest that invasion and civil war could temporarily weaken social control. We are told that during Alaric's siege of Rome in the winter of 408–9 'almost all the slaves who were in Rome, poured out of the city to join the barbarians'; and a few years later, during a similar siege, a slave revolt on a smaller scale occurred in the south Gaulish town of Bazas.[24] These slaves had little to lose, and some of them, in happier times, may have been warriors from beyond the frontiers—it is not surprising that they took advantage of Roman weakness to try and join the invading armies. In Rome and Bazas, order was rapidly re-established once the immediate military emergency had passed. But in northern Gaul and Spain, decades of political and military uncertainty created conditions in which the *Bacaudae* could be active over a prolonged period of time. However, they too disappear from the record when a degree of peace returned to these regions in the second half of the fifth century. The *Bacaudae* and other social dissenters seem to have been a product, as well as a cause, of turbulent times.

By contrast with the West, the eastern empire was relatively untroubled by civil wars and internal unrest during the period of the invasions, and this greater domestic stability was undoubtedly a very important factor in its survival.[25] If the eastern empire had faced internal distractions in the years immediately following the Gothic victory at Hadrianopolis in 378, similar to those that the West faced in the period following the 406–7 barbarian crossing of the Rhine, it might well have gone under. There is no very obvious reason for this greater stability in the East, beyond good luck and good management. In particular, through the dangerous and difficult years after Hadrianopolis, the eastern empire had the good fortune to be ruled by a competent and well-tried military figure, Theodosius (emperor 379–95), who was specifically chosen and appointed from outside the ranks of the imperial family to deal with the crisis. By contrast, the ruler of the West during the years of crisis that followed the Gothic entry into Italy in 401 and the great crossing of the Rhine in 406 was the young

Honorius, who came to the throne only through the chance of blood and succession, and who never earned any esteem as a military or a political leader (Fig. 3.4). Whereas the figure of Theodosius encouraged a healthy respect for the imperial person, that of Honorius, dominated as he was by his military commanders, probably encouraged civil war.

It is unlikely that the East was innately and structurally much more cohesive than the West. If only briefly, it was, for instance, very seriously

3.4 The emperor Honorius trying to look like a military leader, on an ivory plaque of AD 406. In elaborate armour, he holds an orb surmounted by a Victory, and a standard with the words 'In the name of Christ, may you always be victorious'. Reality was less glorious—Honorius himself never took the field; and his armies triumphed over very few enemies other than usurpers.

rocked by the revolt of two Germanic generals in East Roman service, Tribigild and Gainas, in 399–400. Their revolt devastated many of the provinces of the empire, and threatened Constantinople itself. Victory over these rebels was thought significant enough to merit the building of a great spiral column, similar in size and design to Trajan's column in Rome, which dominated the skyline of the eastern capital until its demolition in the early eighteenth century. Violent social unrest too was not a western monopoly; in the right circumstances it could also erupt in the East. During the rebellion of Tribigild, his army marched through some of the provinces of Asia Minor, modern Turkey. Although this was an area of the empire that had long been at peace, and that seems to have been prospering in the years around 400, we are told that Tribigild's force was soon swelled by 'such a mass of slaves and outcasts that the whole of Asia was in grave danger, while Lydia was in utter confusion, with almost everyone fleeing to the coast and sailing across to the islands or elsewhere with their whole families.'[26] The East was not immune from internal problems; but, for reasons we shall explore towards the end of this chapter, it was lucky enough to be largely protected from the external invasions that often served as a trigger for civil war and social strife.

The Failure of Self-Help

As we have seen, the revolts by the *Bacaudae* in the West can partly be understood as an attempt by desperate provincials to defend themselves, after the central government had failed to protect them. Roman civilians had to relearn the arts of war in this period, and slowly they did so. As early as 407/8 two wealthy landowners in Spain raised a force of slaves from their own estates, in support of their relative the emperor Honorius. But it would, of course, take time to convert a disarmed and demilitarized population into an effective fighting force; our two Spanish landowners may indeed have chosen to arm slaves rather than peasants, because some of them were recently captured barbarians with experience of war before their enslavement. In Italy it was only in 440, in the face of a new seaborne threat from the Vandals, that the emperor Valentinian III formally revoked the law that banned Roman civilians from bearing arms. Once armed and habituated to war, local forces could achieve success: by the 470s one Gallic aristocrat was leading local resistance against the Gothic besiegers of Clermont; and a decade later another had emerged as the independent ruler of Soissons in the north. But for most of the West the remilitarization of society came too late.[27]

Interestingly, the most successful resistance to Germanic invasion was in fact offered by the least romanized areas of the empire: the Basque country; Brittany; and western Britain. Brittany and the Basque country were only ever half pacified by the invaders, while north Wales can lay claim to being the very last part of the Roman empire to fall to the barbarians—when it fell to the English under Edward I in 1282. It seems that it was in these 'backward' parts of the empire that people found it easiest to re-establish tribal structures and effective military resistance. This is a point of some interest, because it parallels a phenomenon we shall meet in Chapter 6, when looking at the economy. Sophistication and specialization, characteristic of most of the Roman world, were fine, as long as they worked: Romans bought their pots from professional potters, and bought their defence from professional soldiers. From both they got a quality product—much better than if they had had to do their soldiering and potting themselves. However, when disaster struck and there were no more trained soldiers and no more expert potters around, the general population lacked the skills and structures needed to create alternative military and economic systems. In these circumstances, it was in fact better to be a little 'backward'.

Were the Germanic Tribes Getting Stronger?

Unlike the Romans, who relied for their military strength on a professional army (and therefore on tax), freeborn Germanic males looked on fighting as a duty, a mark of status, and, perhaps, even a pleasure. As a result, large numbers of them were practised in warfare—a very much higher proportion of the population than amongst the Romans. Within reach of the Rhine and Danube frontiers lived tens of thousands of men who had been brought up to think of war as a glorious and manly pursuit, and who had the physique and basic training to put these ideals into practice. Fortunately for the Romans, their innate bellicosity was, however, to a large extent counterbalanced by another, closely related, feature of tribal societies—disunity, caused by fierce feuds, both between tribes and within them. At the end of the first century, the historian and commentator Tacitus fully appreciated the importance for the Romans of Germanic disunity. He hoped 'that it may last and persist amongst the barbarians, that if they can not love us, at least they should hate themselves . . . for Fortune can give us no better gift than discord amongst our enemies'. Similarly, at a slightly earlier date, the philosopher Seneca remarked on the exceptional valour and love of warfare of the barbarians, and pointed to the great danger that there would be for Rome if these strengths were ever joined by reason (*ratio*) and discipline (*disciplina*).[28]

ooo

For the Germanic peoples, unity or disunity was the crucial variable in military strength; while for the Romans, as we have seen, it was the abundance or shortage of cash. Already, before the later fourth century, there had been a tendency for the small Germanic tribes of early imperial times to coalesce into larger political and military groupings. But events at the end of this century and the beginning of the next unquestionably accelerated and consolidated the trend. In 376 a disparate and very large number of Goths were forced by the Huns to seek refuge across the Danube and inside the empire. By 378 they had been compelled by Roman hostility to unite into the formidable army that defeated Valens at Hadrianopolis. At the very end of 406 substantial numbers of Vandals, Alans, and Sueves crossed the Rhine into Gaul. All these groups entered a still functioning empire, and, therefore, a very hostile environment. In this world, survival depended on staying together in large numbers. Furthermore, invading armies were able to pick up and assimilate other adventurers, ready to seek a better life in the service of a successful war band. We have already met the soldiers of the dead Stilicho and the slaves of Rome, who joined the Goths in Italy in 408; but even as early as 376–8 discontents and fortune-seekers were swelling Gothic ranks, soon after they had crossed into the empire—the historian Ammianus Marcellinus tells us that their numbers were increased significantly, not only by fleeing Gothic slaves, but also by miners escaping the harsh conditions of the state's gold mines and by people oppressed by the burden of imperial taxation.[29]

The invaders had no sense of pan-Germanic solidarity, and were happy, when it was to their own advantage, to fight other Germanic peoples in the name of Rome.[30] But they also seem to have been well aware that to fall back into the small groups that were characteristic of their life beyond the Rhine and Danube would quite simply be military and political suicide. This is not to say that Roman diplomacy could never divide an invading group. In around 414 the Roman defenders of Bazas in southern

Gaul were able to detach a group of Alans (under their own king) from the
Gothic besiegers, persuading them instead to join the defence of the city:

> The boundaries of the city are walled about by Alan soldiery,
> With pledges given and accepted, ready to fight
> For us, whom they so recently were besieging as an enemy.[31]

However, within the fifth-century West, evidence of invading groups
coalescing is commoner than evidence of them splitting apart. In 418 a
powerful Alan force was crushingly defeated in Spain by the Visigoths.
The few survivors, we are told, fled and, 'forgetting their previous
independence, subjected themselves to the rule of Gunderic, king of the
Vandals'.[32]

These Alans knew that in their weakened state they could not survive in
Spain alone; while the Vandals were equally well aware of the additional
fighting power that some fierce Alan warriors could offer. The alliance of
Vandals and Alans that followed survived for over 100 years, and was one
of the mainstays of the Germanic conquest of Africa, even though in this
case the two peoples apparently never fully merged. Right up to the fall of
his African kingdom in 533, the Vandal ruler styled himself 'King of the
Vandals and Alans'—presumably, either the Alans wished to retain an
independent identity, or the dominant Vandals were reluctant to adopt
them fully as their own.[33]

Groupings and alliances of this kind were encouraged by the dangerous
circumstances of life within the fifth-century West. They were also greatly
facilitated by the possibilities of rich pickings; a large army had much more
chance of gaining booty and conquests than a small one. When the Vandals left Spain in 429, for their great adventure in Africa, the Alans were
with them, and so too were others—a whole unnamed 'Gothic tribe', as
well as 'persons from other tribes'.[34] Both need and greed encouraged the
formation of large armies. This was not good news for the Romans.

The Limits of Germanic Strength

Individual Germanic groups gained greater unity in the fourth and fifth
centuries, and hence greater strength. But it is also important to put the
unity of these single groups in the context of broader Germanic disunity.
Some accounts of the invasions, and a map like Fig. 1.2 (on p. 6), seem
to be describing successive campaigns in a single war, with the systematic

and progressive seizure of territory by the various armies of a united Germanic coalition. If this had really been the case, the West would almost certainly have fallen definitively in the very early fifth century, and far less of the structures of imperial times would have survived into the post-Roman period. The reality was very much more messy and confused, leaving considerable space for Roman survival. The different groups of incomers were never united, and fought each other, sometimes bitterly, as often as they fought the 'Romans'—just as the Roman side often gave civil strife priority over warfare against the invaders.[35] When looked at in detail, the 'Germanic invasions' of the fifth century break down into a complex mosaic of different groups, some imperial, some local, and some Germanic, each jockeying for position against or in alliance with the others, with the Germanic groups eventually coming out on top.

Some incursions, such as the long migration of a Gothic army through the Balkans, Italy, Gaul, and Spain between 376 and 419 (Fig. 3.5), were indeed quite unlike the systematic annexations of neighbouring territory that we expect of a true 'invasion'. These Goths on entering the empire left their homelands for good. They were, according to circumstance (and often concurrently), refugees, immigrants, allies, and conquerors, moving within the heart of an empire that in the early fifth century was still very powerful. Recent historians have been quite correct to emphasize the desire of these Goths to be settled officially and securely by the Roman authorities. What the Goths sought was not the destruction of the empire, but a share of its wealth and a safe home within it, and many of their violent acts began as efforts to persuade the imperial authorities to improve the terms of agreement between them.[36]

The experience of the Goths also underlines the crucial fact that a degree of accommodation between Germanic incomers and Roman natives was often possible. The incoming peoples were not ideologically opposed to Rome—they wanted to enjoy a slice of the empire rather than to destroy the whole thing. Emperors and provincials could, and often did, come to agreements with the invaders. For instance, even the Vandals, the traditional 'bad boys' of this period, were very happy to negotiate treaty arrangements, once they were in a strong enough negotiating position.[37] Indeed it is a striking but true fact, that emperors found it easier to make treaties with invading Germanic armies—who would be content with grants of money or land—than with rivals in civil wars—who were normally after their heads.

53

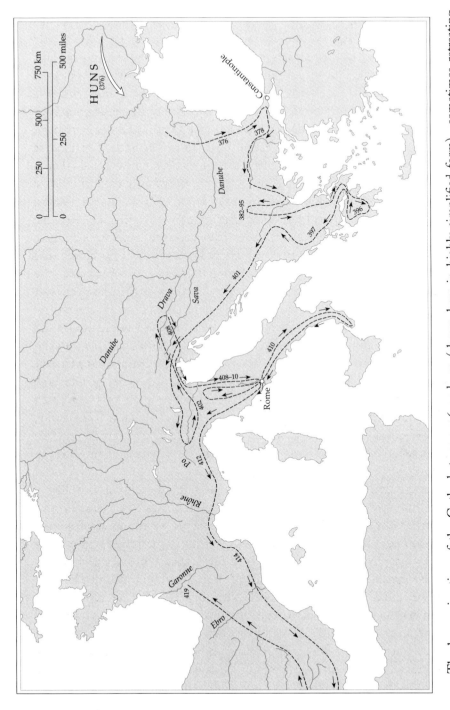

3.5 The long migration of the Goths between 376 and 419 (shown here in highly simplified form)—sometimes retreating (whether before Huns or imperial troops), sometimes advancing triumphantly, and sometimes settled as allies of the empire.

Selling out the Provincials

Because the military position of the imperial government in the fifth century was weak, and because the Germanic invaders could be appeased, the Romans on occasion made treaties with particular groups, formally granting them territory on which to settle in return for their alliance. Four such agreements are recorded in fifth-century Gaul: with the Visigoths, who were given part of Aquitaine, centred on the valley of the Garonne, in 419; with the Burgundians, settled on the upper Rhône near Lake Geneva in about 443; with a group of Alans, granted 'empty lands' around Valence in about 440; and with another Alan group some two years later, settled in an unspecified part of northern Gaul (Fig. 3.6).[38]

In recent scholarship these treaties have received a disproportionate amount of attention, and have been paraded as evidence of a new-found spirit of cooperation between incoming Germanic peoples and the Romans, both those at the centre of power and those in the provinces. But is it really likely that Roman provincials were cheered by the arrival on their doorsteps of large numbers of heavily armed barbarians under the command of their own king? To understand these treaties, we need to appreciate the circumstances of the time, and to distinguish between the needs and desires of the local provincials, who actually had to host the settlers, and those of a distant imperial government that made the arrangements.

I doubt very much that the inhabitants of the Garonne valley in 419 were happy to have the Visigothic army settled amongst them; but the government in Italy, which was under considerable military and financial pressure, might well have agreed this settlement, as a temporary solution to a number of pressing problems. It bought an important alliance at a time when the imperial finances were in a parlous condition. At the same time it removed a roving and powerful army from the Mediterranean heartlands of the empire, converting it into a settled ally on the fringes of a reduced imperial core. Siting these allies in Aquitaine meant that they could be called upon to fight other invaders, in both Spain and Gaul. They could also help contain the revolt of the *Bacaudae*, which had recently erupted to the north, in the region of the Loire. It is even possible that the settlement of these Germanic troops was in part a punishment on the aristocracy of Aquitaine, for recent disloyalty to the emperor. Some or all of these considerations may have weighed with the imperial government

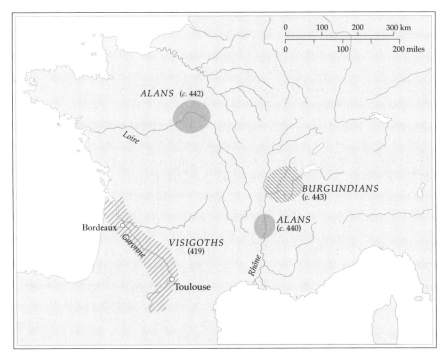

3.6 The areas of Gaul granted to Germanic armies by formal treaty (the location and extent of each territory are only very approximately known).

when settling the Visigoths in Aquitaine, particularly if the arrangement was envisaged as only temporary—until the Roman military position improved. The 419 settlement was almost certainly modelled on earlier arrangements made with Gothic armies in the Balkans, none of which had proved permanent.[39]

The interests of the centre when settling Germanic peoples, and those of the locals who had to live with the arrangements, certainly did not always coincide. The granting to some Alans of lands in northern Gaul in about 442, on the orders of the Roman general Aetius, was resisted in vain by at least some of the local inhabitants: 'The Alans, to whom lands in northern Gaul had been assigned by the patrician Aetius to be divided with the inhabitants, subdued by force of arms those who resisted, and, ejecting the owners, forcibly took possession of the land.' But, from the point of view of Aetius and the imperial government, the same settlement offered several potential advantages. It settled one dangerous group of invaders away from southern Gaul (where Roman power and resources were concentrated); it provided at least the prospect of an available ally; and it cowed the inhabitants of northern Gaul, many of whom had recently been in open revolt against the empire.[40] All this, as our text makes very clear, cost the locals a very great deal. But the cost to the central government was negligible or non-existent, since it is unlikely that this area of Gaul was any longer providing significant tax revenues or military levies for the emperor. If things went well (which they did not), the settlement of these Alans might even have been a small step along the path of reasserting imperial control in northern Gaul.

The imperial government was entirely capable of selling its provincial subjects downriver, in the interests of short-term political and military gain. In 475, despite earlier heroic resistance to the Visigoths, Clermont was surrendered to them by the imperial government, in exchange for the more important towns of Arles and Marseille. Sidonius Apollinaris, bishop of Clermont and a leader of the resistance to the Visigoths, recorded his bitterness: 'We have been enslaved, as the price of other people's security.'[41] Sidonius' opposition to this policy of appeasement proved correct—within a year, Arles and Marseille had fallen back into Visigothic hands, this time definitively.

ooo

It may have been the intention of the imperial government that Roman rule would continue within the territories where Germanic peoples were settled by treaty. For instance, this appears to have been the hope in Aquitaine in 419: the imperial government planned to go on ruling the Garonne valley through the normal structures of provincial civilian administration; the newly settled Visigoths were, in theory, a friendly and obedient force settled on territory that was still Roman.[42]

But, whatever the intention, the introduction of large numbers of heavily armed and experienced fighters under the rule of their own king in reality led to the rapid transfer of effective power. In the 420s, Paulinus of Pella, a Roman aristocrat from near Bordeaux, tried to regain some lost estates within the area of Visigothic settlement. He did not seek redress from the imperial government in Italy, nor from a Roman official in Bordeaux, but attempted to exploit his sons' personal contacts with the newly settled Goths and with the Gothic king. At about the same time, the Goths were also showing signs of a decidedly independent foreign policy.

They aided the Roman state on several occasions in campaigns against Vandals and Alans in Spain; but in the 420s and 430s they launched a series of attacks on Arles, the seat of the Roman Prefect of the Gauls, with the apparent aim of extorting more land or resources from the empire.[43] Already in the 420s Aquitaine was an independent Visigothic state, rather than a Roman province that happened to be hosting an allied army. Whatever the original intentions of the imperial government, effective power had been ceded to the Visigoths, and, as it happened, this situation was never reversed.

Was the Fall of the West Inevitable?

All empires have, sooner or later, come to an end; so it is a reasonable assumption that the Roman empire was destined at some point to fall or to disintegrate. But this does not mean that the fall of the West had to occur during the fifth century; indeed, at a number of points along the line, things might have gone differently, and the Roman position might have improved, rather than worsened. Bad luck, or bad judgement, played a very important part in what actually happened. For instance, had the emperor Valens won a stunning victory at Hadrianopolis in 378 (perhaps by waiting for the western reinforcements that were already on their way), the 'Gothic problem' might have been solved, and a firm example would have been set to other barbarians beyond the Danube and Rhine. Similarly, had Stilicho in 402 followed up victories in northern Italy over the Goths with their crushing defeat, rather than allowing them to retreat back into the Balkans, it is much less likely that another Germanic group in 405–6, and the Vandals, Alans, and Sueves in 406, would have taken their chances within the western empire.[44]

Even after things had started to go seriously wrong for the West in 407, the downhill slide was not necessarily irreversible. A few successes could have begun an improvement in imperial fortunes, as they had done in the second half of the third century. Indeed, in the period 411–21, under the generalship of Constantius and before his premature death, there was a partial revival of Roman fortunes, with the pacification of Italy and the reassertion of imperial control over much of southern Gaul and parts of Spain. It is true that the subsequent Vandal attack on Africa in 429, the eventual fall of Carthage in 439, and the beginning of Vandal sea-raiding were devastating blows that removed the western empire's last secure and lucrative tax base. But even these events were not necessarily fatal—major expeditions against the Vandals were planned in 441 and 468, with considerable eastern assistance, as well as an independent western effort in 460.[45] All three failed miserably—that of 468 ending in a disastrous defeat at sea—but, had any of them succeeded, the recovery of African resources, and the reassertion of imperial prestige, might have enabled the empire to extend its successes into other regions (as indeed eventually happened when Justinian crushingly defeated the Vandals in 533, and went on to reconquer Italy).

If events had fallen out differently, it is even possible to envisage a resurgent western empire under a successful Germanic dynasty. Theoderic the Ostrogoth ruled Italy and adjacent parts of the Danubian provinces and Balkans from 493; from 511 he also effectively controlled the Visigothic kingdom in Spain and many of the former Visigothic territories in southern Gaul, where he reinstated the traditional Roman office of 'Praetorian Prefect for the Gauls' based in Arles. This looks like the beginnings of a revived western empire, under Germanic kings. As things turned out, all this was brought to an end by Justinian's invasion of Italy in 535. But, given better luck, later Ostrogothic kings might have been able to expand on this early success; and—who knows?—might have revived the imperial title in the West centuries before Charlemagne in 800.[46]

How did the East Survive?

The eastern half of the Roman empire survived the Germanic and Hunnic attacks of this period, to flourish in the fifth and early sixth centuries; indeed it was only a thousand years later, with the Turkish capture of Constantinople in 1453, that it came to an end. No account of the fall of the western empire can be fully satisfactory if it does not discuss how the East managed to resist very similar external pressure. Here, I believe, it was primarily good fortune, rather than innately greater strength, that was decisive.[47]

Certainly any theory that the East was always much stronger than the West is demolished by the fact that it was the *eastern* field army that was defeated and massacred at Hadrianopolis in 378. This defeat provoked a profound and immediate eastern crisis: the Balkans were devastated; Constantinople itself was threatened (though saved by the presence of some Arab troops); and Gothic soldiers within the Roman army were slaughtered as a precautionary measure. The loss with all its equipment of perhaps two-thirds of the eastern field army took years of expenditure and effort to repair. Indeed, until the Goths under Alaric entered Italy in 401, it was the eastern emperors, not the western, who occasionally needed military help from the other half of the empire (in 377, 378, 381, 395, and 397). In dealing with the Goths, after their entry into the empire in 376, the eastern emperors alternated between a policy of alliance and one of aggression; but their ambitions after 380 seem to have been limited to containing the Gothic menace, with little hope of destroying it or driving it right out of imperial territory.[48]

The eastern empire was also notably unsuccessful against a fifth-century menace in the Balkans, the Huns, who brought with them the additional problem that they were good at storming cities. The eastern armies never convincingly defeated the Huns in open battle, and suffered some notable disasters, such as the fall and sack of the great fortress town of Naissus in 441; seven years later, an envoy from Constantinople found the city still depopulated and had difficulty finding a place to camp, because the area around was littered with the bones of those killed in the disaster. In 447 the Hunnic leader Attila was able to raise the rate of annual tribute paid to him by the eastern emperor to 2,100 pounds of gold (with a further 6,000 pounds of gold owing as arrears), a sum sufficient to build almost six churches a year the size of S. Vitale in Ravenna. According to our source for this raise in tribute, which is admittedly far from dispassionate, Roman taxpayers were driven to suicide by the resultant misery. It was in fact a western army, under Aetius, though at this date primarily made up of independent Germanic allies, that eventually inflicted a significant defeat on Attila, at the battle of the Catalaunian Fields in 451.[49]

The decisive factor that weighed in favour of the East was not the greater power of its armies and their consequent greater success in battle, but a single chance of geography—a thin band of sea (the Bosphorus, Sea of Marmara, and Dardanelles), in places less than 700 metres wide, that separates Asia from Europe. During the fifth century, this natural line of defence was given considerable human support, through the construction of fortifications that turned Constantinople into the greatest fortress of the Roman world. Standing on the Bosphorus's European shore, Constantinople became a bulwark against enemies in the Balkans, defended as it was by formidable defensive works—the 'Long Walls', sealing off the whole peninsula that led to the straits and to the city, and then the extraordinary triple land-walls of Constantinople itself (Fig. 3.2, at p. 35). But it was the sea, and Roman naval domination, that were decisive for the survival of the eastern empire—invaders from the north could have bypassed Constantinople, to wreak havoc on the interior of the empire, except that the straits and the Roman navy presented an insurmountable obstacle. It is not surprising that in 419 a law was issued in the East threatening death to 'those who have betrayed to the barbarians the art, previously unknown to them, of building ships'. (Fig. 3.7).[50]

The straits protected the largest part of the eastern empire's tax base. Although the Goths and Huns were repeatedly able to devastate the Balkans and Greece, even as far as the Peloponnese, the presence of the sea meant that they were never able to cross into Asia Minor. Consequently the richest provinces of the East, from Constantinople to the Nile, were

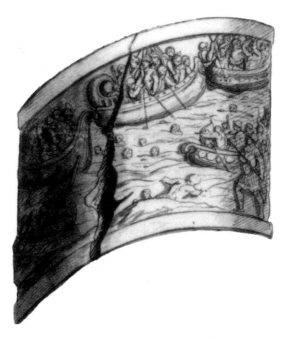

3.7 The advantages of sea power and a thin strip of water. During a military rebellion in 399–400, rebellious troops attempted to cross the Bosphorus on makeshift rafts; but were caught and slaughtered from imperial ships. The scene is shown here on the column erected in Constantinople to commemorate the defeat of the rebels. (This column was destroyed in the eighteenth century, but its reliefs are known from drawings, like this one, made before its destruction.)

untouched by the troubles of the late fourth and fifth centuries, except for one daring raid in 395 by a group of Huns, over the Caucasus, through Armenia, and into Syria. By far the largest part of the eastern empire's tax base (probably well over two-thirds) was safe, and, indeed, during the fifth century enjoyed unprecedented prosperity. The loss of territory and security in the Balkans was serious, and always threatened Constantinople, which during the fifth and sixth centuries became the fixed residence and capital of the eastern emperors. But it was not disastrous. Within an eastern empire safely supplied by the secure provinces of Asia Minor, the Levant, and Egypt, there could even be a debate as to whether it was better to fight the invaders from the North, or to buy them off with gold and Balkan lands.[51]

War and devastation might of course have been carried into the heart of the eastern empire by other means, and two further factors were needed to guarantee the survival of the East: freedom from civil war, which we have explored above; and peace on the Persian frontier. At the end of the fourth, and throughout the fifth century, the empire was at peace with Persia, except for brief periods of hostility in 421–2 and 441–2. This was partly through good fortune (the Persians often had their own serious problems elsewhere), but also partly through good management. In marked contrast to the experience of the third and fourth centuries, both the Persians and the Romans during the fifth century seem to have realized that war was not always in their best interests, and that negotiated and peaceful settlements over differences were both possible and desirable. The Romans even contributed intermittently to the cost of defence of the Persian 'Caspian Gates', a vital route through the Caucasus, which it was in the interest of both empires to hold against invaders from the steppes.

Peace with Persia, at the end of the fourth and through most of the fifth centuries, was undoubtedly of great importance to the survival and well-being of the eastern Roman empire, since, as we have seen, it was impossible to fight successfully on more than one front at a time. Indeed, the Huns took advantage of the two occasions when the empire did get embroiled in Persian wars, in 421–2 and in 441–2 (when there was also a major expedition against Vandal Africa), and immediately launched successful campaigns in the Balkans.[52]

ooo

The history of the eastern empire might have been completely different if there was no band of sea separating modern Europe and Asia. In fact, if the Goths had been able to follow up their stunning victory at Hadrianopolis in 378 with campaigns and raids deep into Asia Minor and Syria, the East might well have fallen long before the West. Geography, with a little human help, saved it.

A similar advantage operated also in the western empire; but unfortunately to lesser effect, and for a much shorter period of time. Thanks to the sea, and Roman naval domination, Africa and the Mediter- ranean islands (including the rich island of Sicily) were protected from the initial devastation. After sacking Rome in 410, the Goths tried to reach Sicily, but were forced to retreat after marching right to the toe of Italy, where they were unable to cross the Straits of Messina. Five years later, they marched to the foot of Spain, hoping to cross to North Africa, but at the Straits of Gibraltar they were again forced to turn back. Roman naval power in the West could hold these narrow strips of sea as effectively as the eastern navy held the Bosphorus and Dardanelles. Unfortunately, however, the West's safe haven (Africa, Sicily, and the other islands) was very much smaller than the equivalent secure provinces in the East, and will have produced a much smaller income: whereas over two-thirds of the East's tax base was safe, in the West the figure was probably under a third. Even more unfortunately, this too was lost in the years following the successful crossing of the Straits of Gibraltar by the Vandals in 429. By 439 they had conquered Carthage and the richest provinces of Africa, and soon afterwards they began a period of conquest and raiding by sea that severely disrupted Sicily and the other West Mediterranean islands.[53]

At one level—because it seems to mock human endeavour (as well as historians' attempts to impose order on the past)—I am very reluctant to believe that a chance geographical difference is central to explaining the remarkable situation at the end of the fifth century (undreamed of only 100 years earlier): an eastern empire, richer and more powerful than ever before; and a western empire that had entirely disappeared. However, the evidence is very strong that a thin band of water, reinforced by sea power and supported by peace on other fronts, was the eastern empire's greatest defence. Whereas, without this advantage, a series of invasions at the start of the fifth century plunged the West into a vicious spiral of devastation, loss of revenue, and bitter internecine strife—from which it never recovered.

IV

LIVING UNDER THE NEW MASTERS

THE CHRONICLER HYDATIUS, describing the way in which Spain was divided up amongst the Vandals, Sueves, and Alans in 411, after two years of warfare, attributed the new situation to God's benevolence: 'After the provinces of Spain had been devastated by the blows I have described, through the mercy of God the barbarians turned to the making of peace, and divided the provinces for settlement by lot amongst themselves. . . . Those Spaniards . . . who had survived the disasters, subjected themselves to slavery under the barbarians who ruled the various provinces.'[1] After two terrible years of warfare and looting, barbarian settlement at least brought a degree of peace.

Hydatius' picture of 'slavery under the barbarians' is in fact exaggerated. Once the violence was over, in large parts of the former western empire a great deal of the social structure, and much of the administrative and cultural framework of imperial times, re-emerged and flourished. In looking at a Germanic kingdom, such as that established by the Ostrogoths at the end of the fifth century in Italy—where games continued in the circus and amphitheatre, and ancient Roman families vied for office—it is even possible to wonder if anything had really changed. However, Hydatius was also right that peace and Germanic rule came at a heavy price.

The Cost of Peace

The new arrivals demanded and obtained a share of the empire's capital wealth, which at this date meant primarily land. We know for certain that many of the great landowners of post-Roman times were of Germanic descent, even though we have very little information as to how exactly they had obtained their wealth at the expense of its previous owners. However, just occasionally we know a little more. We have already met some land-owners in northern Gaul, who in about 442 attempted to resist a settle-ment of Alans by treaty, and lost everything for their pains. In Africa, with the Vandal conquest, we hear of aristocrats who lost all their property and fled abroad: in 451 the western emperor Valentinian III issued a law grant-ing to 'the dignitaries and landowners of Africa, who have been stripped bare by the devastation of the enemy', lands in neighbouring provinces that were still under imperial control. Elsewhere the information, although grim, is very much vaguer. Gildas, in sixth-century Britain, for instance tells us how

> a number of the wretched survivors were caught in the mountains and butchered wholesale. Others, their spirits broken by hunger, went to sur-render to the enemy; they were fated to be slaves for ever . . . Others made for lands beyond the sea; beneath the swelling sails they loudly wailed, singing a psalm . . . 'You have given us like sheep for eating and scattered us among the heathen.'

Gildas's story, although undoubtedly greatly exaggerated, does find partial support in evidence of emigration by Britons, who left their homeland in this period to settle in Brittany across the Channel.[2]

In a few areas of the empire, of which Italy is the only sizeable one, there was an organized and formal division of resources between the incomers and the native population. In 476 a coup in Italy, led by the general Odoacer, deposed the last emperor in the West, and distributed 'a third of the land' of the peninsula amongst Odoacer's Germanic soldiery. As so often in this period, the evidence we have for this allocation is not quite full enough to show beyond doubt what the rebellious soldiery received; and there has recently been a major scholarly debate, between those who believe that only tax revenue was granted into barbarian hands, and those who stick to the idea that land itself was distributed.[3] If one thinks that tax alone was granted, the initial allocation of resources in Italy will have been painless to Italian landowners. Only the state will have suffered, through the loss of tax revenue; but even this loss will have been balanced by the ending of the need to salary the army.

Personally I am convinced that some land was taken away from Italian landowners in 476, and that the settlement therefore hurt. I believe this, because a number of different texts talk of the division of 'land', 'the soil', and 'estates', not of tax; and because there is also explicit mention of 'losses' suffered by the Roman population. For instance, when describing the allocation of resources to the Ostrogoths in Italy, an official letter, which is undoubtedly seeking to minimize the impact of the settlement on the Romans of Italy, still speaks of how '*losses* have increased the friendship of the two peoples, and *a share of the land* purchased a defender'.[4] With a very great deal of ingenuity, references to the Germanic troops receiving land can be interpreted as a figurative way of describing grants of taxation. But, if the settlement had really involved only the transfer of taxation revenue from the state to the settlers, why is this not lauded explicitly, and why are 'losses' mentioned?

Whatever the original allocation of resources to the new Germanic masters, no one disputes that throughout the empire they very rapidly added to their landed wealth through the astute use or abuse of power. Ultimate power was, of course, now in Germanic hands, even though the new rulers were often happy to share much of their authority with Roman ministers. At a local level, the degree of power-sharing with the Roman aristocracy probably varied. For instance, in early sixth-century Italy there were large numbers of Ostrogoths settled in the North, to defend against any further invasion, and here their power and authority must have been keenly felt. But the new rulers were only very lightly scattered across southern Italy and Sicily; when Justinian's general Belisarius invaded Italy from the South in 535–6, it was only when he reached Naples, a third of the way up the peninsula, that he encountered resistance from a town with a substantial Gothic garrison. But under the Ostrogoths all cities, at least in theory, had Gothic 'counts of the city' in charge of a military garrison, and 'counts of the Goths' with authority over any Gothic inhabitants. These 'counts of the Goths' also wielded one very significant power over the natives of Italy—the final say in any dispute that might arise between a Roman and a Goth.[5] As in recent colonial states, like British India, native magistrates in Ostrogothic Italy were not allowed to judge a member of the ruling race.

Unsurprisingly, and with good Roman precedent behind them, the Germanic settlers rapidly used their power to acquire more wealth. We are told, for instance, that Theodahad, nephew of Theoderic the Ostrogothic king of Italy, was a man who 'had gained possession of most of the lands of Tuscany, and was eager by violent methods to wrest the remainder from its owners', and that for him 'to have a neighbour seemed a kind of

misfortune'. Theodahad, as a close relative of the king, was exceptionally
well placed to abuse power and build up massive estates; but at a local level
there must have been many other Goths quietly lining their pockets
through their monopoly of military power, and the political immunity that
this gave them. We learn, for instance, of two unfortunate Italian smallholders dispossessed and enslaved by a powerful Goth, Tanca. In theory
this particular story had a happy ending; an official was ordered to investi-
gate Tanca's activities: 'the whole truth of the case between the parties is to
be examined, and you are to dispense a justice that accords with law, and
corresponds to your character.' However, the man receiving these high-
minded instructions was another Goth, Cunigast, who, we happen to
know, himself acquired a reputation for abusing power. The Roman aristocrat Boethius wrote of him: 'how many times have I stood in the way of
Cunigast when he made an assault on the wealth of some helpless person.'[6] History does not record the fate of our two Italian smallholders, but,
in the hands of Tanca and Cunigast, the cards were stacked firmly against
them.

Working with the New Masters

Germanic rule, once peace was established, was not an unmitigated disaster
for all the native population. Above all, as we have seen at the start of this
chapter, the foundation of the new kingdoms certainly restored a degree of
stability to the West, allowing normal life to resume its course, though
under new masters. The Ostrogoths in Italy very explicitly presented their
rule in this light: 'While the army of Goths wages war, let the Roman live
in peace.'[7] However, it is worth remembering that this was 'peace' in the
context of the dying or dead empire, and relative to the dreadful conditions
of much of the fifth century. In the fourth century, before the invasions of
the West began, there had never been any question of needing large numbers of troops under arms far from the frontiers in areas like Italy, let alone
of allowing them to rule the peninsula. If the settlement of the Germanic
armies was a satisfactory way to re-establish stability, it was satisfactory
faute de mieux.

Fortunately, the invaders entered the empire in groups that were small
enough to leave plenty to share with the locals. Furthermore, in order for
their regimes to operate smoothly, the new rulers needed and wanted
Roman aristocratic administrators and supporters. The author of a sermon

delivered in the southern Gallic town of Riez, shortly after its surrender to the Visigoths in about 477, was putting a brave face on things, but not being entirely untruthful, when he said of the conquerors: 'Behold, the whole world trembles before the clamour of this most powerful race, and yet, he who was considered a barbarian, comes to you with a Roman spirit . . .'.[8] The Germanic peoples entered the empire with no ideology that they wished to impose, and found it most advantageous and profitable to work closely within the well-established and sophisticated structures of Roman life. The Romans as a group unquestionably lost both wealth and power in order to meet the needs of a new, and dominant, Germanic aristocracy. But they did not lose everything, and many individual Romans were able to prosper under the new dispensation.

In many regions, despite some expropriation and loss, Roman aristocratic families continued wealthy and influential under Germanic rule. In southern and central Italy, for instance, the overwhelming impression is of aristocratic continuity, at least into the sixth century; in Gaul too many important families are known to have kept at least part of their wealth and status, particularly in the south. Even in areas where brutal expropriation occurred, such as Vandal Africa and Anglo-Saxon Britain, it is either demonstrably untrue, or very unlikely, that all native landowners were dispossessed. A certain Victorianus of Hadrumentum, who was certainly not of Vandal descent, was, we are told, 'as wealthy as any man in Africa' in 484, and had risen in Vandal service to the office of 'proconsul of Carthage'. In the late seventh century King Ine of Wessex set down laws for his own Saxon people and for Britons under his rule. These laws include a reference to Britons (called by their English name 'Welshmen') with substantial estates and considerable legal status: 'A Welshman, if he has five hides, is a man of a six-hundred [shilling] wergild.' Even in Britain the incomers had not dispossessed everyone.[9]

Smallholders, and in particular dependent tenants, perhaps managed to hold onto their land even more effectively than the aristocracy, because the numbers involved in the invasions and migrations were substantial, but not overwhelming. A large Germanic group probably numbered a few tens of thousands, while regions like Italy and Roman Africa had populations of several millions. In the case of the Vandals, we are told that their leader Geiseric had them counted at the moment of their crossing into Africa in 429, and that they numbered 80,000, including children, the old, and slaves. This figure is almost certainly a considerable exaggeration, since

Geiseric is said to have ordered the census for a specific purpose of making 'the reputation of his people a source of dread'.[10]

In the case of the Anglo-Saxons and others who bordered Roman territory by land or sea, the number of immigrants was probably substantially larger, since here the initial conquests could readily be followed up by secondary migration. However, except perhaps in regions that were right on the frontiers, it is unlikely that the numbers involved were so large as to dispossess many at the level of the peasantry. Many smallholders in the new kingdoms probably continued to hold their land much as before, except that much of the tax and rent that they paid will now have gone to enrich Germanic masters. In the south of the Vandals' African kingdom, forty-five written tablets from the end of the fifth century were discovered in the 1920s. These revealed Roman smallholders, with leases held by right of a centuries-old Roman law—in this area, except that the leases were now dated by the regnal year of a Vandal king, nothing obvious had changed for the local farmers.[11]

ooo

Most of the new rulers ran their kingdoms in a style that closely imitated that of the empire, and that required Roman administrators to make it function. Except in Britain and parts of the Balkans, most of the basic structures of society, which needed experienced Romans to maintain them (the Christian Church, the cities, secular administration, Roman law, and so on), persisted under Germanic rule, at least in the early days. Indeed, in some parts of the former empire, the new rulers took explicit pride in maintaining Roman ways—as Ostrogothic propaganda in early sixth-century Italy expressed it, 'The glory of the Goths is to protect the civil life.'[12] Under the Ostrogoths, the entire administrative and the legal structure of the Roman state—which was, of course, both efficient and profitable—was maintained, and the traditional civilian offices continued in aristocratic Roman hands. The early Germanic Kings of Italy, and elsewhere, even minted their gold coins in the name of the reigning emperor in the East, as though the Roman empire was still in existence (Fig. 4.1).

When they did brutal things to their subjects, as they sometimes did, Germanic kings often chose to do them in a very Roman way and for very Roman reasons. The Vandal king Huneric (477–84)—an Arian Christian, like the rest of his people—was, according to one's point of view, either a heretic and a savage persecutor of the native Catholic majority of Africa,

4.1 The empire lives on in the West, if only in name. Gold coin issued by the Ostrogothic king of Italy, Theoderic. It bears the bust and name of the eastern emperor, Anastasius, and is identical to those issued by Anastasius himself. The only indication that this is a coin produced in an independent Germanic kingdom is the tiny mint mark of Ravenna on the reverse of the coin (next to the cross held by the angel).

or a caring and orthodox ruler who wished to lift his subjects from the appalling doctrinal errors in which they wallowed. He instituted his attacks on Catholicism in a purely Roman style, issuing edicts in Latin, which spelled out his own titles to rule, the errors of the 'homo-ousian' heretics (as he termed the Catholics), and the divine justice of his own position: 'In this matter our Clemency has followed the will of divine judgement . . .'.

Such 'Roman' rule required Roman servants, both at the level of humble clerks and functionaries, and at the level of aristocratic administrators. Of the humbler servants, admittedly, we know very little, though a story, again from Vandal Africa under Huneric, does shed some light on them. The king was apparently particularly concerned to stamp out any possibility of Vandal conversions to Catholicism; to this end he ordered that no one in Vandal dress should be allowed to enter a Catholic church, and posted armed men to enforce the rule with considerable brutality. This order was vehemently opposed by the Catholic bishop of Carthage, Eugenius, 'because a large number of our Catholics came to church dressed in their [Vandal] clothes, since they worked in the royal household'.[13]

It was important for Germanic kings to work closely with aristocratic Roman ministers and advisers, both to ensure the smooth and profitable running of their administrations, and to be confident of local political support. All the new kingdoms from which evidence survives provide examples of a mutually advantageous arrangement between Germanic kings and members of the local aristocracy: the king gave native aristocrats access to power, security of tenure for their lands and status, and grants of privileges and wealth; the aristocrats, in return, gave service and support, both at court and in the localities. Even from Anglo-Saxon Britain we have evidence of this kind of arrangement. The laws of Ine tell us of the king's 'horse-Welshmen', Britons who had entered the West-Saxon king's service as mounted warriors, and had thereby gained a privileged legal status.[14]

On the Continent, the examples of cooperation between local Roman aristocrats and Germanic kings are myriad. Unfortunately, it is in the nature of our sources that we have very little detailed evidence of what precisely these Roman servants of the new rulers gained from their service. But it is very obvious that a Roman like Cassiodorus, one of the principal ministers of Theoderic and his successors as kings of Italy, must have been richly rewarded by his masters. The disintegration of the unified empire, and its replacement by a scatter of Germanic courts, indeed gave provincial Romans readier access to influence and power than they had held in the fourth century, when there was only one imperial court, often at a great distance. Paulinus of Pella, for instance, a landowner of south-western Gaul, was awarded the important office of 'Count of the Private Largesse' by a puppet-emperor created by the Visigoths during their stay in southern Gaul in 412–16. This was a marked step up in the world for a provincial Gallic aristocrat; though, sadly for Paulinus, his ambition came badly unstuck when the Goths withdrew from southern Gaul and the emperor in Italy, Honorius, reasserted his power. However, the settlement of the Visigoths around Toulouse and Bordeaux in 419 again gave Paulinus hope: two of his sons went to live amongst the Goths in Bordeaux, in the hope of furthering the family's interests. Again, sadly, these hopes of power and influence proved transitory: both sons died young, one of them having gained 'both the friendship and the anger of the king'. Others, however, were luckier—Paulinus tells us that at the time he was writing, in around 458, 'we see many flourishing under Gothic favour'.[15]

Most of the aristocrats who are known to have entered Germanic service in the fifth and early sixth centuries still did so in the traditional Roman way, as civilians. In the later fifth century Sidonius Apollinaris, the doyen of learned aristocratic standards in Gaul, wrote to Syagrius, the great-grandson of a Roman consul of the same name. Syagrius junior had very sensibly entered Burgundian service, and was in demand as a translator and legal expert. His role as a 'new Solon to the Burgundians' had given him considerable influence amongst his new masters: 'you are loved, frequented, and sought after; you delight, and you are chosen; you are consulted, you make decisions, and you are listened to.' However, there were also Romans who, from quite an early date, entered the service of the new kings as warriors. Italy enjoyed peace for most of the fifth and early sixth centuries; it was therefore also one of the very last regions where the late-Roman tradition of a demilitarized aristocracy persisted. But even here there were Romans, like a certain Cyprianus, who served their new Gothic masters loyally and fully in a military as well as a civilian capacity.[16]

In imagining a regime such as that of the Ostrogoths in early sixth-century Italy, we should certainly not imagine a hard-and-fast horizontal division of power and resources, with everyone above the line a Goth, and everyone below a Roman. Romans like Cyprianus and Cassiodorus were very wealthy, and were major powers in the land, able to lord it over many a humble Goth. On the other hand, we should also never forget that both royal power and almost all military might lay in the hands of Goths, and that in cases of legal dispute between a Goth and a Roman it was always a Gothic judge who presided over the court. Elsewhere in the West, the formal advantaging of the newcomers was sometimes even starker. In the Frankish *Salic Law* of around 500, Romans were offered the protection of a *wergild* (blood-price), alongside their Frankish neighbours. One group of Romans, members of the king's retinue, had higher *wergilds* than those of ordinary free Franks. But, and this is very telling, Franks in the royal retinue were judged to be worth exactly double the amount of an equivalent Roman; while 'ordinary' Roman landowners (not in royal service) were similarly valued at exactly half the price of a normal free Frank.

> But if anyone kills a free Frank . . . let him be liable for . . . 200 *solidi*.
> But if a Roman landowner . . . is killed, let him . . . be held liable for . . . 100 *solidi*.

In Ine's Wessex, some 200 years later, the situation was similar: a Briton in royal service had a higher blood-price than an ordinary Saxon, but a much lower one than a Saxon of equivalent standing. The advantages of wealth and royal patronage meant that within all the new kingdoms some natives

were far higher up the pecking order of society than many Germanic
settlers. But, in the case of settlers and natives of equal wealth and position, there existed structures, both formal and informal, that favoured the
newcomer.[17]

Theoderic's Moustache and Germanic Identity

Eventually, of course, the distinction between Germanic rulers and
Roman subjects became blurred, and finally disappeared altogether. But
the change was undoubtedly very slow. It is also very difficult to document,
because our sources rarely record the kind of detail—such as which language people were speaking—that we need to know in order to chart
cultural separation and eventual cultural assimilation. For instance,
Ostrogothic Italy is much the best documented of all the early Germanic
kingdoms; but it is only from scattered snippets of information that we
learn the important, if unsurprising, fact that Goths continued to speak
their native Gothic while resident in Italy, and that some Romans chose
to learn the language of their new masters.[18] Cassiodorus tells us that
the loyal Roman servant of the Ostrogothic kings, Cyprianus (whom
we have met above), had himself learned Gothic, and had also educated
his two young sons in the same language. Gothic was presumably the
favoured language of the Gothic elite, which it was advantageous to
have learned. Procopius, in his history of Justinian's conquest of Italy in
the 530s and 540s, happens to tell two stories that reveal ordinary
Ostrogoths communicating amongst themselves in Gothic some forty
years after their people had arrived in Italy. One story, set during the
siege of Rome in 537–8, involves a Gothic soldier talking to his com-
rades 'in their native language'. The other, set in 536, describes how a
soldier in Justinian's army, Bessas 'a Goth by birth', talked to two
enemy soldiers defending Naples (presumably Ostrogoths) 'in the language of the Goths'. Gothic as a spoken language was still in normal
use amongst the Ostrogoths of Italy during the 530s. The Goths in Italy
were still some way from assimilating fully with the Latin-speaking
majority.[19]

There is also a very interesting piece of evidence to show that King
Theoderic himself, and one of his successors, continued to feel different
from their Roman subjects, almost certainly because they still felt 'Gothic'.
The only certain representation that we have of Theoderic is on a gold

medallion, known as the 'Senigallia medallion' (Fig. 4.2). He is shown here in very Roman mode: identified by a Latin inscription and Roman titles; wearing a cuirass and cloak (in the manner of contemporary coin portraits of east-Roman emperors); and bearing an orb surmounted by a Victory. But he is also shown with long hair covering his ears, and, most significantly, with a moustache. There is no representation that I know of, from any century, that shows a Roman, or indeed a Greek, with a moustache (unless it is accompanied by a beard); and there is not even a word in the Latin language for 'moustache'. Contemporaries, whether Romans or Goths, will have interpreted Theoderic's moustache as a sign of his un-Romanness, indeed of his Gothicness; and, in doing so, they will surely have been right. As late as 534–6, one of his successors, Theodahad, is also shown on coinage sporting a prominent moustache (Fig. 4.3). Theodahad, according to Procopius, was an unwarlike man, learned in Latin literature and Platonic philosophy; in these respects he had clearly

4.2 Gold medallion with the bust, and in the name, of Theoderic. The inscription on the reverse, 'King Theoderic victor over foreign peoples' (*victor gentium*), is an implicit claim that the Ostrogoths were less foreign, and therefore more Roman, than other Germanic tribes.

4.3 A philosopher-king with a Gothic moustache. Copper coin of the Ostrogothic king Theodahad (534–6). The design on the reverse is closely modelled on coins of the first century AD, down to the claim that this was issued 'by decree of the Senate' (*Senatus consultu*, the 'SC' that appears on either side of the Victory).

moved towards 'Romanness'. But even the learned Theodahad kept his Gothic moustache.[20]

Penetrating the smokescreen of Latin culture is particularly difficult for Ostrogothic Italy, where Theoderic's minister Cassiodorus produced for his masters a studied image of Gothic Romanness. The Goths are presented in most contemporary texts as upholders of Roman culture, and as a force for spreading it to other, less civilized peoples. For instance, Theoderic, in a letter penned by Cassiodorus, hoped that a lyre-player sent to Clovis, king of the Franks, would 'perform a feat like that of Orpheus, when his sweet sound tames the savage hearts of the barbarians'. Sentiments like these, of course, implied that the Goths themselves were not barbarians. Ostrogothic propaganda even extended this patronizing treatment of other Germanic peoples to their own 'cousins', the Visigoths of Gaul and Spain. In about 510, soon after he had taken over control of a large part of southern Gaul from the Visigoths, Theoderic wrote to his new Gallic subjects, describing his own rule as 'Roman' and regulated by law, and contrasting it explicitly with the unregulated 'barbarian' rule of the Visigoths: 'You who have been restored to it after many years should gladly obey Roman custom . . . And therefore, as men by God's favour recalled to ancient liberty, clothe yourself in the morals of the toga, cast off barbarism, throw aside savagery of mind, for it is wrong for you, in my just times, to live by alien ways.' Only very rarely, as with Theoderic's moustache, does a different reality show through—one that reveals the survival of a Gothic identity, which, of course, the Romans would have had no hesitation in branding as 'barbarian'.[21]

To a lesser extent, the same problem of penetrating a very Roman public face is also present in other kingdoms. The Visigothic king Euric (466–84), for instance, did some very Roman things: he patronized a Latin poet, Lampridius; and his regime helped restore the great Roman bridge at Mérida in Spain, recording this achievement in a Latin verse inscription. It is only by chance, in the *Life* of the saintly Italian bishop Epiphanius (who was sent on an embassy to Euric), that we are treated to a vignette of life at the Visigothic court of Toulouse, which suggests a different reality. In this story, Euric, while in the presence of the ambassadors from Italy, talks Gothic to his fellow courtiers, 'burbling some unintelligible native mutterings'. He eventually replies to Epiphanius, who has been trying to gauge the king's mood through his facial expressions, only through an interpreter. The story does not prove that Euric could not speak Latin— he may have been deliberately seeking to confuse and annoy Epiphanius— but it does show that Gothic was still very much a live language at his court, more than fifty years after the Visigoths had arrived in Aquitaine.[22]

It is clear that important and easily identifiable differences between the Germanic incomers and their Roman subjects persisted for many years after the initial settlements. By the start of the sixth century, the Visigoths had ruled parts of Gaul for over eighty years. As far as we can tell, after an initial seizure of resources, they had not been particularly oppressive masters; certainly, they had not attempted to encourage the spread of their own Arian Christian beliefs in the brutal manner that the Vandals had occasionally used in Africa. There is also evidence of a degree of integration between Goths and natives. Individual Roman aristocrats are well attested in Visigothic service, such as Leo of Narbonne, who rose to be a close counsellor of Euric II (466–84); and some Goths had adopted very Roman ways—in around 480, Ruricius of Limoges, a landowner in Aquitaine, addressed a letter to a fellow landowner, with all the elaborate courtesy and stylistic tricks that are familiar in the correspondence of this period between highly educated Romans. The recipient of this letter of friendship, however, was a man named 'Freda', almost certainly a Goth by birth. A little later, in 507, a noble Roman, Apollinaris—despite being the

son of the man who had vehemently resented the Visigothic takeover of
Clermont in 475—led a large force of Romans from the Auvergne to fight
on the Visigoths' side against the Franks. At first sight, the Visigoths in
around 500 seem completely assimilated and integrated.[23]

However, in the very early sixth century, probably in the face of an ever-
increasing threat from the Franks, the Visigothic king did two interesting
things. First, he issued a solemn compendium of Roman law (known as
the *Breviarium* of Alaric), to be used in the judging of Romans living
under Visigothic rule. This, we are told in its preamble, was produced after
extensive consultation, with all departures in wording from original
imperial texts being approved by a group of bishops and 'selected men
amongst our provincials'. Secondly, he allowed, indeed almost certainly
encouraged, the holding of a great council of the Catholic churches under
his rule in Gaul, at Agde in 506. This even involved recalling from exile
the leading Catholic bishop—and president of the council—Caesarius of
Arles. The assembled bishops duly prayed for their royal master, despite
his Arian beliefs:

> The holy synod met in the city of Agde, in the name of the Lord, and with
> the permission of our master, the most glorious, most magnificent and most
> pious king. Kneeling on the ground we prayed to the Lord for his rule, his
> longevity and his people, that God might extend in good fortune, govern in
> justice, and protect in courage, the kingdom of him who granted us the
> right to meet here together.

An even greater council was planned for the following year (507), to be
held at the royal capital of Toulouse and to be attended by Catholic
bishops from Spain as well as Gaul. The *Breviarium* and the Council of
Agde show Visigothic rule in Gaul at its most benign; but they also show
that, right up to its final defeat in 507, it was still alien rule, over Roman
subjects who were readily identifiable as different from the Visigoths
through their adherence to Roman law and to Catholic Christianity.[24]
Indeed, it was not until 587, over 200 years after their first arrival in the
empire in 376, that the Visigoths finally abandoned their Arianism and
converted to Catholic Christianity.

Generally within the new kingdoms, despite differences, those of
Roman and those of Germanic descent lived peacefully side by side. The
Romans had little choice in the matter, and the Germanic peoples had no
need and no particular wish to be unpleasant. However, times of stress

could inflame ethnic tension, just as they can today, with bloody consequences. In 552 the Goths in Italy suffered two important reverses in quick succession at the hands of the invading army of Justinian: a defeat in open battle and the loss of the city of Rome. Embittered by these events and by the obvious favour shown to Justinian's army by Italy's Roman aristocracy, the defeated Goths destroyed 'without mercy' those Romans they met during their retreat, and, more specifically, killed any patricians they found in the cities of Campania, and slaughtered in cold blood 300 aristocratic Roman children whom they were holding as hostages. Distrust of their parents had made these children prisoners; bitterness killed them.[25] When placed under stress, the apparently peaceful coexistence of Goths and Romans in Italy collapsed into bloodshed.

Moustachioed Romans and Pen-Wielding Barbarians: The Making of Single Peoples

There is no reason to believe, as people once did, that ethnic behaviour and identity are genetically transmitted, and therefore immutable. But experience suggests that a great deal of an individual's identity is acquired during childhood and early youth, from parents, the wider family, and companions, and that this identity, once acquired, is not easily forgotten. This being so, individuals have never been entirely free to choose what they wish to be; old identities, even inconvenient ones, die hard. Furthermore, for a change of identity to be successful, this requires, not only mental and cultural adjustments on the part of the person making the shift, but also the acceptance of that person into the group they wish to join. As we know from modern experience, acceptance is by no means always freely given, and often has to be 'earned' over time—for instance, as an Englishman, I am not sure that, even if I had lived my life in Scotland, I could ever have earned acceptance as a Scot. Individuals and groups can successfully change their identities, even dramatically; but to do so they have to overcome barriers, both in their own minds and in those of the group they wish to join. This takes time, often several generations.[26]

Modern experience also suggests, unsurprisingly, that some changes of identity are very much easier to make than others. It is, for instance, simple for me to be 'British', and, although I am now too old to change, it would once have been comparatively simple to become an 'American'. A great deal of scholarly ink has been used recently to show how flexible and changeable various Germanic tribal identities were in the post-Roman West, suggesting that individuals and groups could fairly easily and rapidly change their allegiance from one Germanic tribe to another. However, changes such as these *within* the broad 'Germanic' family of peoples—say, from being an Alaman to a Frank, or a Sueve to a Visigoth—may have been amongst the easier transitions to make, though I doubt that even such comparatively simple transformations could have been effected rapidly.

The verse epitaph of Droctulft, a Sueve who served in the Byzantine army in Italy in the later sixth century, is very interesting in this regard. It tells us that Droctulft was born a Sueve, but brought up amongst the Lombards, before abandoning his adoptive people to fight against them on behalf of the Byzantines. We are also specifically told that he sported a long beard, which may well have been a mark of his adopted Lombard identity (the 'Longobards', or Lombards, were known precisely for this feature). However, at the time of his death, according to his epitaph, 'he considered [Byzantine] Ravenna to be his homeland'. Droctulft's epitaph shows that it was indeed possible to change allegiance, in his case more than once (from Sueve to Lombard, and from Lombard to Byzantine Roman)—but it also shows that an individual's past, and his former identities, right back to his distant birth and parentage, were not necessarily forgotten; in Droctulft's case they travelled with him to the grave.[27]

The barrier between 'Romans', within the empire, and 'barbarians', outside it, had been a formidable one in the fourth century and earlier, and we should therefore not expect the distinction between Germanic incomers and their Roman subjects to vanish in a hurry—though in time we would expect the differences to become attenuated, and eventually to disappear. In Frankish Gaul, as we have seen from the *Salic Law*, the distinction between Romans and Franks was still very significant in around AD 500, with Romans holding different (and inferior) blood-prices from their Frankish neighbours. However, this distinction appears to have blurred by the time of Gregory of Tours, who in the late sixth century wrote a long history of his own times and a large number of miracle stories, full of lively and circumstantial detail, which very seldom mention whether someone was a Roman or a Frank. People in Frankish Gaul, whatever their ancestry, were apparently slowly adopting a common identity; indeed, by the end of the seventh century there were no 'Romans' left in northern Gaul, only people who considered themselves 'Franks'.[28]

Unfortunately, our sources seldom give us more than the barest hint of how such assimilation came about. In part it must have happened through a process of Roman subjects wishing to better themselves, by adopting some of the culture, and eventually the identity, of their new masters. Earlier in this chapter we have seen the Catholic Romans of Carthage who worked in the Vandal court and wore Vandal dress (though, they may, of course, have done so reluctantly and at the behest of their employers). A more extreme, and obviously voluntary, case of cultural movement into the Germanic ruling class is that of Cyprianus and his sons in Ostrogothic Italy. He was himself ambitious enough to learn Gothic, and ambitious enough for his children to train them in the same skill. This achievement was praised by his Gothic masters as a sure sign of the young men's future devoted service: 'The boys are of Roman stock, yet speak our language, clearly showing the future loyalty that they will hold towards us, whose speech they now are seen to have adopted.' Unfortunately, we do not know the names of these boys who were being so carefully groomed for success under Ostrogothic rule. It is entirely possible, indeed quite likely, that their upwardly mobile father gave them Gothic names.[29]

However, there were problems for Romans who wanted to adopt Germanic culture—in particular, a centuries-old, deeply ingrained certainty that their own ways were immeasurably superior to those of the barbarians. In Ostrogothic Italy, the learned Ennodius mocked Jovinianus, a Roman who sported both a Roman cloak and a 'Gothic beard' (very possibly a moustache in the style of Theoderic and Theodahad). Jovinianus' Roman dress and Gothic facial hair are to us a fascinating example of two ethnic groups beginning to fuse into one; but, for Ennodius, Jovinianus was 'mixing discordant offspring in a hostile alliance', and his beard gave him a 'barbarian appearance'. Ennodius' scorn illustrates the barriers that still defended Roman ways. Similarly, when Sidonius Apollinaris wrote to Syagrius, the Roman noble who had entered Burgundian service and had learnt their language to do so, he mocked and reproved him, gently but firmly, for this achievement. He reminded Syagrius of his distinguished Roman ancestry and his education in Latin literature and rhetoric, and told him what he and others thought of his new-found skills: 'You cannot guess how much I and others laugh when I hear that in your presence the barbarian is frightened to commit a barbarism in his own language.' Germanic languages, with their lack of a written history or literature, were not for gentlemen.[30]

Faith in the superiority of Roman culture was, to some extent, shared by the Germanic peoples themselves. Their presentation of their rule in a very Roman guise was partly aimed at their local Roman subjects, but it almost certainly also pleased the rulers themselves. In Ostrogothic Italy, as we have seen, Theoderic and his successors were happy to present themselves as the upholders of Roman culture, and to see this as a vital difference between themselves and the true barbarians beyond. Indeed, even when we get a glimpse of underlying 'Gothicness' (as with Theoderic's moustache, or Cyprianus' wish to teach his children the Gothic language), it is always presented in a very 'Roman' way. The praise that Cyprianus received for bringing up his children to speak Gothic was penned in the elegant Latin of Cassiodorus, and Theoderic's hair and moustache were carefully crimped for presentation on an otherwise entirely 'Roman' object (Fig.4.2, at p. 73). It was inevitable that Roman ways, honed and perfected by hundreds of years of effortless superiority, would be very beguiling to the new Germanic masters of the West, and would emerge even in unlikely contexts. In the Frankish kingdom of the 570s, Chilperic is recorded to have built circuses for chariot-racing at Soissons and Paris in clear emulation of Roman practice. At this late date and in this northern clime, he was almost certainly satisfying his own vanity far more than the expectations of his subjects.[31]

If we look at the two large Germanic kingdoms that survived to the end of the sixth century, those of the Visigoths and of the Franks, what seems to have happened is that the indigenous Roman population eventually adopted the identity of their masters, and became 'Visigoths' or 'Franks' (from which 'Français' and 'French' derive); but at the same time these masters adopted the culture of their subjects—in particular dropping their native language and religion in favour of those of their subjects. The explanation, I think, is that both groups moved 'upwards': the Romans into the political identity of their Germanic masters; the Germanic peoples into the more sophisticated cultural framework of their Roman subjects.[32]

Romans were indeed skilled in encouraging barbarians to adopt their ways. In about 477, the same Sidonius Apollinaris who laughed at Syagrius for his excellent grasp of Burgundian wrote to a Frankish count of Trier, Arbogastes. Arbogastes had written a polished letter in Latin to

Sidonius, requesting a theological work from his pen. Sidonius politely and humbly declined the request, but he complimented Arbogastes fulsomely on his excellent Latin:

> You plead that you only trifle with refinement, when you have drunk deep at the spring of Roman eloquence; and, though the waters you now drink are those of the Moselle, the words you pour forth are those of the Tiber. You are the companion of barbarians, but ignorant of barbarisms. In words and deeds, you are equal to our leaders of old, who wielded the pen as often as they did the sword.[33]

Arbogastes governed a city of the Rhineland, where the survival of Roman culture was under serious threat. Sidonius was writing, not just to praise him, but also to strengthen his literary resolve. Similarly, in the 480s the bishop of Reims, Remigius, wrote to Clovis, the new Frankish king of the region in which his see lay. Remigius, of course, also wrote in Latin, the language of high culture and history, and he congratulated Clovis on taking over 'the governance of Belgica Secunda'. This was not strictly true: the Roman province of Belgica Secunda had long ceased to exist.[34] But Remigius was not only flattering Clovis; by presenting him in a Roman light, he was also gently steering him towards a particular view of his command—later in the same letter he encouraged the king (at this date a pagan) to heed the advice of his bishops. The tactic worked; later in his reign Clovis was baptized into the Catholic faith by Remigius himself.

∞

What happened to Germanic culture in the post-Roman West is significantly and radically different from what happened to the culture of the Arabs, after their successful invasion of the Near East and North Africa in the seventh century, and this difference is worth exploring. In many respects the Arab and Germanic conquests look similar—both were carried out predominantly by fierce tribesmen, and both took over the territory of ancient and sophisticated empires. At first Arab rule also resembled that of the post-Roman Germanic states in the West—with a small military elite lording it over a large population that continued to live very much as before.

However, the long-term cultural impact of the Arab invasions was much more radical than that of the Germanic conquerors in the West. As in Gaul, where the conquered indigenous population eventually assumed the identity of 'Franks', so in the Near East and North Africa almost everyone eventually became an 'Arab'. But, in so doing, they also adopted both the religion and the language of the conquerors, Islam and Arabic. It is as though the people of Gaul, the ancestors of the French, had adopted the paganism and the Germanic language of the Franks. One reason for this difference must lie in the fact that the Arab conquerors, though few in number, entered the empire under the banner of a new religion whose sacred text was in Arabic. This religion then proved itself both right and powerful, by giving the Arabs stunning victories over both the Persians and the East Romans. In these circumstances, the Arabs were not going to convert to Christianity, nor were they going to abandon their language, although they were very happy to adopt other sophisticated features of east-Roman life, exemplified by the mosaiced and marbled dwellings of their rulers. Islam and Arabic remained at the core of the conquerors' identity, so it was those amongst the conquered native population who wished to become 'Arabs' who had to change their religion and their language.

Unlike the Arabs, the Germanic invaders entered the empire with a highly flexible cultural identity. It was possible for a Frank to be very much a Frank, while speaking a Latin-based language and worshipping at the shrine of a Gallo-Roman saint like St Martin of Tours. Culturally, the Germanic invaders were very accommodating in the long term. But it is also worth remembering that, when it came to their political identity, it was the Gallo-Romans who eventually had to adjust to becoming 'Franks'. The fusion of peoples that emerged out of the Germanic settlements took centuries to develop, and was something of a compromise—it was not a simple question of the Germanic peoples sinking rapidly and without trace into the Roman subsoil.

ooo

Some of the recent literature on the Germanic settlements reads like an account of a tea party at the Roman vicarage. A shy newcomer to the village, who is a useful prospect for the cricket team, is invited in. There is a brief moment of awkwardness, while the host finds an empty chair and pours a fresh cup of tea; but the conversation, and village life, soon flow on. The accommodation that was reached between invaders and invaded in the fifth- and sixth-century West was very much more difficult, and more interesting, than this. The new arrival had not been invited, and he brought with him a large family; they ignored the bread and butter, and headed straight for the cake stand. Invader and invaded did eventually settle down together, and did adjust to each other's ways—but the process of mutual accommodation was painful for the natives, was to take a very long time, and, as we shall see in Part Two, left the vicarage in very poor shape.

PART TWO

THE END OF A CIVILIZATION

V

THE DISAPPEARANCE
OF COMFORT

I T IS CURRENTLY deeply unfashionable to state that anything like a
'crisis' or a 'decline' occurred at the end of the Roman empire, let alone
that a 'civilization' collapsed and a 'dark age' ensued. The new ortho-
doxy is that the Roman world, in both East and West, was slowly, and
essentially painlessly, 'transformed' into a medieval form. However, there
is an insuperable problem with this new view: it does not fit the mass of
archaeological evidence now available, which shows a startling decline in
western standards of living during the fifth to seventh centuries.[1] This was
a change that affected everyone, from peasants to kings, even the bodies of
saints resting in their churches. It was no mere transformation—it was
decline on a scale that can reasonably be described as 'the end of a
civilization'.

The Fruits of the Roman Economy

The Romans produced goods, including mundane items, to a very high
quality, and in huge quantities; and then spread them widely, through all
levels of society. Because so little detailed written evidence survives for
these humble aspects of daily life, it used to be assumed that few goods
moved far from home, and that economic complexity in the Roman period
was essentially there to satisfy the needs of the state and the whims of the
elite, with little impact on the broad mass of society.[2] However, painstaking work by archaeologists has slowly transformed this picture, through
the excavation of hundreds of sites, and the systematic documentation and
study of the artefacts found on them. This research has revealed a
sophisticated world, in which a north-Italian peasant of the Roman
period might eat off tableware from the area near Naples, store liquids

in an amphora from North Africa, and sleep under a tiled roof. Almost all archaeologists, and most historians, now believe that the Roman economy was characterized, not only by an impressive luxury market, but also by a very substantial middle and lower market for high-quality functional products.[3]

By far the fullest and most telling evidence comes from the study of the different types of pottery found in such abundance on Roman sites: functional kitchenwares, used in the preparation of food; fine table-wares, for its presentation and consumption; and amphorae, the large jars used throughout the Mediterranean for the transport and storage of liquids, such as wine and oil.[4] Pottery reports make for dry reading, but they contain a mass of data that we can readily exploit to shed light on the Roman economy and its impact on daily life. We can tell when and where pots were made, from their shape and fabric, and assess the levels of expertise that went into their manufacture; and we can tell how far they travelled and the status of the consumers who used them, by charting their presence on domestic sites.[5] Furthermore, the picture we can build up for pottery also provides an insight into the production and exchange of other goods, for which much less archaeological evidence survives. Pots, although not normally the heroes of history books, deserve our attention.

Three features of Roman pottery are remarkable, and not to be found again for many centuries in the West: its excellent quality and considerable standardization; the massive quantities in which it was produced; and its widespread diffusion, not only geographically (sometimes being transported over many hundreds of miles), but also socially (so that it reached, not just the rich, but also the poor). In the areas of the Roman world that I know best, central and northern Italy, after the end of the Roman world, this level of sophistication is not seen again until perhaps the fourteenth century, some 800 years later.

The high quality of Roman pottery is very easy to illustrate with pieces of tableware, or indeed kitchenware and amphora, in the hand, but impossible to do justice to on the page, even when words can be backed up by photographs and drawings. Most Roman pottery is light and smooth to the touch, and very tough, although, like all pottery, it shatters if dropped on a hard surface. It is generally made with carefully selected and purified clay, worked to thin-walled and standardized shapes on a fast wheel, and fired in kilns capable of ensuring a consistent finish. With handmade pottery, inevitably there are slight differences between individual vessels of the same design, and occasional minor blemishes. But what strikes the eye and the touch most immediately and most powerfully with Roman pottery is its consistently high quality.

This is not just an aesthetic consideration, but also a practical one. These vessels are solid (brittle, but not friable), they are pleasant and easy to handle (being light and smooth), and, with their hard and sometimes glossy surfaces, they hold liquids well and are easy to wash. Furthermore, their regular and standardized shapes will have made them simple to stack and store. When people today are shown a very ordinary Roman pot, and, in particular, are allowed to handle it, they often comment on how 'modern' it looks and feels, and need to be convinced of its true age.

An impression of modernity is achieved not only by a sophisticated quality and finish, but also by a remarkable consistency between different vessels of the same design. Like many people, I find Roman pottery predictable to the point of being rather dull; but this consistency does have its advantages. A fragment of a Roman pot can very often be matched, with the help of the right manual, to a specific production site at a particular moment in time. This is because thousands of potsherds of identical colour and appearance (down to tiny details) have already been excavated on other sites, some of them in datable contexts. For example, a fragment of pottery discovered on the island of Iona off the Scottish mainland can, despite the apparent implausibility of the link, be attributed with confidence to a sixth-century date and a production site, thousands of miles away by sea, in modern Tunisia.[6] Later, we shall see how such uniformity was achieved.

When considering quantities, we would ideally like to have some estimates for overall production from particular potteries, and for overall consumption at specific settlements. Unfortunately, it is in the nature of the archaeological evidence, which is almost invariably only a sample of what once existed, that such figures will always be elusive. However, no one who has ever worked in the field would question the abundance of Roman pottery, particularly in the Mediterranean region (Fig. 5.1). On Roman settlements (above all urban sites), the labour that archaeologists have to put into the washing, sorting, and storing of potsherds constitutes a high proportion of the total man-hours involved in the initial process of excavation. At the moment of study and publication, the amount of time

5.1 The scale of Roman production and consumption. The industrial container in the corner of this excavation trench at Caesarea (in modern Israel) is full of Roman potsherds.

(and pages) colonized by the pottery rises yet higher. Even the storage of such an abundance can be a major headache. I well remember as a child, sometime around 1960, helping to dump into a river (where they would not pollute the archaeological record) boxes and boxes of Roman pottery recovered in field survey north of Rome, which had simply outgrown the available storage space.[7] Archaeologists collect, wash, mark, sort, store, study, draw, and publish the thousands upon thousands of Roman potsherds discovered in excavation and field survey, and thereby develop a healthy respect for the impressive quantity (and quality) of pottery in circulation in ancient times. Sadly, it is very difficult to translate this experience satisfactorily into the words (let alone numbers) that will convince all others.

Only rarely can we derive any 'real' quantities from deposits of broken pots.[8] However, there is one exceptional dump, which does represent a very large part of a site's total history of consumption, and for which an estimate of quantity has been produced. On the left bank of the Tiber in

Rome, by one of the river ports of the ancient city, is a substantial hill some 50 metres high, Monte Testaccio—'Pottery Mountain' is a reasonable translation into English (Fig. 5.2). It is made up entirely of broken oil amphorae, mainly of the second and third centuries AD and primarily from the province of Baetica in south-western Spain. It has been estimated that Monte Testaccio contains the remains of some 53 million amphorae, in

5.2 The hill near the Tiber, known as Monte Testaccio, which is made up entirely of broken amphorae (some 53 million in all), imported from southern Spain. It is shown here in a view of the city of 1625.

which around six thousand million (6,000,000,000) litres of oil were imported into the city from overseas.[9] Imports into imperial Rome were supported by the full might of the state and were therefore quite exceptional—but the size of operations at Monte Testaccio, and the productivity and complexity that lay behind them, none the less cannot fail to impress. This was a society with similarities to our own—moving goods on a gigantic scale, manufacturing high-quality containers to do so, and occasionally, as here, even discarding them on delivery. Like us, the Romans enjoy the dubious distinction of creating a mountain of good-quality rubbish.[10]

Roman pottery was transported not only in large quantities, but often also over substantial distances. Many Roman pots, in particular amphorae and the fine-wares designed for use at table, could travel hundreds of miles—all over the Mediterranean, and also, as we have seen in the case of a find from Iona, further afield (Fig. 5.4 at p. 98).[11] Other regional products have more limited, but still impressive, distributions (Fig. 5.3). But maps that show the myriad find spots of a particular type of pottery tell only part of the story. For our purposes, when trying to measure the scale and reach of the ancient economy, and the impact of its disappearance, what is more significant than any geographical spread is the access that different levels of society had to good-quality products.

In all but the remotest regions of the empire, Roman pottery of a high standard is common on the sites of humble villages and isolated farmsteads. For example, excavation of a tiny farmstead, in the hills behind the Roman city of Luna in Italy, which was occupied between the second century BC and the first century AD, produced the following range of pottery vessels: the huge storage jars (*dolia*), characteristic of the ancient world; coarse kitchenwares that were probably locally made (for the most part fast-wheel turned, but including some vessels that were hand-shaped); other kitchenwares imported from potteries along the West coast of Italy; amphorae from this same coastal area (with a few sherds also from southern Italy and Africa); and, finally, the fine glossy tablewares of Campania near Naples and of Arezzo in the Arno valley.[12] The amphorae need not have been holding their original contents when they reached this farmstead, so they are not necessarily evidence of the consumption of south-Italian and African wine or oil at this site; but the table- and kitchenwares must have been here in their primary function. The list is not unimpressive for a peasant household.

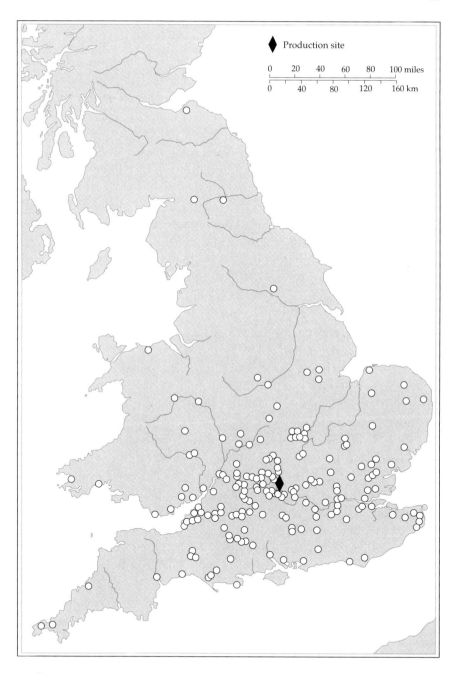

5.3 Regional distribution. The diffusion of pottery manufactured in the third and fourth centuries at a production site just outside modern Oxford.

The Solid Roofs of Antiquity

The picture I have so far presented derives entirely from the evidence of pottery. The sceptic can argue that ceramics play only a minor role in daily life, and that pottery production and distribution are a small part of any economy. This is, however, true only up to a point. Pottery in most cultures is vital in relation to one of our primary needs, food. Ceramic vessels, of different shapes and sizes, play an essential part in the storage, preparation, cooking, and consumption of foodstuffs. They certainly did so in Roman times, even more than they do today, since their importance for storage and cooking has declined considerably in modern times, with the invention of cardboard and plastics, and with the spread of cheap metalware and glass. Furthermore, in the ancient Mediterranean, pottery played a particularly important role, because amphorae, not barrels, were the normal containers for the transport and domestic storage of liquids. There is every reason to see pottery vessels as central to the daily life of Roman times.

I am also convinced that the broad picture that we can reconstruct from pottery can reasonably be applied to the wider economy. Pots are low-value, high-bulk items, with the additional disadvantage of being brittle—in other words, no one has ever made a large profit from making a single pot (except for quite exceptional art objects), and they are difficult and expensive to pack and transport, being heavy, bulky, and easy to break. If, despite these disadvantages, vessels (both fine tablewares and more functional items) were being made to a high standard and in large quantities, and if they were travelling widely and percolating through even the lower levels of society—as they were in the Roman period—then it is much more likely than not that other goods, whose distribution we cannot document with the same confidence, were doing the same. If good-quality pottery was reaching even peasant households, then the same is almost certainly true of other goods, made of materials that rarely survive in the archaeological record, like cloth, wood, basketwork, leather, and metal. There is, for instance, no reason to suppose that the huge markets in clothing, footware, and tools were less sophisticated than that in pottery.

There is also some fascinating recent evidence from the ice cap of Greenland, that seems to confirm, for metalworking, the general picture from pottery, that manufacturing in the Roman period was on a grand scale. Snow, as it descends to earth, collects and traps atmospheric

pollution; in the Arctic it then forms a distinct annual layer, distinguish-
able from that of other years by a partial thaw in the summer and a
subsequent refreezing. By coring into the ice cap and analysing the
samples, it is therefore possible to reconstruct the history of atmospheric
pollution through the ages. This research has shown that lead and copper
pollution—produced by the smelting of lead, copper, and silver—were
both very high during the Roman period, falling back in the post-Roman
centuries to levels that are much closer to those of prehistoric times. Only
in around the sixteenth and seventeenth centuries did levels of pollution
again attain those of Roman times.[13] As with Monte Testaccio, we can pay
the Romans the double-edged compliment of noting their modernity.

Further confirmation for this view can be found in an even humbler
item, which also survives well in the soil but has received less scholarly
attention than pottery—the roof tile. In some parts of the Roman world
tiles were so common that they go almost unnoticed by modern archaeologists. When I thought it would be interesting to compare the use in
Italy of roof tiles in Roman and post-Roman times, I found no general
discussion of the availability of brick and tile in the Roman period. But I
did encounter an unspoken and general assumption that tiles were quite
normal throughout the peninsula, even in out-of-the-way places and in
very humble settings. Archaeologists surveying the countryside around
Gubbio, in the central Italian Apennines, for example, divided the Roman
rural sites they discovered into four categories, depending on the quality
and quantity of their surface remains. Of these categories, the very lowest
type was considered to represent the remains of mere 'sheds'. However,
even these 'sheds', at the very bottom of the building hierarchy and in an
upland area, had tiled roofs. Indeed, in some parts of Italy, a tiled roof, like
good-quality pottery, was already a common feature in pre-Roman times.
For instance, in southern Italy around the Greek city of Metapontion, a
field survey was able to map over 400 ancient farmsteads, discovered from
surface remains, 'above all roof tiles'.[14]

Excavation has confirmed the impression from surface finds that in
ancient Italy even very humble structures often had tiled roofs. The farmstead behind Luna that produced such a diverse range of pottery had a
roof that was at least partly of tiles; while further south, in a remote
Apennine setting (near Campobasso in Molise), an even smaller farmstead, of the second century BC, also had a tiled roof. Even buildings
intended only for storage or for animals may well often have been tiled: a

Roman structure in the hills near Gubbio had a roof of tiles, but is thought to have been only a barn or stable.[15]

Because they are so common, tiles are, as we have seen, taken for granted by archaeologists working in many parts of the Roman world. But, of course, their very frequency is extraordinary, and well worthy of note. Tiles can be made locally in much of the Roman world, but they still require a large kiln, a lot of clay, a great deal of fuel, and no little expertise. After they have been manufactured, carrying them, even over short distances, without the advantages of mechanized transport, is also no mean feat. On many of the sites where they have been found, they can only have arrived laboriously, a few at a time, loaded onto pack animals. The roofs we have been looking at may not seem very important, but they represented a substantial investment in the infrastructure of rural life.

A tiled roof may appeal in part because it is thought to be smart and fashionable, but it also has considerable practical advantages over roofs in perishable materials, such as thatch or wooden shingles. Above all, it will last much longer, and, if made of standardized well-fired tiles, as Roman roofs were, will provide more consistent protection from the rain—with minor upkeep, a tiled roof can function well for centuries; whereas even today a professionally laid thatch roof, of straw grown specifically for its durability, will need to be entirely remade every thirty years or so.[16] A tiled roof is also much less likely to catch fire, and to attract insects, than wooden shingles or thatch. In Roman Italy, indeed in parts of pre-Roman Italy, many peasants, and perhaps even some animals, lived under tiled roofs. After the Roman period, sophisticated conditions such as these did not return until quite recent times: as with good-quality pottery, I suspect it is only in late medieval Italy that tiles again became as common as they had been in the Roman period.

How was such Sophistication Achieved?

Because I am particularly interested in the impact of economic change on daily life, I have concentrated so far on Roman artefacts at the consumer end—the range and quality of the products available, and the type of person who might have access to them. However, to believe in the impressive picture I have outlined, we need also to look briefly at production and distribution. Again it is pottery that provides our most complete and convincing evidence. An influential study by the archaeologist David Peacock, which combined archaeological evidence with modern ethnographic data, divided Roman pottery production into a number of different categories: at its simplest, 'household production', characterized by a rough appearance and very basic technology (without the use of a wheel or kiln); 'workshop industries', making kiln-fired, good-quality, wheel-turned pottery; and, finally, some 'giant fine-ware producers', whose output can reasonably be termed 'industrial' in scale.[17] Both workshop industries and the giant producers required skilled, specialist labour; and, to survive, had to sell their goods in quantity, often over substantial distances.

These different types of production coexisted, in various combinations and proportions, within the Roman world. For instance, whereas in the Mediterranean the 'industrial' producers dominated the market for tablewares, in later Roman Britain, pottery was primarily made by smaller workshop industries, with a regional (though sometimes not inconsiderable) distribution (Fig. 5.3, at p. 93). But in neither Britain nor the Mediterranean did these more sophisticated products entirely displace simple 'household production'.

Unsurprisingly, it is the really large Roman pottery industries that produce the most striking evidence of complex and sophisticated production methods. The best evidence of all comes from the potteries that flourished between AD 20 and 120 at la Graufesenque, near Millau, in what was then southern Gaul. Like the fine tablewares of other giant producers, pots from la Graufesenque were distributed very widely through the empire, and indeed even beyond it (Fig. 5.4). But, in this case, we are also fortunate to have some telling evidence excavated at the production site itself, in particular, a large number of graffiti scratched onto broken potsherds. One group of these almost certainly records the stacking of huge communal kilns on behalf of different individual workshops, so that each could recover their own vessels at the end of the firing (Fig. 7.9, at p. 161). Independent workshops were shaping and decorating their own pots—though to common designs—and were then pooling the costs and expertise needed for the vital and technically difficult process of firing.[18]

More impressive still are the contents of a deep refuse pit from the same site (Fig. 5.5). This contained the remains of about 10,000 vessels, over 1,000 of them undamaged when excavated. These were rejected 'seconds' (some of them with a hole deliberately punched through their base, to prevent them from slipping into circulation), which did not quite match

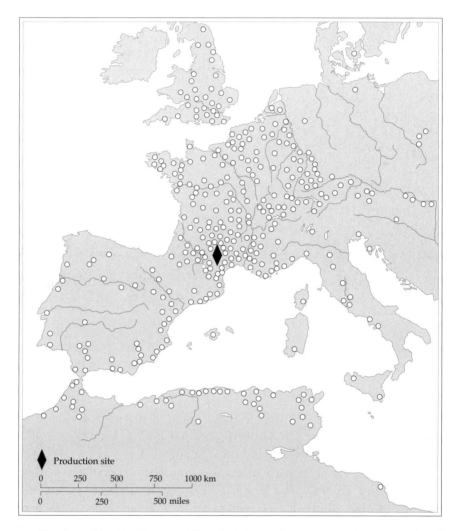

5.4 Empire-wide distribution. The diffusion of one type of mass-produced Roman pottery—find spots of the tableware manufactured at la Graufesenque (near Millau in southern France).

the standards expected, and which the potters at la Graufesenque discarded in order to maintain the quality and consistency of their product.[19] Their pride in these features, and the premium that consumers would place on their wares, is also suggested by the prominent makers' stamps that many south-Gaulish vessels bear (from la Graufesenque and elsewhere). It is not

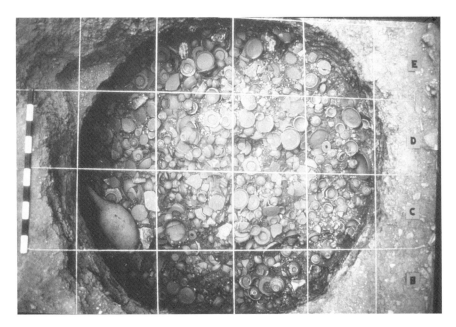

5.5 Quality control. A refuse pit at the pottery-production site of la Graufesenque. The pit was about 3 metres deep and 2.3 metres in diameter, and (as is clear from the photograph) filled with pottery 'seconds', discarded as substandard.

too fanciful to see these stamps as a guarantee of quality and status, like 'Royal Worcester' or 'Meissen' in a modern context.

In the Mediterranean region, the manufacture of tablewares during imperial times was always dominated by a few major producers, who operated on a similar vast scale, and, presumably, with similar sophistication to that documented at la Graufesenque. In other areas, Roman production was on a smaller scale, such as that exemplified by the various potteries of later Roman Britain, with small kilns, less evidence of quality control, and networks of distribution that are best described as 'regional' (Fig. 5.3, at p. 93).[20] However, even smaller industries will have required considerable skills and some specialization in order to flourish, including, for example: the selection and preparation of clays and decorative slips; the making and maintenance of tools and kilns; the primary shaping of the vessels on the wheel; their refinement when half-dry; their decoration; the collection and preparation of fuel; the stacking and firing of the kilns; and the packing of the finished goods for transport. From unworked clay to finished product, a pot will have passed through many different processes and several different hands, each with its own expert role to play.

To reach the consumer then required a network of merchants and traders, and a transport infrastructure of roads, wagons, and pack animals, or sometimes of boats, ships, river- and sea-ports. How exactly all this worked we will never know, because we have so few written records from the Roman period to document it; but the archaeological testimony of goods spread widely around their region of production, and sometimes further afield, is testimony enough to the fact that complex mechanisms of distribution did exist to link a potter at his kiln with a farmer needing a new bowl to eat from. Occasionally a lucky archaeological find takes us closer to the process, like the discovery of a case of south-Gaulish table-ware still waiting to be unpacked in a shop at Pompeii, or the many wrecks of the Roman period that have been found in the Mediterranean still carefully loaded with their cargoes (Fig. 5.6). Wrecks filled with amphorae are so common that two scholars have recently wondered whether the volume of Mediterranean trade in the second century AD was again matched before the nineteenth century.[21]

∞

I am keen to emphasize that in Roman times good-quality articles were available even to humble consumers, and that production and distribution were complex and sophisticated. In many ways, this is a world like our own; but it is also important to try and be a little more specific. Although this is inevitably a guess, I think we are looking at a world that is roughly comparable, in terms of the range and quality of goods available, to that of the thirteenth to fifteenth centuries, rather than at a mirror image of our own times. The Roman period was not characterized by the consumer frenzy and globalized production of the modern developed world, where mechanized production and transport, and access to cheap labour overseas, have produced mountains of relatively inexpensive goods, often manufactured thousands of miles away.

In Roman times machines still played only a relatively small part in manufacture, restricting the quantity of goods that could be made; and everything was transported by humans and animals, or, at best, by the wind and the currents. Consequently, goods imported from a distance were inevitably more expensive and more prestigious than local products.

5.6 Roman transport: a shipwreck, loaded with amphorae, under excavation off the south coast of France.

A seventh-century bishop of Alexandria in Egypt, for instance, reinforced his reputation for asceticism by consistently refusing to drink wine imported from Palestine, preferring to consume a local vintage, although 'its taste is nothing to boast of and its price is low'.[22] Although some goods travelled remarkable distances, the majority of consumption was certainly local and regional—Roman pottery, for instance, is always much commoner near its production site than in more distant areas. What is striking, however, from the archaeological evidence, is how many people were able to buy at least a few of the more expensive products from afar.

Making and Moving Goods for the State

Whether all this production and distribution were motivated primarily by the desire for profit, or generated by the needs of the state, has been the source of much debate amongst historians. A consensus in the 1960s, that the state was the prime mover in the Roman economy, has been challenged—in my opinion successfully—by an explosion of archaeological work, uncovering goods and patterns of distribution that are impossible, or at least very difficult, to explain in terms of state activity. For example, it would take a lot of special pleading to see, in the distribution map of 'Oxford ware' pottery within late Roman Britain (as shown in Fig. 5.3, at p. 93), a pattern of production for the Roman state: the area where the potteries were sited played no role in the administration of Britannia, and it is on domestic sites in the demilitarized south of the province that the vast majority of Oxford ware is found. The pattern that the find spots of this pottery form looks straightforwardly commercial, with a fairly even spread of goods around the kiln sites, falling off with distance and hence increased transport costs.[23]

However, even if many, myself included, would now choose to prioritize the role of the merchant over that of the state, no one would want to deny that the impact of state distribution was also considerable. Monte Testaccio alone testifies to a massive state effort with a wide impact: on Spanish olive-growers; on amphora-manufacturers; on shippers; and, of course, on the consumers of Rome itself, who thereby had their supply of olive oil guaranteed. The needs of the imperial capitals, like Rome and Constantinople, and of an army of around half a million men, stationed mainly on the Rhine and Danube and on the frontier with Persia, were very considerable, and the impressive structures that the Roman state set up to supply them are at least partially known from written records. We have, for instance, a list from around AD 400 of the imperial manufactories (*fabricae*), making goods specifically for the use of state employees.[24] They were scattered through the empire (though most were located within comparatively easy reach of the frontiers, where the army was based), and they produced above all clothing and weaponry. In northern Italy, for example, there were *fabricae* for woollen cloth at Milan and Aquileia, for linen at

Ravenna, for shields at Cremona and Verona, for body armour at Mantua, for bows at Pavia, and, finally, for arrows at Concordia. The sheer number of these *fabricae* is impressive; but considerable administrative coordination must also have been required to collect, transport, and distribute their disparate finished products. Somehow an archer facing the barbarians across the Rhine had to be united with his bow from Pavia and his arrows from Concordia, as well as his socks from Milan or Aquileia.

The distributive activities of the state and of private commerce have sometimes been seen as in conflict with each other; but in at least some circumstances they almost certainly worked together to mutual advantage. For instance, the state coerced and encouraged shipping between Africa and Italy, and built and maintained the great harbour works at Carthage and Ostia, because it needed to feed the city of Rome with huge quantities of African grain. But these grain ships and facilities were also available for commercial and more general use. In the case of some products, the link with this state grain trade was almost certainly a close one. At least some of the fine African pottery, which dominated the market for tablewares in the late Roman West, probably travelled out of Carthage as far as Rome, as a secondary cargo in the ships carrying grain for the imperial capital; and more of it probably travelled because African shippers had state privileges, which enabled them to move goods at a lower cost. One remarkable example of the symbiotic relationship that could exist between state and commercial distribution is found in the Italian-made bricks used frequently in buildings of early imperial times in Carthage. Moving bricks hundreds of miles overseas does not normally make commercial sense—presumably these Italian bricks reached Africa because empty grain ships were unstable without ballast, and this was a ballast that could turn a small profit.[25]

The state, and commercial enterprise, both created their own sophisticated networks of production and distribution, sometime with a close relationship between the two. Indeed from the point of view of the consumer, who is the main focus of my interest, it matters little whether an African dish reached him by way of private enterprise, by way of the state, or by way of a bit of both. What matters is that the ancient world had an array of complex structures in place, which somehow got a high-quality dish from Africa to its provincial user.

The state may also have encouraged private commerce in more subtle ways. For instance, the first- and second-century finds from the fortress of

Vindolanda on Hadrian's Wall are remarkable, not only for their state of preservation, but also for the rich variety of objects to which they testify. Letters and lists survive from Vindolanda that make it clear that a plethora of objects, often dispatched from elsewhere, were in routine use by the soldiery and their families. One letter, for instance, refers to the sending of socks, sandals, and underpants; another to the dispatch of wooden articles, ranging from bed boards to cart axles. The shoes that have been recovered from this site range from standard but solid military boots, doubtless army issue, to a delicately shaped woman's slipper, probably the property of the camp commander's wife, which is prominently stamped with its maker's name—the equivalent, surely, in both style and status to a modern Gucci shoe. It has rightly been suggested that this fortress, in the remotest part of a distant province of the empire, served as a beacon of Mediterranean sophistication in a consumer darkness. In defending the north of Britain, the state brought in, not only soldiers with money in their pockets, but also a mass of solidly made objects, and a tempting display of southern consumer culture.[26]

The End of Complexity

In the post-Roman West, almost all this material sophistication disappeared. Specialized production and all but the most local distribution became rare, unless for luxury goods; and the impressive range and quantity of high-quality functional goods, which had characterized the Roman period, vanished, or, at the very least, were drastically reduced. The middle and lower markets, which under the Romans had absorbed huge quantities of basic, but good-quality, items, seem to have almost entirely disappeared.

Pottery, again, provides us with the fullest picture.[27] In some regions, like the whole of Britain and parts of coastal Spain, all sophistication in the production and trading of pottery seems to have disappeared altogether: only vessels shaped without the use of the wheel were available, without any functional or aesthetic refinement. In Britain, most pottery was not only very basic, but also lamentably friable and impractical (Fig. 5.7). In other areas, such as the north of Italy, some solid wheel-turned pots continued to be made and some soapstone vessels imported, but decorated tablewares entirely, or almost entirely, disappeared; and, even amongst kitchenwares, the range of vessels being manufactured was

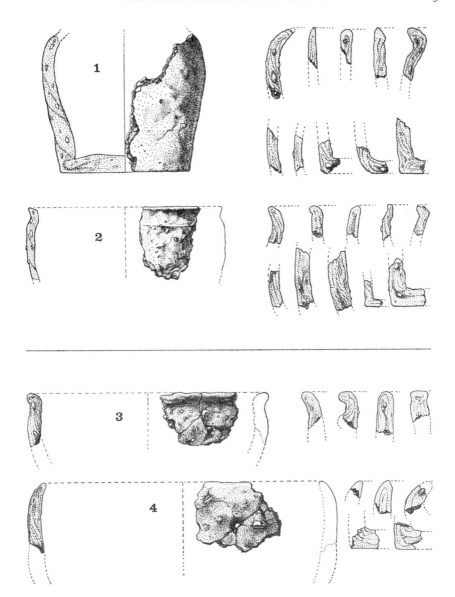

5.7 Pottery fit for a king? Sixth- and seventh-century pots from Yeavering, a rural palace of the Anglo-Saxon kings of Northumbria. The vessels were hand-shaped, out of poorly processed clay, and were only lightly fired (so that they are very friable).

gradually reduced to only a very few basic shapes. By the seventh century, the standard vessel of northern Italy was the *olla* (a simple bulbous cooking pot), whereas in Roman times this was only one vessel type in an impressive *batterie de cuisine* (jugs, plates, bowls, serving dishes, mixing and grinding bowls, casseroles, lids, amphorae, and others).

In some limited areas, the story of pottery production in the post-Roman centuries is more complex and sophisticated, but always within an overall context of unmistakable and marked decline. The great tableware producers of Roman North Africa continued to make (and export) their wares throughout the fifth and sixth centuries, and indeed into the latter half of the seventh. But the number of pots exported and their distribution became gradually more-and-more restricted—both geographically (to sites on the coast, and eventually, even there, only to a very few privileged centres like Rome), and socially (so that African pottery, once ubiquitous, by the sixth century is found only in elite settlements).[28] Furthermore, the range of vessel forms and their quality also gradually declined. From my own experience of excavating in the port town of Luna in northern Italy, I know that, while sherds of third- and fourth-century African pottery are two a penny on the site, fragments of sixth-century vessels are rare enough to be exciting.

Some regional potteries also survived into post-Roman times. For instance, in southern Italy and the Rhineland wheel-turned pottery of a practical nature, sometimes decorated with features like incised combing or red paint, continued to be made and distributed quite widely through the fifth, sixth, and seventh centuries. But even these products display neither the high quality of many earlier Roman wares, nor the range of vessel types once available. There is no area of the post-Roman West that I know of where the range of pottery available in the sixth and seventh centuries matches that of the Roman period, and in most areas the decline in quality is startling.

Furthermore, it was not only quality and diversity that declined; the overall quantities of pottery in circulation also fell dramatically. This fact is very difficult to demonstrate conclusively; but it will be familiar to anyone who has worked on a post-Roman site—mountains of Roman pottery are reduced to a few interesting but unassuming boxes of post-Roman sherds. In both excavation and field survey, while Roman pottery is so abundant that it can be a positive nuisance, post-Roman wares of any kind are almost invariably very scarce.

Within this generally bleak picture there were a few islands of greater sophistication. The seventh- and eighth-century city of Rome has recently been shown to have had a ceramic history considerably more complex than that of most of the West. Rome continued to import amphorae and table-wares from Africa even in the late seventh century, and it was here, in the eighth century, that one of the very first medieval glazed wares was developed. These features are impressive, suggesting the survival within the city of something close to a Roman-style ceramic economy. But, even in this exceptional case, a marked decline from earlier times is evident, if we look at overall quantities. The post-Roman imports are known primar-ily from a rubbish dump of this period, excavated on the site of the ancient Crypta Balbi in the centre of the city, which produced around 100,000 seventh-century potsherds, including some African tableware and the remains of an estimated 500 imported amphorae.[29] For the post-Roman West, this is a very impressive deposit of pottery—so far unparalleled anywhere else in its size and its diversity—and it points to a continuity of trans-Mediterranean trade into the late seventh century, which was unsuspected until recently. But it also needs to be put into perspective. Imports on this scale and of this diversity would be wholly unremarkable even in a provincial city of Roman times, and 500 amphorae is probably a little less than half the load of one seventh-century cargo ship.[30]

Furthermore, the Crypta Balbi dump was almost certainly produced by a rich monastery, whose inhabitants belonged to the city's elite. On the evidence that we have at present, during the sixth and seventh centuries, even in Rome high-quality pottery and imported amphorae were available only to the rich: what had once been widely diffused products had become luxury items. For instance, the survey of a massive swathe of countryside immediately north of Rome discovered large quantities of imported tablewares of the Roman period, on humble as well as aristocratic sites; but almost none, on any site, from the sixth and seventh centuries.[31] Even in the few places, like Rome, where pottery imports and production remained exceptionally buoyant, the middle and lower markets for good-quality goods, which were such a feature of earlier times, had wholly disappeared.

This picture of western decline in the manufacture and availability of pottery is placed in sharp relief by the totally different story of what happened in the fifth- and sixth-century East. Here, the fourth, fifth, and sixth centuries saw the appearance and diffusion of new tablewares, manufactured in Cyprus and Phocaea (in the north-west of modern Turkey), and of new types of amphora, to transport the wine and oil of different areas of the Levant and Aegean. These products are found in large quantities throughout the eastern Mediterranean, even on comparatively humble rural sites, and were also exported westwards to Africa and beyond. On this evidence, the fifth- and sixth-century East resembled the West of earlier Roman times, rather than its much bleaker contemporary situation. These very different histories in East and West raise the obvious question of why such a divergence had occurred—an issue I shall address in the next chapter.

∞

The evidence of other products reinforces the picture of western decline provided by pottery. For instance, in Britain—as ever an extreme case—every one of the building crafts introduced by the Romans, the mundane as well as the luxury ones, disappeared completely during the fifth century. There is no evidence whatsoever of the continued quarrying of building stone, nor of the preparation of mortar, nor of the manufacture and use of bricks and tiles. All new buildings in the fifth and sixth centuries, whether in Anglo-Saxon or unconquered British areas, were either of wood and other perishable materials or of drystone walling, and all were roofed in wood or thatch.

In Northumbria at the very end of the seventh century, a reforming abbot, Benedict Biscop, wished to build churches 'in the Roman manner' at his newly founded monasteries of Jarrow and Monkwearmouth—in other words, in the mortared stone with which he had become familiar during two pilgrimages to Rome. In order to reintroduce this technology, he brought in artisans from Gaul, including glaziers to decorate the windows (the latter described as 'craftsmen as yet unknown in Britain').[32] The resulting buildings, which survive in part, are tiny by Roman or later medieval standards, and their windows are mere slits in the stonework, but they represent the heroic reintroduction of stone building and glazing into a region that had not seen anything of the kind for about three centuries. In a world of wooden houses, Biscop's solid churches, with their windows of coloured glass, must have been deeply impressive.

In the Mediterranean region, the decline in building techniques and quality was not quite so drastic—what we witness here, as with the history of pottery production, is a dramatic shrinkage, rather than a complete disappearance. Domestic housing in post-Roman Italy, whether in town or countryside, seems to have been almost exclusively of perishable materials. Houses, which in the Roman period had been primarily of stone and brick, disappeared, to be replaced by settlements constructed almost entirely of wood. Even the dwellings of the landed aristocracy became much more ephemeral, and far less comfortable: archaeologists, despite considerable efforts, have so far failed to find any continuity into the late-sixth and seventh centuries of the impressive rural and urban houses that had been a ubiquitous feature of the Roman period—with their solid walls, and marble and mosaic floors, and their refinements such as under-floor heating and piped water. At present it seems that in Italy only kings and bishops continued to live in such Roman-style comfort.[33]

A limited tradition of building in mortared stone and brick did survive in Italy and elsewhere, primarily for the construction of churches, but it was on a scale that was dwarfed by the standing buildings of the Roman period (Fig. 7.4, at p. 149). Furthermore, as far as we can tell, even when stone and brick were used, the vast majority of it was not newly quarried or fired, but was second-hand material, only very superficially reshaped to fit its new purpose. In the early medieval churches of Italy, the brickwork has none of the regularity of Roman and later medieval times, and the columns, bases, and capitals were not newly worked, but were ancient marbles reused without any recarving, even if they made up a very disparate set. New carving was restricted to the small marble elements, such as chancel screens, altar canopies, and pulpits, that were the focus of the liturgy.[34]

As with pottery, the change was most complete, and significant, in the lower and middle markets. In the fifth and sixth centuries, tiles, which, as we have seen, had been very widely available in Roman Italy, disappear from all but a few elite buildings.[35] It may have been as much as a thousand years later, perhaps in the fourteenth or fifteenth centuries, that roof tiles again became as readily available and as widely diffused in Italy as they had been in Roman times. In the meantime, the vast majority of the population made do with roofing materials that were impermanent, inflammable, and insect-infested. Furthermore, this change in roofing was not an isolated phenomenon, but symptomatic of a much wider decline in domestic building standards—early medieval flooring, for instance, in all but palaces and churches, seems to have been generally of simple beaten earth.

ooo

It is possible to question the full bleakness of my picture, with drafty timber walls, rotting and leaking roofs, and dirty floors typifying post-Roman housing in both Britain and Italy. There is no absolute rule that says that a thatched roof, or a timber building, is inferior to one of solider materials. Although now a luxury 'heritage' item (because it has to be renewed on a regular basis, at considerable cost), the thatch of modern England works well as a roofing material, and even offers better insulation against heat and cold than tiles or slates; and the timber houses of Scandinavia and north America are as sophisticated and comfortable as any brick building. It is therefore possible to argue that the change that happened at the end of the Roman period, from the use of solid building materials to perishable ones, was not a step backwards into discomfort, as I have portrayed it, but a step sideways into a different way of living, motivated by cultural choice.

Precisely because post-Roman buildings were made of perishable materials, we know very little for certain about what they were really like. They are generally documented only from the holes left in the subsoil by their supporting timbers. Above these holes, depending on our inclinations, it is possible to imagine superstructures of very varying sophistication and complexity (Fig. 5.8). If we want, we can carve the wooden posts, insert wooden floors, and, of course, also fill these imagined superstructures with intricately made objects, like wall hangings and furniture—again all in perishable materials, and hence also absent from the archaeological record. Personally, given the generally very poor quality of post-Roman pottery, the product we can most readily compare with its Roman equivalent, I think that post-Roman houses were, for the most part, pretty basic. But I have to admit that I cannot prove this conclusively.

A World without Small Change

The almost total disappearance of coinage from daily use in the post-Roman West is further powerful evidence of a remarkable change in levels of economic sophistication. In Roman times, a complex and abundant coinage was a standard feature of daily life, in three metals, gold, silver, and copper. Gold and silver pieces, which were of considerable value and therefore seldom casually lost, are rarely found outside hoards. But Roman copper coins are common on archaeological sites in almost all areas of the empire. For instance, excavation of a fairly remote fourth-century

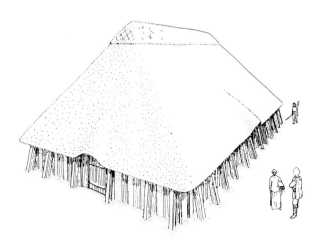

5.8 Elaborately decorated residence, or simple wooden house? Alternative reconstructions, both of which are possible, of the same seventh-century building excavated at Cowdery's Down in Hampshire.

Romano-British farmstead, at Bradley Hill in Somerset, produced seventy-eight copper coins, of which sixty-nine were scattered finds, lost individually by the ancient inhabitants. Finds like these, along with textual evidence, show that coins were readily available and widely used to facilitate economic exchange, at a mundane as well as an elevated level.[36]

In Britain new coins ceased to reach the island, except in tiny quantities, at the beginning of the fifth century. There is, of course, a possibility that the millions of copper coins that were circulating during the fourth century continued in use, and examples of these are indeed sometimes found in post-Roman settlements and burials. However, almost all the later settlements where Roman coins are found had a pre-existing Roman phase, which makes it impossible to know whether these coins were still being used to facilitate exchange, or whether they were inert relics from a former age. If we look at post-Roman sites without an earlier Roman phase, where the possibility of confusion does not exist, scattered coins are either exceedingly rare or not present at all. For example, the large and impressive coastal fortress of Tintagel in Cornwall, a centre of very considerable political and economic importance in the post-Roman fifth and sixth centuries, has produced none of the scattered coins that would demonstrate that they were still in regular use when the settlement was at its height.[37] Tintagel was a site of far greater importance and size than the fourth-century farmstead at Bradley Hill, but it is at Bradley Hill that coins were in everyday use. Like wheel-turned pottery, coinage, once common, had effectively disappeared from fifth- and sixth-century Britain.

In the western Mediterranean, the decline of coinage, as with other items, is less total and less sudden. Many of the new Germanic rulers of the West issued their own gold coins, and some minted also in silver, often closely imitating the currency of the contemporary east-Roman empire (e.g. Fig. 4.1, at p. 69). In Vandal Africa and Ostrogothic Italy, the new regimes also produced coins in copper (e.g. Fig. 4.3, at p. 74). These issues, although very much rarer amongst excavated finds than fourth-century Roman imperial coins, were not insignificant—for instance, it is thought that the large copper coins of late fifth-century Italy were the inspiration for a major reform of the east-Roman coinage some years later. Elsewhere in the West, however, the regular issuing of copper coins had already ceased during the fifth century. The only exceptions known at present are two local copper coinages, both probably of the sixth century:

one minted in the area around Seville in Visigothic Spain; the other in the main entrepôt for Frankish trade with the Mediterranean, Marseille.[38]

Even these coinages disappeared during the sixth century. During the seventh century, new copper coins in the West were minted only in areas ruled by the East Romans (such as Ravenna, Rome, and Sicily). But even these coins must have had only a limited production and circulation, since they are rarely found in excavation (Fig. 5.9A). Evidence of an abundant copper coinage of the seventh and early eighth centuries has so far been found only in one city, Rome, much of it in the form of local 'unofficial' issues—though there are hints that Sicily too may have had substantial numbers of coins in circulation.[39] The overall picture from the West, therefore, is of the use of copper coins becoming scarcer through the fifth and sixth centuries, and minimal by the seventh, though this trend is more gradual and less dramatic in Italy, at least from Rome southwards.

As with pottery, the history of coinage in the eastern Mediterranean is very different. Here new copper coins are common throughout the sixth century, and well into the seventh (Fig. 5.9B–E). In the Aegean region, however, during the seventh century new coins became very scarce, except in Constantinople itself (Fig. 5.9B, C, D). Only further south, in the Levantine provinces, did copper coins continue to be common (Fig. 5.9E).[40] Again these differences call out for explanation, and will be explored in the next chapter.

ooo

There is admittedly no straightforward correlation between the presence or absence of new coins, and levels of economic sophistication. There is, as we have seen, always the possibility that large numbers of older coins continued in circulation, even when new ones were not available; and in the Mediterranean region, unlike in Britain, the presence of Roman coins in later hoards proves beyond doubt that old money could remain in use for centuries. Furthermore, because rulers were under no obligation to mint coins as a service to their subjects, the stimulus behind a new issue may often have been political ambition, and not commercial need. For instance, after his conquest of Ravenna in 751, the Lombard king Aistulf issued a copper coinage of the size and design of the previous Byzantine coins of the city, substituting his own name and bust for that of the emperor.[41] Nowhere else in Italy did the Lombards ever mint in copper.

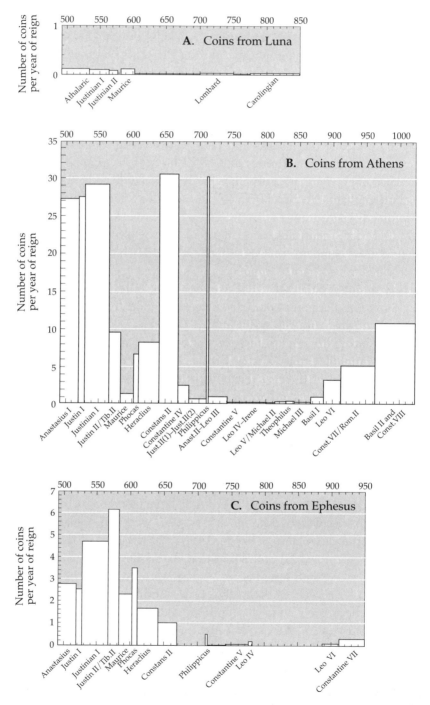

5.9 The availability of small change. Finds of newly minted copper coins (shown as numbers of coins per year) from different sites in the western and eastern Mediterranean: A—the town of Luna (in Liguria, Italy); B—Athens in Greece; C—Ephesus on the Aegean coast of modern Turkey;

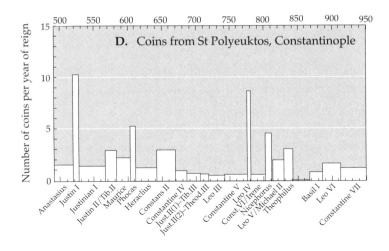

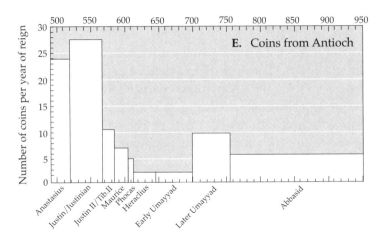

D—Constantinople (specifically, from the excavation of the church of St Poly-euktos); E—Antioch in Syria. (Note that the vertical axis for each histogram is different.)

The Ravenna issue by Aistulf was a one off, and almost certainly an act of ideological bravado, rather than an attempt to meet any real economic need.

However, for a number of reasons, it would be a serious mistake to ignore the information that coin finds can give. Coins offer some considerable advantages as evidence. First, they can usually be closely dated. Secondly, unlike most other artefacts (including pottery), coins have attracted the attention of archaeologists for a very long time; and, as a result, the coin finds from a large number of excavations have been published accurately and in full. With coins, we have available some substantial and reliable databases of evidence, which, with due caution, can readily be compared across the whole area of the former Roman world (as in Fig. 5.9).

Thirdly, coinage is undoubtedly a great facilitator of commercial exchange—copper coins, in particular, for small transactions. In the absence of coinage, raw bullion for major purchases, and barter for minor ones, can admittedly be much more sophisticated than we might initially suppose.[42] But barter requires two things that coinage can circumvent: the need for both sides to know, at the moment of agreement, exactly what they want from the other party; and, particularly in the case of an exchange that involves one party being 'paid back' in the future, a strong degree of trust between those who are doing the exchanging. If I want to exchange one of my cows for a regular supply of eggs over the next five years, I can do this, but only if I trust the chicken-farmer. Barter suits small face-to-face communities, in which trust either already exists between parties, or can be readily enforced through community pressure. But it does not encourage the development of complex economies, where goods and money need to circulate impersonally. In a monied economy, I can exchange my cow for coins, and only later, and perhaps in a distant place, decide when and how to spend them. I need only trust the coins that I receive.

The pattern of availability or absence of copper coins does coincide closely with the picture of receding economic complexity provided by other data: of a decline that hit the northern provinces of the empire around AD 400; but which did not touch the eastern Mediterranean until some 200 years later; and which even then did not affect the Arab Levant and Egypt. It is striking that, within this broad pattern, there are three local issues of copper coins in the West, all of them in areas where we have reasons to suppose that a somewhat more sophisticated economy survived:

sixth-century south-western Spain, at the heart of the Visigothic kingdom; sixth-century Marseille, the gateway port for the Frankish kingdoms; and seventh- and early eighth-century papal Rome. The few regions that still needed copper coins produced them; their absence elsewhere must be symptomatic of a western economy that had changed dramatically from Roman times.

A Return to Prehistory?

The economic change that I have outlined was an extraordinary one. What we observe at the end of the Roman world is not a 'recession' or—to use a term that has recently been suggested—an 'abatement', with an essentially similar economy continuing to work at a reduced pace. Instead what we see is a remarkable qualitative change, with the disappearance of entire industries and commercial networks. The economy of the post-Roman West is not that of the fourth century reduced in scale, but a very different and far less sophisticated entity.[43]

This is at its starkest and most obvious in Britain. A number of basic skills disappeared entirely during the fifth century, to be reintroduced only centuries later. Some of these, such as the technique of building in mortared stone or brick, can perhaps be seen as products of specifically Roman styles of display, and therefore peculiarly susceptible to political and cultural change. But for other crafts, explanations in terms of cultural change, rather than economic decline, are impossible to uphold. All over Britain the art of making pottery on a wheel disappeared in the early fifth century, and was not reintroduced for almost 300 years. The potter's wheel is not an instrument of cultural identity. Rather, it is a functional innovation that facilitates the rapid production of thin-walled ceramics; and yet it disappeared from Britain. Presumably, though I would be the first to admit that it is hard to credit, this was because there were no longer enough consumers around to sustain any specialized potting.

Sophistication in production and exchange did survive in post-Roman Britain, but only at the very highest levels of society and the highest level of artefacts. In the early seventh century an East Anglian ruler was buried at Sutton Hoo with an extraordinarily rich and exotic accompaniment of treasure: silver and copper dishes from the eastern Mediterranean; an enamelled bronze bowl, probably from West Britain; some splendid weaponry, some of it perhaps from Scandinavia; gold coins from the

Frankish kingdoms; and some wonderful native gold jewellery, incorporating garnets and millefiore glasswork from the Continent (or, possibly, from even further afield). The jewellery, which was certainly made in Anglo-Saxon Britain, displays levels of craftsmanship and design that are extraordinarily accomplished and sophisticated (Fig. 5.10 above). But these are all rare elite items, made or imported for the highest levels of society. At this level, beautiful objects were still being made, and traded or gifted across long distances. What had totally disappeared, however, were the good-quality, low-value items, made in bulk, and available so widely in the Roman period. An object from the Sutton Hoo ship burial that attracts very little attention in its British Museum showcase speaks volumes: the pottery bottle (Fig. 5.10 below). In the context of seventh-century East Anglia, it was almost certainly a high-status item, imported from abroad (since it was shaped on a wheel, at a time when all pottery in Britain was hand-formed). But in any context of the Roman period, even a rural peasant context, it would be entirely unremarkable, or notable only for its porous fabric and rough finish. The economy that sustained and supplied a massive middle and lower market for low-value functional goods had disappeared, leaving sophisticated production and exchange only for a tiny number of high-status objects.[44]

It may initially be hard to believe, but post-Roman Britain in fact sank to a level of economic complexity well below that of the pre-Roman Iron Age. Southern Britain, in the years before the Roman conquest of AD 43, was importing quantities of Gaulish wine and Gaulish pottery; it had its own native pottery industries with regional distribution of their wares; it even had native silver coinages, which may well have been used to facilitate exchange, as well as for purposes of prestige and gift-giving.[45] The settlement pattern of later iron-age Britain also reflects emerging economic complexity, with substantial coastal settlements, like Hengistbury in modern Hampshire, which were at least partly dependent on trade. None of these features can be found reliably in fifth- and sixth-century post-Roman Britain. It is really only in about AD 700, three centuries after the disintegration of the Romano-British economy, that southern Britain crawled back to the level of economic complexity found in the pre-Roman Iron Age, with evidence of pots imported from the Continent, the first substantial and wheel-turned Anglo-Saxon pottery industry (at Ipswich), the striking of silver coins, and the emergence of coastal trading towns, such as Hamwic (Saxon Southampton) and London.[46] All these features

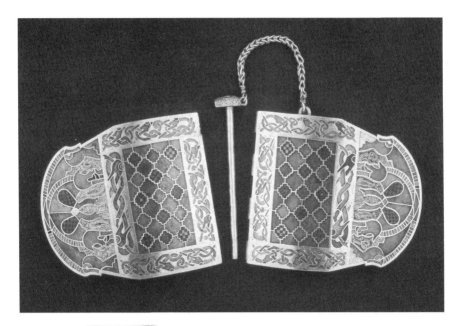

5.10 The decline of low-value products. Above, one of two gold shoulder-clasps, decorated with glass and garnets; and, below, a pottery bottle. Both were buried with an East Anglian king at Sutton Hoo in around AD 625.

were new, or only just beginning, in around AD 700; but all had existed in southern Britain during the pre-Roman Iron Age.

In the western Mediterranean, the economic regression was by no means as total as it was in Britain. As we have seen, some trade, some trading towns, some coinage, and some local and regional industries persisted throughout the post-Roman centuries. But it must be remembered that in the Mediterranean world the level of economic complexity and sophistication reached in the Roman period was very considerably higher than anything ever attained in Britain. The fall in economic complexity may in fact have been as remarkable as that in Britain; but, since in the Mediterranean it started from a much higher point, it also bottomed out at a higher level. If, as we have done for Britain, we compare pre-Roman and post-Roman Mediterranean economies, in some areas at least a very similar picture can be found to that sketched out above—of a regression, taking the economy way below levels of complexity reached in the pre-Roman period. In southern and central Italy, for example, both the Greek colonies and the Etruscan territories have provided much more evidence of trade and sophisticated native industries than can be found in post-Roman Italy. The pre-Roman past, in the temples of Agrigento and Paestum, the tombs of Cerveteri and Tarquinia, and a mass of imported and native pottery and jewellery, has left enough material remains to serve as a major tourist attraction. The same cannot be said of the immediately post-Roman centuries.

The case of central and southern Italy raises a very important point. The complex system of production and distribution, whose disappearance we have been considering, was an older and more deeply rooted phenomenon than an exclusively 'Roman' economy. Rather, it was an 'ancient' economy that in the eastern and southern Mediterranean was flourishing long before Rome became at all significant, and that even in the northwestern Mediterranean was developing steadily before the centuries of Roman domination. It is true that in some distant northern provinces— the interior of the Balkans, northern Gaul, the Rhineland, and Britain— Roman power and economic complexity were more or less chronologically coterminous. But, even in these regions, as we have seen in looking at iron-age Britain, the result of the Roman conquest was perhaps more to intensify older developments than completely to change the direction of economic life. What was destroyed in the post-Roman centuries, and then only very slowly re-created, was a sophisticated world with very deep roots indeed. How could such a remarkable change have happened?

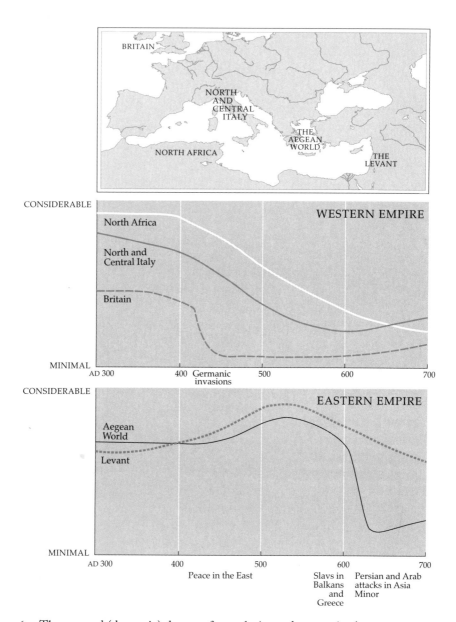

6.1 The ups and (dramatic) downs of complexity and prosperity, between AD 300 and AD 700, in five regions of the Roman world: Britain; northern and central Italy; the Roman provinces of central North Africa; the islands and coastal provinces of the Aegean; and the 'Levant' (the region between modern Turkey to the north, and Egypt to the south).

VI

WHY THE DEMISE
OF COMFORT?

W<small>E WILL NEVER</small> know precisely why the sophisticated economy that had developed under the Romans unravelled. The archaeological evidence, which is all we really have, can tell us what happened, and when; but on its own cannot provide explanations as to why change occurred. A friable Anglo-Saxon hand-shaped pot is eloquent testimony to a dramatic fall in living standards, but it cannot tell us what had destroyed the industries that only a few decades earlier had spread high-quality wares throughout southern Britain. However, what we can do is chart the progress of decline against other known events and changes in the Roman world, to see whether there are any likely connections.

Patterns of Change

There was no single moment, nor even a single century of collapse. The ancient economy disappeared at different times and at varying speeds across the empire. If, for the sake of simple and ready comparison, we show this process in graph form for five separate regions of the empire—from Roman complexity in around AD 300, to the dramatically simpler world of around 700—we can immediately see substantial differences, but also some similarities, between what happened in different areas (Fig. 6.1). Inevitably, this graph is a gross simplification of a mass of difficult, and sometimes disputed, archaeological evidence, but I hope the basic patterns that I have shown are reasonably close to the evidence currently available, and therefore more helpful than harmful.[1]

There is general agreement that Roman Britain's sophisticated economy disappeared remarkably quickly and remarkably early. There may already have been considerable decline in the later fourth century, but, if so, this was a recession, rather than a complete collapse: new coins were still in widespread use and a number of sophisticated industries still active. In the early fifth century all this disappeared, and, as we have seen in the previous chapter, Britain reverted to a level of economic simplicity similar to that of the Bronze Age, with no coinage, and only hand-shaped pots and wooden buildings.[2]

Further south, in the provinces of the western Mediterranean, the change was much slower and more gradual, and is consequently difficult to chart in detail. But it would be reasonable to summarize the change in both Italy and North Africa as a slow decline, starting in the fifth century (possibly earlier in Italy), and continuing on a steady downward path into the seventh. Whereas in Britain the low point had already been reached in the fifth century, in Italy and North Africa it probably did not occur until almost two centuries later, at the very end of the sixth century, or even, in the case of Africa, well into the seventh.[3]

Turning to the eastern Mediterranean, we find a very different story. The best that can be said of any western province after the early fifth century is that some regions continued to exhibit a measure of economic complexity, although always within a broad context of decline. By contrast, throughout almost the whole of the eastern empire, from central Greece to Egypt, the fifth and early sixth centuries were a period of remarkable expansion. We know that settlement not only increased in this period, but was also prosperous, because it left behind a mass of newly built rural houses, often in stone, as well as a rash of churches and monasteries across the landscape (Fig. 6.2). New coins were abundant and widely diffused (Fig. 5.9B–E, at pp. 114–15), and new potteries, supplying distant as well as local markets, developed on the west coast of modern Turkey, in Cyprus, and in Egypt. Furthermore, new types of amphora appeared, in which the wine and oil of the Levant and of the Aegean were transported both within the region, and outside it, even as far as Britain and the upper Danube. If we measure 'Golden Ages' in terms of material remains, the fifth and sixth centuries were certainly golden for most of the eastern Mediterranean, in many areas leaving archaeological traces that are more numerous and more impressive than those of the earlier Roman empire.[4]

In the Aegean, this prosperity came to a sudden and very dramatic end in the years around AD 600.[5] Great cities such as Corinth, Athens,

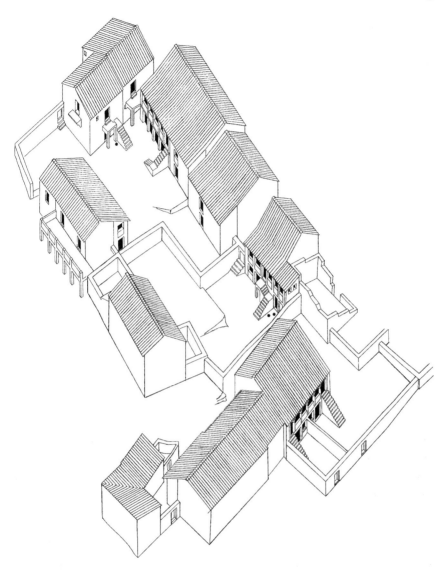

6.2 Farmers' houses of the fourth to sixth centuries, in the north Syrian village of
Déhès. The walls are of carefully squared local limestone, and have often survived
to their full height; the roofs, which have fallen in, are known from excavation to
have been tiled. In plan and size, these are quite humble structures, the dwellings
of very 'ordinary' farmers, with animals and storage below, and a couple of rooms
for the humans above. But their solidity and functional comfort are impressive,
and they must have been made by professional builders—hundreds of similar
houses survive, some reroofed and reoccupied in modern times.

Ephesus, and Aphrodisias, which had dominated the region since long before the arrival of the Romans, shrank to a fraction of their former size—the recent excavations at Aphrodisias suggest that the greater part of the city became in the early seventh century an abandoned ghost town, peopled only by its marble statues.[6] The tablewares and new coins, which had been such a prominent feature of the fifth and sixth centuries, disappeared with a suddenness similar to the experience of Britain some two centuries earlier (Fig. 5.9B, C at p. 114). It is possible, for instance, that in parts of seventh-century Greece only rough hand-shaped pottery was in use.[7] The imperial capital, Constantinople, may have been the only exception to this generally bleak picture. Here, for instance, new copper coins continued to be produced and to be used (Fig. 5.9D), and a new glazed tableware was developed during the seventh century to replace the fine-wares of earlier times. But even Constantinople shrank dramatically in both wealth and population from the booming centre of perhaps half-a-million people of the years around AD 500. Seventh-century Constantinople still stood out as a great city; but this was mainly thanks to buildings from its past, and because the other great cities of the Aegean, like Ephesus, had declined even more calamitously.[8]

By AD 700 there was only one area of the former Roman world that had not experienced overwhelming economic decline—the provinces of the Levant, and neighbouring Egypt, conquered by the Arabs in the 630s and 640s. Here sophisticated potteries continued to flourish at centres like Jerash (in modern Jordan), and new copper coins were produced in quantity (Fig. 5.9E, at p. 115). Even on an inland village site, Déhès in northern Syria, copper coins and good-quality pottery were still common items throughout the seventh and eighth centuries—whereas in the contemporary Aegean and western Mediterranean they had more or less disappeared from use, even in major trading cities. In Arab Baysān, ancient Scythopolis (in modern Israel), a section of porticoed shopping street was completely rebuilt in the second quarter of the eighth century by order of the Caliph, who recorded his work in two elegant mosaic inscriptions, with Arabic letters of gold tesserae set against a deep-blue background: 'In the name of Allāh, the Compassionate, the Merciful, Hishām, servant of Allāh, Commander of the faithful, ordered this building to be built . . .' (Fig. 6.3). By Roman standards Hishām's new market building is quite small, but it suggests a level of sophistication and prosperity quite unparalleled in the rundown provinces of the rest of the old empire.[9]

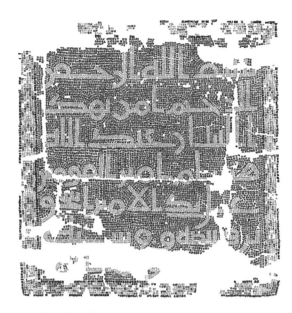

6.3 Early eighth-century porticoed shops in the Arab city of Baysān. The mosaic inscription, set on the front of the building, recorded its construction under the Caliph Hishām in 737/8.

The End of an Empire and the End of an Economy

Even the most cursory glance at my graphs shows that there must have been a close connection between the unravelling of the Roman empire and the disintegration of the ancient economy. This link between economic and political decline has been explored by many historians over the years; but most have concentrated on the period *before* the fall of the empire, in order to explore whether declining prosperity weakened the Roman capacity to resist invasion. This question remains important, and I have discussed it earlier in this book (pp. 41–2). My focus here, however, will be on what happened *after* the invasions began. The evidence available very strongly suggests that political and military difficulties destroyed regional economies, irrespective of whether they were flourishing or already in decline.

The death of complexity in Britain in the early fifth century must certainly have been closely related to the withdrawal of Roman power from the province, since the two things happened at more or less at the same time. The only uncertainties in Britain are whether the later fourth century already saw serious economic problems developing, and exactly how fast change occurred.[10] One of the characteristics of the post-Roman archaeological record, here, and elsewhere, is the disappearance of any closely datable items, such as coins, and, in an archaeological record without chronological pointers, change may seem more rapid than it actually was.

Further south, in the western Mediterranean, decline is much more gradual, and cannot be so obviously and immediately attributed to specific political and military events. My graph for Italy and North Africa shows two straight lines, turning down at the beginning of the fifth century, and thereafter heading slowly but surely downhill, implying an inexorable and steady loss of complexity, which began with the invasion of the West. In truth, the start of economic decline in Africa and Italy cannot yet be fixed with such precision, and its progress, once under way, is also open to debate. It is very possible that descent was, in reality, far from smooth, and characterized by periods of recovery and periods of steep fall.

However, if we look at the broad pattern of decline through the fifth and sixth centuries in both Africa and Italy, and particularly if we then compare this with what was happening in the eastern Mediterranean, a close link between political and economic developments seems unavoidable. In both the Aegean world and the Levant, the economy was expanding in both size and complexity through the fifth and into the sixth century, in other words moving in exactly the opposite direction to that of the West (Fig. 6.1, at p. 122). Politically and militarily, this was a period of unusual peace and stability in the East, except in the troubled north Balkans close to the Danube frontier, a peace that was seriously shattered only by a major Persian invasion in 540. It seems very much more likely than not that the different political and military histories of the East and the West played a decisive role in their divergent economic fortunes.

This supposition is confirmed by what happened in Greece at the end of the sixth century, and in Asia Minor (modern Turkey) during the first half of the seventh. East Roman military power and political control crumbled and almost disappeared, first in Greece, in the face of Slav and Avar invasions; and then in Asia Minor, before Persian and Arab invasions and raiding. In 626, and again in 674–8 and 716–18, even Constantinople itself was besieged. Unlike Rome and the West in the fifth century, the capital city and the rump of its empire survived, but by the skin of their teeth. It cannot be coincidence that during the troubled decades around AD 600, the sophistication of the late-antique Aegean world evaporated.[11]

As we have seen, the only parts of the former Roman world that still look economically developed at the end of the seventh century are the Levantine provinces (and neighbouring Egypt, whose economic history is known primarily from written sources). Yet again this suggests a close connection between stability, on the one hand, and prosperity, on the other—these regions were overrun by the Arabs without prolonged fighting, and until 750 benefited from Arab rule, as the peaceful heartlands of a new empire centred on Damascus.

oOo

All regions, except Egypt and the Levant, suffered from the disintegration of the Roman empire, but distinctions between the precise histories of different areas show that the impact of change varied quite considerably. In Britain in the early fifth century, and in the Aegean world around AD 600, collapse seems to have happened suddenly and rapidly, as though caused by a series of devastating blows. But in Italy and Africa change was much more gradual, as if brought about by the slow decline and death of complex systems.

These different trajectories make considerable sense. The Aegean was hit by repeated invasion and raiding at the very end of the sixth century, and throughout the seventh—first by Slavs and Avars (in Greece), then by Persians (in Asia Minor), and finally by Arabs (on both land and sea). On several occasions, imperial power was limited effectively to the walled area of Constantinople itself; and even this was nearly lost—in 626 the city probably survived a campaign by allied Persian and Avar armies only because the Persians were unable to cross the Bosphorus and help in a joint assault on the walls. A remarkable collection of miracle stories from Thessalonica, the second city of the empire, gives us some idea of the realities of life here during the difficult years of the seventh century. The city was repeatedly besieged by Slavs and Avars, and its territory subjected to periodic raids. According to our source, only the miraculous powers of Saint Demetrius saved Thessalonica from famine and from falling to the enemy.[12] The picture is remarkably similar to that from Noricum 200 years earlier, in the *Life* of Severinus. It is not hard to believe that conditions like these caused economic havoc.

We know much less about exactly what happened inside fifth-century Britain, because the written record is so poor, but just the list of known troublemakers is impressive: Irish raiding and settling in the West; Picts invading from the North; Anglo-Saxons (and others) pushing inland from the South and East; as well as internal warfare between competing sub-Roman kingdoms. In these circumstances, production, transport, and marketing will all have been very seriously affected, as will the all-important spending power of the consumer. Furthermore, in Britain there were very few protracted intervals of calm, in which a recovery could get under way.

By contrast, Italy enjoyed prolonged periods of respite during the fifth and early sixth centuries, and Africa suffered comparatively little from disruption after its conquest by the Vandals in 429–39. It is, therefore, not surprising that we do not see in these regions the vertiginous drop in sophistication documented in fifth-century Britain and the seventh-century Aegean. What probably occurred in Italy and Africa was the slow unwinding of a Mediterranean-wide imperial and commercial system, hurried on its way by particular difficulties—such as the Gothic Wars and Lombard invasions in sixth-century Italy, and Berber raiding in North

Africa.[13] The historian of the Gothic Wars, Procopius, who was an eye-witness to much of the campaigning in Italy, gives us some indication of the harm done here by this fighting. He tells an evocative story of how the Ostrogothic king Theodahad, at the beginning of the wars, sought out a Jewish prophet to tell him how things would work out. The seer took three groups of ten pigs, assigned a group each to the Goths, the invading East Romans, and the native Italians, and shut them up in separate huts for a number of days without food. When the huts were opened, only two pigs in the Gothic hut were still alive, while only a few had died amongst the East Romans. In the Italian hut, half the pigs were dead, and the rest had lost all their bristles. We do not need to believe the literal truth of this story; but Procopius was a witness to the impact of the Gothic Wars in Italy, and his tale must at least have rung true.[14]

Financial and commercial links across the Mediterranean forged during the Roman period (or even earlier) meant that regions like Italy and Africa suffered not only their own parochial troubles, but also, to a more limited extent, from the problems of other areas. Italy's connections with the rest of the Mediterranean were partly based on the peninsula's position as the traditional heart of Roman power—a privilege that inevitably died with the empire. Italy's aristocracy, for instance, lost a great slice of its spending power when Africa fell to the Vandals in 429–39, since many Italian landowners held extensive African estates.[15] According to the *Life* of a pious Italian aristocrat, Melania, who gave away her wealth at the start of the fifth century, one of her African estates, near the small city of Thagaste, was 'larger than the town itself, with a bath-building, many craftsmen (goldsmiths, silversmiths, and coppersmiths), and two bishops, one for our own faith, the other for the heretics'. With the resources from her African properties, Melania and her husband were able to build and support two large monasteries, one for 130 holy virgins, the other for 80 men.[16] Wealth like this was lost to the Italian aristocracy at the Vandal Conquest, which also, of course, deprived Italy and its resident emperor of all the taxes paid by Africa, and of the substantial levy of grain used to feed the city of Rome.

The effect on Africa of the empire's disintegration was less immediate and perhaps mainly commercial. The African provinces during the third and fourth centuries had exported large quantities of fine tablewares and olive oil throughout the western Mediterranean. This trade continued into the fifth and sixth centuries, and indeed into the seventh, and was perhaps never substantially disrupted at its African end. But the quantity of goods exported gradually shrank, until by the seventh century it was only a trickle in comparison to fourth-century levels.[17] This decline is probably best explained in terms of the disintegration of a system of privileged trade, fostered by the empire, and by the gradual impoverishment of consumers on the northern shores of the Mediterranean, badly hit by the insecurity of the fifth and sixth centuries. In good times, close links between the different shores of the Mediterranean brought complexity and wealth; but in bad times, they meant that the problems of one region could have a damaging effect on the prosperity of another.

ooo

The Roman empire had encouraged and facilitated economic development in a number of different ways, both direct and indirect. The Roman state itself ordered the production and distribution of many goods; and, above all, collected and redistributed vast quantities of money raised in taxation. The demise of the state will have hit many areas directly and hard—when, for instance, the professional army along the Rhine and Danube disintegrated during the fifth century, the spending power in the frontier region of tens of thousands of soldiers (salaried with gold from all over the empire) also disappeared, as did the manufactories in areas like northern Italy that had made their equipment. Thereafter soldiers were local men, carrying their own, less extensive equipment—as a fighting force these men may or may not have been as effective as the Roman army, but they were certainly much less significant as a motor of the economy. The effect of the disintegration of the Roman state cannot have been wholly dissimilar to that caused by the dismemberment of the Soviet command economy after 1989. The Soviet structure was, of course, a far larger, more complex, and all-inclusive machine than the Roman. But most of the former Communist bloc has faced the problems of adjustment to a new world in a context of peace, whereas, for the Romans of the West, the end of the state economy coincided with a prolonged period of invasion and civil war.

The emperors also maintained, primarily for their own purposes, much of the infrastructure that facilitated trade: above all a single, abundant, and empire-wide currency; and an impressive network of harbours, bridges, and roads. The Roman state minted coins less for the good of its subjects than to facilitate the process of taxing them; and roads and bridges were repaired mainly in order to speed up the movement of troops and government envoys. But coins in fact passed through the hands of merchants, traders, and ordinary citizens far more often than those of the taxman; and carts and pack animals travelled the roads much more frequently than did the legions.[18] With the end of the empire, investment in these facilities fell dramatically: in Roman times, for instance, there had been a continuous process of upgrading and repairing the road network, commemorated by the erection of dated milestones; there is no evidence that this continued in any systematic way beyond the early sixth century.[19]

Security was undoubtedly the greatest boon provided by Rome. Peace was not constant through the Roman period, being occasionally shattered by civil wars, and in the third century by a serious and prolonged period of Persian and Germanic invasion. However, the 500 years between Pompey's defeat of the pirates in 67 BC and the Vandal seizure of Carthage and its fleet in AD 439 comprise the longest period of peace the Mediterranean sea has ever enjoyed. On land, meanwhile, it is a remarkable fact that few cities of the early empire were walled—a state of affairs not repeated in most of Europe and the Mediterranean until the late nineteenth century, and then only because high explosives had rendered walls ineffective as a form of defence. The security of Roman times provided the ideal conditions for economic growth.

ooo

The dismembering of the Roman state, and the ending of centuries of security, were the crucial factors in destroying the sophisticated economy of ancient times; but there were also other problems that played a subsidiary role. In 541, for instance, bubonic plague reached the Mediterranean from Egypt, and spread inexorably through the former Roman world, reoccurring on several occasions over subsequent decades. The historian Evagrius, a resident of Antioch in Syria, interrupted the flow of his narrative to give an account of how the disease had affected his own family. As a boy, on the plague's first appearance in the empire, he himself had been struck down, but was lucky enough to survive. Later, however, on its return, it was to kill his first wife and several of his children, as well as other members of his wider family. Just two years before writing, when the plague visited Antioch for a fourth time, he lost both his daughter and her son. There is little reason to doubt that this occurrence and recurrence of disease were not just a personal tragedy, for people like

Evagrius, but also a substantial demographic blow to the population of the empire.[20]

It has also been argued recently, on the evidence of both written accounts and of tree-ring data, that for over a year in 536–7 the sun was obscured, perhaps as the result of an asteroid strike, with disastrous consequences for the growing season.[21] Disasters like these certainly did happen, with terrible consequences for many individuals; but it is probably right to see them as subsidiary, rather than primary, causes of the decline of the ancient economy. Acts of God tend to occur in all periods of history, but their effects are generally long-lasting only when an economy is already in trouble. Stable economies can survive intermittent crises, even on a grand scale, because they seldom affect the underlying structures of society.[22] For instance, the Black Death in fourteenth-century England is known to have killed between a third and half the total population, which is an extraordinarily high figure. But it did not destroy the structures of English life, and therefore did not in fact blow later medieval England's economy substantially off course. The Roman world could have recovered from acts of God; what it could not survive were the prolonged troubles of the end of the empire, and the definitive dissolution of the Roman state.

It was, as we have seen, the fifth-century invasions that caused these difficulties, and brought down the ancient economy in the West. However, this does not mean that the death of the sophisticated ancient world was intended by the Germanic peoples. The invaders entered the empire with a wish to share in its high standard of living, not to destroy it; and we have met, earlier in this book, people like the Ostrogoths living in marble palaces, minting imperial-style coins, and being served by highly educated Roman ministers. But, although the Germanic peoples did not intend it, their invasions, the disruption these caused, and the consequent dismembering of the Roman state were undoubtedly the principal cause of death of the Roman economy. The invaders were not guilty of murder, but they had committed manslaughter.

Experiencing Collapse

The *Life* of Saint Severinus, with its detailed testimony to the fall of Noricum (see pp. 17–20 and Fig. 2.2, at p. 18), provides some eloquent examples of how the daily lives of people in a frontier province were affected by the disintegration of Roman power. It tells of the numerous acts of violence, which made life difficult for producers, distributors, and consumers alike, and it also provides a few snippets of more specific information. At one point, the unfortunate citizens of Batavis begged the saint to intercede with the king of a local Germanic tribe, so that they might be allowed to trade. Even local exchange had apparently been made impossible. Unsurprisingly, the import of goods into Noricum from afar had also become very difficult. At one point, aided by a miracle, Severinus distributed to the poor of Lauriacum a dole of olive oil, which, our source tells us, was brought by merchants to the province only with the greatest of difficulty. For oil to reach Noricum, it had to travel by a dangerous over-land route from Italy or hundreds of miles up the highly disturbed lower Danube. In these circumstances, it is more surprising that the poor of late-fifth-century Noricum still hoped to be given imported olive oil—rather than use animal fat as their lighting, cooking, and washing medium—than to hear that supply had been severely disrupted.[23]

The disappearance of the Roman state meant that the Noricans no longer enjoyed the security they needed to benefit from trade; but it also had another immediate and important impact. The *Life* tells us that, even before Severinus arrived in the province in the 450s, defence had become almost entirely a local responsibility. Only one garrison, that of Batavis, was still receiving pay from the imperial government in Ravenna for its work on the Danube. But, as we have already seen, this was not for long. The pay had to be collected in person by a detachment of the soldiery, who made the round trip, across dangerous countryside and over the Alps, to Ravenna. One year, these voyagers were attacked and slaughtered.[24] No more gold ever reached Noricum from the imperial government. This fascinating story documents the very end of the redistributive process that for centuries had pumped gold from the prosperous and peaceful provinces of the interior of the empire to the frontier regions that bore the brunt of barbarian attack, but thereby also enjoyed the principal fruits of the army's spending.

These stories illustrate disruption, but they also show that economic structures can be very resilient—the citizens of Batavis sought the permission of the local Germanic king to go on trading; some olive oil was still reaching Lauriacum, and even the poor still expected it; and the soldiery of one city were prepared to make a long and dangerous journey to collect their wonted pay. But, in the face of repeated difficulties, even resilient structures will crumble. A period of prolonged respite, helped by neighbouring economies in better shape, might well have led to recovery in Noricum (and elsewhere). But periods of prolonged respite were rare, and no provinces in the West were entirely unaffected by troubles. In these circumstances, the western provinces got caught in a vicious circle of economic decline, from which it would take centuries to regain Roman levels of sophistication.

The Danger of Specialization

I have argued that the end of the ancient economy, and the timing of its collapse, were closely linked to the demise of the Roman empire. However, to understand the full and unexpected scale of the decline—turning sophisticated regions into underdeveloped backwaters—we need to appreciate that economic sophistication has a negative side. If the ancient economy had consisted of a series of simple and essentially autonomous local units, with little specialization of labour within them and very little exchange between them, then parts of it would certainly have survived the troubles of post-Roman times—dented perhaps, but in an essentially recognizable form. However, because the ancient economy was in fact a complicated and interlocked system, its very sophistication rendered it fragile and less adaptable to change.[25]

For bulk, high-quality production to flourish in the way that it did in Roman times, a very large number of people had to be involved, in more-or-less specialized capacities. First, there had to be the skilled manufacturers, able to make goods to a high standard, and in a sufficient quantity to ensure a low unit-cost. Secondly, a sophisticated network of transport and commerce had to exist, in order to distribute these goods efficiently and widely. Finally, a large (and therefore generally scattered) market of consumers was essential, with cash to spend and an inclination to spend it. Furthermore, all this complexity depended on the labour of the hundreds of other people who oiled the wheels of manufacture and commerce by maintaining an infrastructure of coins, roads, boats, wagons, wayside hostelries, and so on.

Economic complexity made mass-produced goods available, but it also made people dependent on specialists or semi-specialists—sometimes working hundreds of miles away—for many of their material needs. This worked very well in stable times, but it rendered consumers extremely vulnerable if for any reason the networks of production and distribution were disrupted, or if they themselves could no longer afford to purchase from a specialist. If specialized production failed, it was not possible to fall back immediately on effective self-help.

Comparison with the contemporary western world is obvious and important. Admittedly, the ancient economy was nowhere near as intricate as that of the developed world in the twenty-first century. We sit in tiny productive pigeon-holes, making our minute and highly specialized contributions to the global economy (in my case, some teaching, and a bit of writing about the end of the Roman world), and we are wholly dependent for our needs on thousands, indeed hundreds of thousands, of other people spread around the globe, each doing their own little thing. We would be quite incapable of meeting our needs locally, even in an emergency. The ancient world had not come as far down the road of specialization and helplessness as we have, but it had come some way.

The enormity of the economic disintegration that occurred at the end of the empire was almost certainly a direct result of this specialization. The post-Roman world reverted to levels of economic simplicity, lower even than those of immediately pre-Roman times, with little movement of goods, poor housing, and only the most basic manufactured items. The sophistication of the Roman period, by spreading high-quality goods widely in society, had destroyed the local skills and local networks that, in pre-Roman times, had provided lower-level economic complexity. It took centuries for people in the former empire to reacquire the skills and the regional networks that would take them back to these pre-Roman levels of sophistication. Ironically, viewed from the perspective of fifth-century Britain and of most of the sixth- and seventh-century Mediterranean, the Roman experience had been highly damaging.

VII

THE DEATH OF A
CIVILIZATION?

THE POTS, TILES, AND COINS that are the protagonists of the last two chapters are not always seen as central to the core of human existence. Indeed, in the rich developed world (where historians flourish), well-made objects have become so much an accepted part of existence that their importance tends to be overlooked, particularly by intellectuals, who often see themselves as somewhat above such mundane things. However, these same high-minded intellectuals record their elevated thoughts on the latest laptop, in a weatherproof room, comfortably clothed, and surrounded by those mass-produced items known as 'books'. Our own experience should teach us every minute of every day how important high-quality functional objects are to our well-being.

So far we have looked at manufactured goods, but the benefits of a sophisticated economy can also be seen at a 'lower', even more basic, level—the production of food—and in the 'higher' reaches of human achievement, such as the spread of literacy and the construction of monumental buildings.

A Vanishing Population

Although we cannot be certain, it is likely that the end of the ancient economy had an impact that was greater even than a dramatic regression in manufacturing. Food production may also have slumped, causing a steep drop in the population. Almost without exception, archaeological surveys in the West have found far fewer rural sites of the fifth, sixth, and seventh centuries AD than of the early empire.[1] In many cases, the apparent decline is startling, from a Roman landscape that was densely settled and cultivated, to a post-Roman world that appears only very sparsely inhabited (Fig. 7.1a, b). Almost all the dots that represent Roman-period settlements disappear, leaving only large empty spaces. At roughly the same time, evidence for occupation in towns also decreases dramatically—the fall in the number of rural settlements was certainly not produced by a flight from the countryside into the cities.

At first sight this evidence seems to point clearly and unequivocally to a *massive* drop in population in the post-Roman centuries, to half or perhaps even a quarter of Roman levels. However, as so often, the picture is not quite as clear as it at first appears. Archaeologists can find people of the past only if they left behind them durable material remains. If these people belonged to a culture like that of Roman times, which produced large quantities of solid building materials and shiny pottery, then their settlements show up very clearly in the modern plough soil, as readily identifiable concentrations of broken tile, fragments of mortar, and potsherds. But, unfortunately, the same is not true of settlements from periods with very few durable objects; and, as we have seen, this is exactly what the post-Roman centuries were like. Wooden houses and thatched roofs predominated, which left no tile and mortar fragments, while early medieval pottery is not only much scarcer than its Roman equivalent, but is also generally a dull brown or grey in colour, and therefore difficult to spot in the plough soil. Post-Roman sites, and thus post-Roman people, are often very difficult to find.

Unfortunately, material remains, although a good index of economic sophistication, are not necessarily a reliable index of levels of population. This important point can be illustrated by comparing a Roman with a post-Roman site in Britain. The small fourth-century Roman farmstead at Bradley Hill in Dorset had a partially tiled roof, and on excavation produced nearly 3,500 sherds of Roman pottery, and, as we have already seen, even seventy-eight coins. Although it may have been inhabited by only two or three families of farmers (perhaps twenty people), for as little as fifty years, they left behind them a lot of archaeological evidence. Even a casual modern observer, walking over the site of this farm, might well have noticed its remains on the surface. By contrast, Yeavering, the great royal estate centre of the sixth- and seventh-century Northumbrian kings, may well have been used for over a century by more than 100 people, including men and women from the very highest ranks of society. But its buildings were constructed entirely of perishable materials, which left no trace in

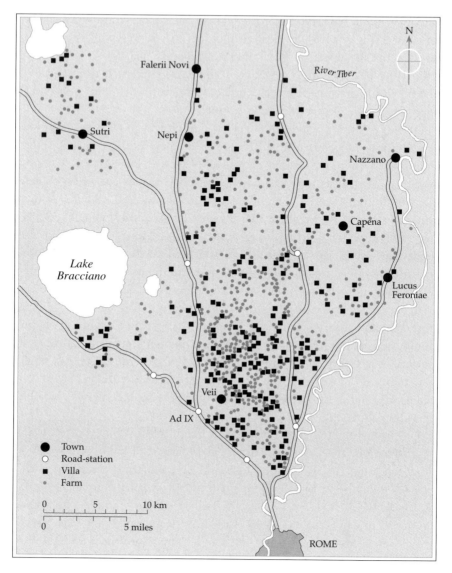

7.1 Disappearing people. Rural settlements north of the city of Rome, in Roman and post-Roman times, as revealed by field survey.
(*a*) Sites occupied in the period around AD 100.

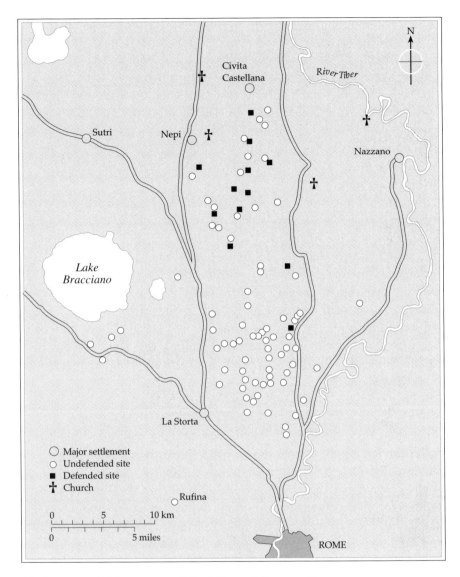

(*b*) Sites revealed by pottery of the fifth to eight centuries AD.

the topsoil; and its pottery was not only very scarce, but also extremely friable and hence liable to fall into dust under the plough (Fig. 5.7, at p. 105). Even a very thorough archaeological field survey could have walked right over Yeavering without noticing any trace of settlement. The site was in fact discovered only because local conditions allowed the post-holes of its timber buildings to be visible from the air.[2] Bearing the example of Yeavering in mind, it is almost certain that, lurking in the large empty spaces of distribution maps like Fig. 7.1b, were a lot of people who are, at present, archaeologically invisible. They were there, but we cannot find them.

Because of these problems with the evidence, we cannot take the apparent lack of post-Roman sites at face value, as unequivocal evidence for a cataclysmic collapse of population in post-Roman times. But, of course, this same evidence does not compel us to assume that population levels remained constant. It is entirely possible that the difficulty we have in finding post-Roman people is due to their being substantially fewer in number, as well as to their leaving fewer material traces. While maintaining a healthy scepticism over the impression of emptiness given by maps like Fig. 7.1b, we should also beware of filling the gaps with fictitious people. Some of the people we cannot see may well never have been there in the first place.

oooo

Since economic complexity definitely increased the quality and quantity of manufactured goods, it is more likely than not that it also increased production of food, and therefore the number of people the land could feed. Archaeological evidence, from periods of prosperity, does indeed seem to show a correlation between increasing sophistication in production and marketing, and a rising population. For instance, as we have seen, the fifth and early sixth centuries in the eastern Mediterranean saw expansion in the production and export of fine pottery, as well as of wine and oil carried in amphorae; in the very same period, there was a rash of new settlements in the East, even in areas where agriculture is difficult, like the limestone hills of northern Syria—where much of the cultivable soil is confined to tiny pockets in the bare rock (Fig. 7.2).[3] Furthermore, as we can tell from the material remains they left behind, the people who inhabited this unpromising terrain were far from scraping a miserable existence on the very edge of subsistence. They had the resources to invest in a spectacular

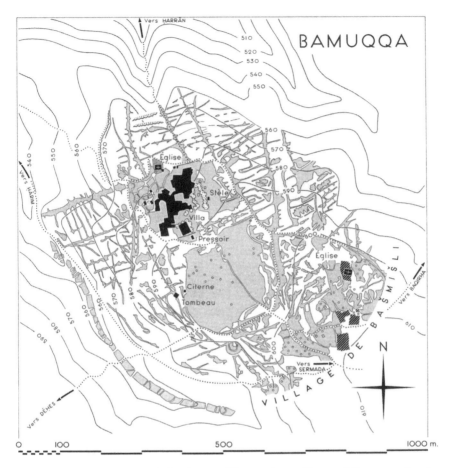

7.2 Prosperity in a difficult landscape. The ancient village of Bamuqqa in the north-Syrian limestone hills. Around the settlement (in black) are shown (in grey) the pockets of cultivable soil, most of them tiny.

series of rural churches, and in some very solid and impressive domestic housing (Fig. 6.2, at p. 125).

In the West, earlier evidence—from first-century Italy, first- and second-century Gaul and Spain, and third- and fourth-century North Africa—all suggests a similarly close link between the development of a market-oriented economy and an increasing density and spread of settlement. For instance, the Roman peasant family near Luna in northern Italy, whom we have already met eating from imported pottery dishes, was living on top of a steep ridge, very ill-suited to conventional agriculture. The successful cultivation of the hillside, and hence the well-being of this peasant household, were almost certainly made possible by the development and export of a prestigious local wine, for which terraced hillside production was perfectly suited.[4]

If we ask ourselves exactly how a complex economy could produce more food than a very basic one, and thereby feed more mouths, two closely related answers can be offered. First, if agricultural products could be readily exported and sold (whether in a regional or an international market), then farmers could specialize in producing those crops for which local conditions were particularly well suited. For instance, the cultivators of the north Syrian hills would be able to exploit the small and unpromising pockets of soil around their villages to grow many more olive trees than they themselves actually needed (Fig. 7.2). The surplus oil could be sold within the wider region, and in the fifth to seventh centuries it could even be exported overseas—as shown by the discovery of amphorae from Syria and its neighbouring provinces throughout the Mediterranean, and even beyond it. Meanwhile, foodstuffs that could not be cultivated locally in quantity, like grain, could be brought in from nearby areas with better arable cultivation, such as the alluvial plains of Mesopotamia. In this way, specialization, coupled with exchange, could markedly increase the productivity of the soil, by allowing it to be used for the crops best suited to local climatic and geological conditions.

Secondly, specialization and the ability to turn crops into cash allowed farmers to invest in improvements, that in turn increased productivity yet further. For instance, the Syrian cultivators of the limestone hills built a large number of solid olive presses around their villages, the remains of which are still standing there today, which allowed them to extract their oil efficiently and locally. At the same time, their counterparts on the plains were able to extend and intensify their arable cultivation by building complex irrigation and water-management systems, involving dams, underground channels, and reservoirs, as well as conventional irrigation ditches.[5] Through capital investment, farmers were able to get much more out of their land.

However, in the conditions of later times, without flourishing international and regional markets, specialization and investment became much more difficult, and the inhabitants of areas like the limestone hills were forced to return to a more mixed, and hence less productive, agriculture. When this happened, the population had to fall. It is indeed thought that parts of the Levant did not regain the levels and density of population that they sustained in late Roman and early Arab times until well into the nineteenth, or even the twentieth century.

Unfortunately, there is no reliable way at present of measuring Roman agricultural output, let alone of comparing it with that of the post-Roman centuries. But we do, from the West, now have some very revealing evidence for the changing size of stock animals. The careful recording of animal leg bones, recovered from datable excavated contexts, has allowed zoologists to estimate the changing size of livestock in different periods. The results are striking. Cattle and, to a lesser extent, other domesticated animals show a marked rise in average size in Roman times (Fig. 7.3). These larger animals, like modern cattle, carried a much greater weight of meat than their pre-Roman ancestors. But to put on this weight they required intensive feeding on good-quality pasture and, probably, plentiful winter fodder.[6] These conditions could be achieved in an economic environment, like that of Roman times, that encouraged some specialization in the use of land and in the deployment of labour. But it appears to have been impossible to sustain this improvement in the more basic conditions of the post-Roman centuries. Cattle size fell back to prehistoric levels.

In the Roman period, the land certainly supported high levels of population, with no evident signs that resources were overstretched—since, even in densely populated areas, peasant households could afford consumer products like imported pottery. To sustain this level of population and affluence, food production must surely have been highly efficient. It is also very possible that in post-Roman times agricultural

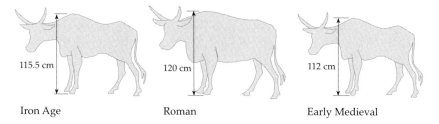

115.5 cm

120 cm

112 cm

Iron Age   Roman   Early Medieval

7.3 The rise and fall of the Roman cow. The approximate size of cattle, from the Iron Age, through Roman times, to the early Middle Ages. The information is based on finds from 21 iron-age, 67 Roman, and 49 early medieval sites.

sophistication disappeared as comprehensively as the manufacturing industries whose miserable fate is so much better documented in the arch-aeological record. On balance, slippery and elusive though the evidence is, I believe it is much more likely than not that the post-Roman period saw a marked decline in agricultural productivity, and therefore in the number of people that the land could sustain. This was decline at the baseline of human existence.

Greater Sophistication, or Greater Exploitation?

The Roman period is sometimes seen as enriching only the elite, rather than enhancing the standard of living of the population at large. Indeed, some scholars claim that the wealthiest and most powerful members of society were enriched specifically at the expense, and to the detriment, of the less privileged. For instance, a recent book on Roman Britain depicts its economy as an instrument of oppression, and explicitly compares Rome's impact on the island to the worst effects of modern imperialism and capitalism. The end of Roman power is celebrated as the end of exploitation: 'The mass of British people could then enjoy a short golden age free from landlords and tax collectors.' Roman economic sophistica-tion had benefited only property-owners and the state; and the 'Dark Ages' that followed its demise were in reality a 'golden age'.[7]

I think this, and similar views, are mistaken. For me, what is most striking about the Roman economy is precisely the fact that it was not solely an elite phenomenon, but one that made basic good-quality items available right down the social scale. As we have seen, good-quality pot-tery was widely available, and in regions like Italy even the comfort of tiled roofs. I would also seriously question the romantic assumption that eco-nomic simplicity necessarily meant a freer and more equal society. There is no reason to believe that, because post-Roman Britain had no coinage, no wheel-turned pottery, and no mortared buildings, it was an egalitarian haven, spared the oppression of landlords and political masters. Tax, admittedly, could no longer be collected in coin; but its less sophisticated equivalent, 'tribute', could perfectly well be extorted in the form of sheaves of corn, pigs, and even slaves.

However, while criticizing those who see the Roman world in very negative terms, I would not want to make the mistake of depicting it in too rosy-tinted a hue. The presence of a more complex economy and of better-quality manufactured goods did not make for a universally happy world, in which no one was oppressed or economically downtrodden—just as the material well-being of the modern western world has by no means solved all its own poverty, let alone the poverty of those strangers abroad on whom we all depend. Many of the most impressive engineering feats of Roman times were carried out by slave labour—for instance, the granite columns of the Pantheon that so impressed me as a child were laboriously hacked out of the rock of the Egyptian desert by convicts and slaves, forced to work in unimaginably harsh and bleak conditions. An observer of the first century BC noted that 'the slaves who work in the mines . . . wear out their bodies day and night . . . dying in large numbers because of the exceptional hardship they endure'.[8]

There were also huge differences of wealth even amongst the free, just as there are today, and greater economic sophistication may well have widened the gap between the rich and the poor. Even in prosperous and highly developed parts of the empire, people at the bottom of society could live abject lives and die in misery. For instance, in Roman Egypt, one of the richest provinces of the empire, new-born children were abandoned on dumps of excrement and rubbish sufficiently often to gain a special name, 'dung-foundlings' (*coprianairetoi*). Some of these infants may have been abandoned by their parents for social reasons (for instance, if born out of wedlock), but others were certainly left to the kindness of strangers only because their parents could not afford to feed them. We know that the rubbish heaps of Egypt contained broken amphorae and fine-ware bowls from all over the Mediterranean; but these will have been of little consolation to the abandoned dung-children of the province and to their wretched parents.[9]

Similarly, however sophisticated Roman agriculture was, harvests could still fail, and, when they did, transport was not cheap or rapid enough to bring in the large quantities of affordable grain that could have saved the poor from starvation. Edessa in Mesopotamia was one of the richest cities of the Roman East, surrounded by prosperous arable farming. But in AD 500 a swarm of locusts consumed the wheat harvest; a later harvest, of millet, also failed. For the poor, disaster followed. The price of bread shot up, and people were forced to sell their few possessions for a pittance in order to buy food. Many tried, in vain, to assuage their hunger with leaves and roots. Those who could, fled the region; but crowds of starving people flocked into Edessa and other cities, to sleep rough and to beg: 'They slept in the colonnades and streets, howling night and day from the pangs of hunger.' Here disease and the cold nights of winter killed large numbers of them; even collecting and burying the dead became a major problem.[10]

Suitable Homes for Saints

If we turn our gaze upwards from the fundamentals of human society, the production and availability of food, to 'higher' things, like the scale of buildings and the spread of literacy, we find a similar dramatic downturn at the end of the Roman world. This is not very surprising, because craftsmanship and skill cannot flourish in a material vacuum: architects, builders, marble-workers, and mosaicists, teachers and writers, all require a degree of economic complexity to sustain them.

In Italy and elsewhere in the Mediterranean, there was an unbroken tradition of some building in mortared brick and stone throughout the post-Roman centuries, as we have seen, and many impressive earlier buildings were also kept in repair. Late sixth-century Anglo-Saxon visitors to Rome, for instance, would have seen things undreamed of in their native Britain, where the Roman buildings had been allowed to decay and all new building was in timber. They would have found a few newly built brick churches, freshly decorated with mosaics and frescos, and, above all, a large number of immensely impressive fourth- and fifth-century basilicas, kept in repair and in continuous use. Old St Peter's, for instance, the fourth-century predecessor of the present basilica, stood proud throughout the Middle Ages—a huge building, around 100 metres long and with five aisles separated by a forest of marble columns.

But, if we look at the new churches of post-Roman Italy, what is most immediately striking about them is how small they are (Fig. 7.4). Buildings of the late sixth, seventh, and early eighth centuries are very rarely over 20 metres long; a modern viewer might well describe them as 'chapels' rather than 'churches'. The embellishment of earlier buildings was also often on a very small scale. Pope John VII, at the beginning of the eighth century, was evidently proud of his decorative works in the basilicas of Rome, since his brief biography lists these in some detail. His principal project may have been the oratory dedicated to Mary the Mother of God, which he built inside St Peter's. His biographer states that he spent on it 'a large sum of gold and silver'. The oratory was demolished when the

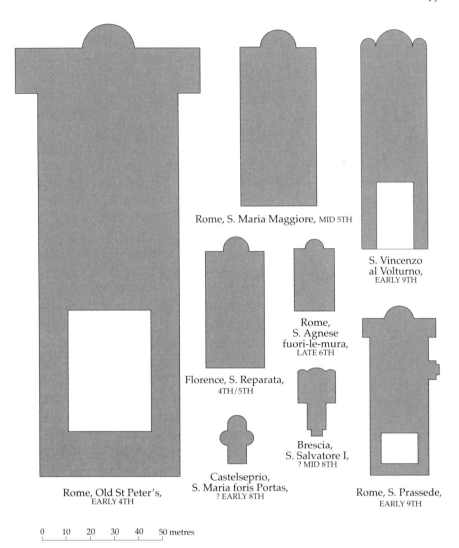

Rome, S. Maria Maggiore, MID 5TH

S. Vincenzo
al Volturno,
EARLY 9TH

Rome,
S. Agnese
fuori-le-mura,
LATE 6TH

Florence, S. Reparata,
4TH/5TH

Brescia,
S. Salvatore I,
? MID 8TH

Castelseprio,
S. Maria foris Portas,
? EARLY 8TH

Rome, Old St Peter's,
EARLY 4TH

Rome, S. Prassede,
EARLY 9TH

0   10   20   30   40   50 metres

7.4 Tight quarters for the saints. The ground-plans of some representative churches in Italy, all drawn to the same scale. The small size of buildings of the sixth to early eighth centuries is very clear—only in the later eighth and ninth centuries do larger churches again appear.

present St Peter's was built, but it survived long enough to be drawn by Renaissance antiquarians, which allows us to see how big a structure an early eighth-century 'large sum' of money could build. By the standards of the Roman period (or of the later Middle Ages) John's oratory was tiny: a few columns (most of them older ones reused), and the embellishment of one wall with a sizeable panel of mosaic.[11]

Evidence from Visigothic Spain, which has much the finest collection of seventh-century churches anywhere in the West, confirms the picture from Italy. The Visigothic churches are built of squared stone blocks and are impressively solid, but all of them are similar in size to the contemporary buildings of Italy. For instance, San Juan de Baños, built by a Visigothic king in the mid-seventh century (and therefore a commission from the very pinnacle of society), is only about 20 metres long, as is the most elaborate church of the period, San Pedro de la Nave near Zamora.[12]

What we see in Italy, Spain, and most of the Mediterranean is a partial survival of the heritage of the past, and a dramatic shrinkage in the scale of new construction (Fig. 7.4). In these areas not every building and skill of the Roman period was lost—it is only in a few exceptional places, like the parts of Britain conquered by the Anglo-Saxons, that anything quite so apocalyptic occurred. On the other hand, all over the West, if God and his saints had had to rely on their newly built quarters, they would have found themselves very cramped indeed.

ooo

This abandonment of building in mortared brick and stone in provinces like Britain, and the very reduced scale of building elsewhere, are sometimes interpreted as the result of cultural choice, rather than economic necessity. According to this argument, the elite were no longer in thrall to the Roman obsession with bricks and marble—as the historian Chris Wickham put it in 1988, 'fine clothes were becoming for kings more precious than good bricks'.[13] The rich in early medieval times, according to this interpretation, were just as well off as the elite of Roman times, but chose to spend their money differently: in particular on jewellery and fine textiles (as clothing and as wall-hangings).

There is, however, one insuperable problem with this argument—the Romans had plenty of jewellery and fine textiles, as well as their splendid buildings. Comparatively little of their jewellery survives, because they very rarely buried it with the dead (unlike the Germanic peoples); but occasional finds, and frequent references and representations in written sources and in art, prove beyond any doubt that elaborate earrings and necklaces were a well-established feature of aristocratic Roman life. There have also been enough spectacular finds of large and elaborately decorated silverware (Fig. 7.5) to prove that rich Romans relished the chance to show off their access to precious metals.[14] Similarly, the sumptuous textiles that survive from Roman Egypt are quite sufficient to dispel any notion that Roman dress was characterized by the homespun toga.

We notice Roman jewellery and precious metalwork less than their post-Roman equivalents, mainly because we are distracted by a mass of other luxury items that disappeared (or became very scarce) after the end of the empire: marbled and mosaiced private houses, in both town and country; baths with piped water and underfloor heating; a plethora of exotic foods, spices, and wines; as well as immensely expensive items of pure waste, like the animals imported for the sole purpose that they should die in the amphitheatre (ideally taking with them a few unfortunate slave 'huntsmen'). Very wealthy Romans even derived status from their costly libraries and their expensive literary education. This was a world where the display of social superiority could be very subtle—while paying out huge sums of money for the barbarian slaves and exotic beasts, whose slaughter in the amphitheatre was necessary to secure his status, a Roman aristocrat could also lay claim to a philosophical education that set him above such vulgar things.

'Here Phoebus the perfume-seller had a really good fuck': The Use of Writing in Roman Times

Sometime shortly before the fatal eruption of Vesuvius in AD 79, this message was scratched onto the wall of a brothel in the centre of Pompeii.[15] It is apparently evidence of a satisfied customer—unless, of course, it is only male posturing. But it is certainly evidence that one tradesman in Pompeii could write, and assumed that other clients could read and would appreciate his account of time and money well spent. Evidence such as this has led to an intense debate over the extent to which the people of Roman times could read and write, and the importance of the written word in their society.[16] In the absence of any statistical evidence, the issue will always be open to discussion, since it will never be possible to come up

7.5 The Roman love of precious metal. The silver treasure of a rich Roman, hidden after about AD 450 and discovered in the late 1970s. The total weight of the silver is 68.5 kilograms.

with reliable figures for the number of people comfortable with literacy, let alone provide a nuanced view of what level of literacy they had attained. The principal evidence we have of people being able to write is the chance survival of texts, like the one above, and these are only a small and an unknowable proportion of what once existed; while, for people being able to read, hard evidence is necessarily even slimmer. There is no way of knowing how many Pompeians could read Phoebus' message.

However, what is striking about the Roman period, and to my mind unparalleled until quite recent times, is the evidence of writing being casually used, in an entirely ephemeral and everyday manner, which was none the less sophisticated. The best evidence for this comes, unsurprisingly, from Pompeii, because the eruption of AD 79 ensured a uniquely good level of preservation of the city's buildings and the various forms of writing that they bore. Over 11,000 inscriptions, of many different kinds, have been recorded within Pompeii, carved, painted, or scratched into its walls. Some of them are very grand and formal, like the dedications of public buildings and the funerary epitaphs, similar to others found all over the Roman world. Inscriptions such as these are not necessarily good evidence of widespread literacy. The enormous numbers that were produced in Roman times could reflect a fashion for this particular medium of display, rather than a dramatic spread of the ability to read and write.

Other Pompeian inscriptions are perhaps more telling, because they display a desire to communicate in a less formal and more ephemeral way with fellow citizens. Walls on the main streets of Pompeii are often decorated with painted messages, whose regular script and layout reveal the work of professional sign-writers. Some are advertisements for events such as games in the amphitheatre; others are endorsements of candidates for civic office, by individuals and groups within the city. These endorsements are highly formulaic, and for the most part decidedly staid: worthy Pompeians declare their support for one candidate or another. However, a fascinating group of three breaks the mould. All support the same candidate for office, a certain Marcus Cerrinius Vatia. One claims to have been painted on behalf of 'all the sleepers' of the city, one by the petty thieves, and one by the 'late drinkers'.[17] Either this Marcus had a very good sense of humour, or he had political opponents prepared to deploy dirty tricks against him. But either way these texts are from a society sophisticated enough, not only to have professionally painted political posters, but also to mock the genre.

Graffiti offer even more striking evidence of the spread and use of writing in Pompeian society. These are found all over the city, scratched into stone or plaster by townspeople with time on their hands and a message to convey to future idlers; in Phoebus the perfume-seller's message we have already met an example from one particularly famous group, the brothel-graffiti (Fig. 7.6). Many of these messages are highly obscure, because we lack the local knowledge needed to understand them; but some, like 'Sabinus hic' (Sabinus [was] here), are both very simple, and entirely familiar.[18]

As with the election posters, graffito-culture in Pompeii was sophisticated enough to poke fun at itself. One verse, which has been found scratched in four different places in the city, always in a different hand, runs as follows:

> Wall, I admire you for not collapsing in ruins
> When you have to support so much tedious writing on you.[19]

Even though we cannot estimate the proportion of Pompeians who were literate (was it 30 per cent, or more; or perhaps only 10 per cent ?), we can say with confidence that writing was an essential, and a day-to-day part of the city's life. Writing was even common enough to be lightly mocked.

Pompeii is uniquely rich in the evidence it offers of a city that used writing at all sorts of different levels, from the grandiose to the completely trivial. It is also likely that it was an unusually literate settlement. A rural village in Italy as well preserved as Pompeii, or a city in a region with less of a literate tradition, would almost certainly produce much less evidence of the use of writing. However, this is not to say that writing, even at an ephemeral and trivial level, failed to reach out-of-the-way regions. Roman Britain has produced far fewer examples of writing than contemporary central Italy; but this has had the advantage that every one of them has been carefully collected and published. The resulting volumes are slim in comparison to the evidence from Pompeii, but none the less impressive. There is an extraordinary variety of different types of inscription: formal dedications and epitaphs on stone; makers-stamps on a wide variety of objects (such as ingots, tiles, metal vessels, pottery, and leather goods); inscribed metal labels and seals; and short, scratched inscriptions, above all to denote ownership, on all kinds of different objects (for instance, 875 on fragments of tableware pottery, and 619 on kitchenwares). The list is truly impressive in its diversity. It includes, for instance, twenty-seven

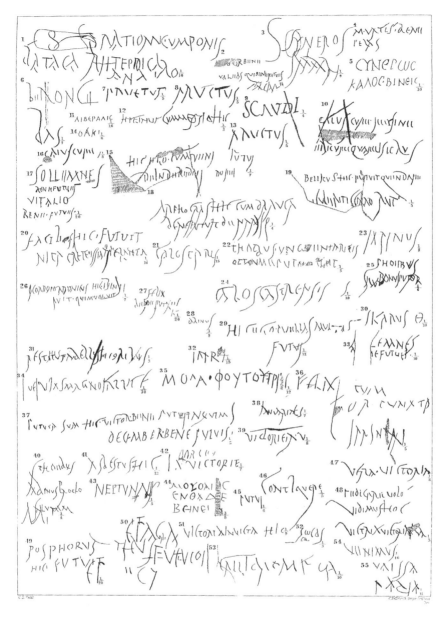

7.6 Brothel-graffiti from Pompeii. That written by Phoebus the perfume-seller is no. 22.

fragments of wooden barrels, branded or scratched with their owner's name or initials, and thirty-one tiny inscribed stamps, that are believed to have been used to mark the salves dispensed by oculists.[20]

The archaeology of Roman Britain is exceptionally well known and fully published. Consequently, it has even been possible to chart the distribution across the province of Roman styluses, the small metal rods used for writing on wax tablets. Nearly 350 of these have been recorded on rural sites, primarily in the richer south-east, but also with a smattering in the North and West. Unsurprisingly, the majority come from villas, the dwellings of the ruling class, but this is by no means exclusively the case—styluses have also been found on a large number of humbler rural settlements, with no aristocratic pretensions. Some use of writing seems to have penetrated even low-status rural sites.[21]

Like Pompeii, Roman Britain has also produced evidence of the very ephemeral and trivial use of writing—the kind that brings individuals from the distant past vividly to life, though often in a highly enigmatic way. A tile from Roman London had an inscription scratched on it while it was drying: 'Austalis has been going off on his own for thirteen days.' Who was Austalis, and who wrote this observation—a tile-worker, an overseer, or perhaps someone just passing through the yard? A second tile, from Silchester, has a one-word message, 'SATIS' (enough), drawn neatly on it with a finger (Fig. 7.7). This was probably the foreman marking up the end of a batch; but, alternatively, we can fantasize that it was a tired worker celebrating the end of a particularly hard day. A third graffito, on a clay water pipe supplying the bath-house of a villa in Lincolnshire, proclaims 'Liber esto' (Be free), the formula with which a slave was emancipated. Was this perhaps the daydream of a slave in the brickyard? We will never know the answer to all these questions; nor will we ever be confident of the status of the people who passed us these messages. But writing in informal and ephemeral use was certainly a feature of Roman Britain.[22]

In Britain, as elsewhere in the Roman world, some sectors of society certainly used writing more extensively than others. The army, in particular, depended heavily on the written word. Some of this military literacy did not require high levels of intellectual achievement. The Roman army shared with modern armed forces an obsession with labelling its equipment, presumably because it also had a way of disappearing out of the storeroom. The resulting very brief inscriptions could be read, or at least recognized, by someone with only the most basic knowledge of letters.

7.7 'SATIS (enough)' drawn with a finger onto a Roman tile from Calleva (Silchester, in Hampshire) while it was drying in the brickyard.

However, many soldiers could manage much more than this. In the 1970s and 1980s hundreds of documents of the late first and early second century AD were discovered at the fortress of Vindolanda on Hadrian's Wall, written in ink on smooth, thin slips of wood (and, exceptionally, preserved in waterlogged conditions). Experts have identified in these documents the handwriting of hundreds of different people. This is perhaps not surprising amongst the letters that were received from outside the fort; but even amongst the texts written at Vindolanda itself, very few were written by the same hand—for instance, a dozen requests for leave are preserved, all written by different people. The officers at Vindolanda were certainly literate; some soldiers in the ranks may also have been.[23]

There is similar evidence of high levels of military literacy from elsewhere in the empire, sometimes of a very ephemeral kind. In 41 BC during the civil war that followed the death of Julius Caesar, Octavian (the future Emperor Augustus) trapped Lucius Antonius and Fulvia (the brother and the wife of Mark Antony), within the walls of the central Italian town of Perugia. A number of lead sling-bolts (roughly the size of hazelnuts), manufactured during the siege that followed, have been recovered in

Perugia; they bear short inscriptions, which both sides carved into their moulds, so that the bolts could be used in a war of words, as well as to inflict death or injury. Some of these inscriptions are fairly tame, wishing victory to one or other side, or commenting on Lucius Antonius' receding hairline (which is also known from his coinage). Others are rather richer in flavour, like the one, fired from Octavian's side, which bluntly asks: 'Lucius Antonius the bald, and Fulvia, show us your arse [L[uci] A[ntoni] calve, Fulvia, culum pan[dite]].'[24] Whoever composed this refined piece of propaganda and had it cast into a sling-bolt certainly expected some of the soldiery on the other side to be able to read.

ooo

If we ask ourselves how the ability to read and write came to be so wide-spread in the Roman world, the answer probably lies in a number of different developments, which all encouraged the use of writing. In particular, there is no doubt that the complex mechanism of the Roman state required literate officials at all levels of its operations. There was no other way that the state could raise taxes in coin or kind from its provincials, assemble the resulting profits, ship them across long distances, and consume or spend them where they were needed. A great many lists and tallies will have been needed to ensure that a gold *solidus* raised in one of the peaceful provinces of the empire, like Egypt or Africa, was then spent effectively to support a soldier on the distant frontiers of Mesopotamia, the Danube, or the Rhine.

In the documents from Vindolanda on Hadrian's Wall, we have already seen one example of the high levels of literacy expected and achieved in state service. A far larger body of evidence, of a very varied kind, has been recovered from Egypt at the other end of the empire, where dry conditions have preserved a mass of administrative records of many different kinds, some of them highly ephemeral. Figure 7.8 is a tiny papyrus receipt, of the late second century AD. It was issued to a certain Sotouetis when he entered the gates of the settlement of Soknopaiou Nesos in the Fayum. The imperial customs official on duty there took 3 per cent of the value of the goods that Sotouetis was carrying, and issued him with this neat receipt, giving it the extra validity of a clay seal in the centre, stamped with the heads of the ruling emperors. This slip of papyrus shows that the wheels of the Roman fiscal and bureaucratic machine ground very fine: what Sotouetis was carrying was a mere six amphorae of wine. Other very

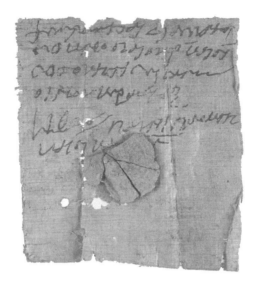

7.8 Literacy and the administration. A tax receipt from Roman Egypt. The document, in papyrus and with a clay seal stamped into the middle, is here reproduced actual size.

similar tax receipts survive, mostly for equally trivial quantities of food-stuffs, being carried in or out of the gates of Soknopaiou Nesos on donkeys and camels. Even at this very low level of Roman bureaucracy, an official had to be able to issue a neat and formal written receipt, and the animal-driver concerned, while probably illiterate himself, presumably used the written document when challenged further along the road over his customs liabilities.[25]

The complex Roman economy certainly also needed the written word in order to function. The dry sands of Egypt have produced a mass of different types of commercial document: requests for goods; contracts for services and products; lists of articles and dues; records of dispatch; receipts of goods and payments; and many more besides. Outside Egypt, most of our evidence consists of chance and scrappy survivals in the arch-aeological record. Fortunately it is sufficient to prove what is anyway obvi-ous—that the written word was necessary for production and trade on the scale achieved in the Roman period. For instance, as we have already seen, over 200 graffiti, scratched onto broken bits of pottery, have been recovered from the massive pottery-production site at la Graufesenque.

The largest single category are lists, often in four columns: first a name (presumed to be the proprietor of a workshop); then a type of vessel; a dimension; and, finally, a number (Fig. 7.9). When the columns of numbers are added up they can total over 30,000. These graffiti are almost certainly the records of the stacking of huge communal kilns—so that, after firing, the individual workshops got back the same vessels that they had put in.[26]

Writing was perhaps even more necessary during the complex and precarious processes of distribution. In the second half of the nineteenth century, the riverside quays on the Saône at Lyons were rebuilt, and in the process the river was dredged. Around 4,000 small seals of the Roman period, mainly in lead, which had once identified and protected bales and crates, were recovered during the dredging. Many of these seals were military or originated at the imperial customs post at Arles, but the great majority bore simple inscriptions (often just the initials of a name), which were almost certainly the identifying marks of individual shippers and producers. Goods passing through Lyons, which was a vital staging post on the route to and from the Mediterranean, needed to be identified, and, in the widely literate Roman period, this was done with small inscribed seals.[27] Amphorae, when they are well preserved, sometimes bear similar evidence of how writing was used to identify goods in transit. Brief painted inscriptions, which survive on the necks of some vessels, very occasionally seem to have been aimed at the consumer (identifying the contents), but generally seem to have served as records during the process of production and shipping.[28]

Writing was also needed at the moment of sale or exchange. A group of graffiti, preserved in a hilltop trading site in modern Austria, shed some light on this. In the period between about 35 BC and AD 45, merchants, dealing above all in the iron goods that were mined and worked in the area, were using two cellars on the site. They covered the walls in over 300 graffiti, with simple messages, like 'Orobius 565 hooks' or 'Surulus 520 hooks'. These must be basic records of sales (or perhaps of goods stored in the cellars).[29]

So far we have looked at the spread of literacy amongst merchants and state officials, both civilian and military; but there was also a pressure on the rich to learn. In the Roman world, the ability to read and write became a prerequisite of upper-class life. In part this was for solidly practical reasons. In a society where government and the economy revolved around

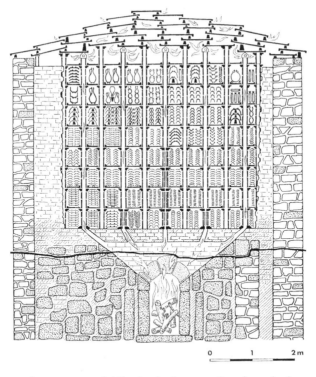

7.9 Literacy and commerce. A kiln-load of pottery listed on the base of a broken potsherd, from the production site at la Graufesenque, in southern France. Below is a cross-section drawing of just such a kiln-load being fired (based on the evidence of similar graffiti and of the excavated remains of one kiln).

writing, there was a very strong incentive for those who controlled power and money to be confident with their letters. But there were also powerful ideological and social pressures encouraging the aristocracy to be fully literate. Reading and writing (and a grounding in classical literary culture) were in Roman times an essential mark of status. Indeed, for the very richest landowners, the senatorial aristocracy, a basic literary education was not considered nearly enough. Males of this class were expected to have a thorough knowledge of the language and literature of the ancient world, and to be expert in oratory and rhetoric, skills that were obtainable only through long and expensive schooling. Thanks to these incentives, illiterates amongst the Roman upper classes were very rare indeed.

The powerful hold that literacy held over the Roman world is exemplified in a striking portrait of a Pompeian couple (Fig. 7.10), of which other similar examples exist. The man has in his hand a papyrus roll, and the woman is holding to her lips a stylus, for writing on the wax tablets that she holds in her other hand. This couple, who did not come from the very highest ranks of the Pompeian aristocracy, probably chose to be depicted in this way as a mark of their status—they belonged to the ranks of those who were literate, and they wished to display the fact. In this sense, the portrait is evidence that literacy was far from universal in Roman Pompeii. But it is none the less an impressive fact, typical of the Roman world and difficult to parallel before modern times, that a provincial couple should have chosen to be painted in a way that very specifically celebrated a close relationship with the written word, on the part of both the man and his wife.

Another indication of how deeply entrenched literacy became amongst the Roman ruling classes is the striking fact that, despite frequent military coups, not until the accession in the East of Justin I in 518 was the empire ruled by someone who is said to have been unable to read or write. Procopius, who wrote soon after his reign, recorded of Justin, an uneducated soldier from the Balkans, that he was 'ignorant of every letter, being as they say unlettered [analphabetos], the first such case amongst the Romans'. Earlier emperors, in particular Maximinus Thrax (235–8), another Balkan soldier, had been made fun of for their lack of educational polish, but the worst that Maximinus' highly derogatory biography accused him of was an ignorance of Greek and a knowledge of Latin that was only newly acquired.[30]

7.10 A Pompeian couple celebrate their literacy. The house where the portrait was found was prosperous, but by no means one of Pompeii's richest dwellings.

'Turo the pilgrim, may you live for ever in God': Early Medieval Literacy

At some date between the mid-seventh and the mid-ninth centuries, a pilgrim with the Germanic name 'Turo' scratched this message into a wall of the pilgrimage shrine of S. Michele sul Gargano on the heel of Italy (Fig. 7.11). The script is laboured enough to be his own work, unlike other

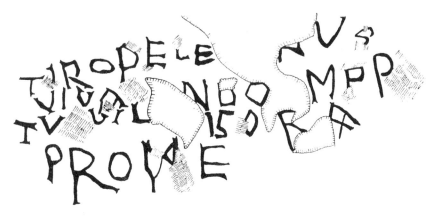

7.11 Turo's scratched message, celebrating his visit to the shrine of S. Michele sul Gargano in southern Italy.

more regular inscriptions at the site, which were probably carved on behalf of visiting pilgrims by more practised hands. Turo added at the end of his inscription: 'You who read this, pray for me.'[31]

Reading and writing, and the importance of the written word, certainly did not disappear in the post-Roman West. Only in some remote provinces did the use of writing vanish completely, as it did in Anglo-Saxon Britain during the fifth century, to be reintroduced by Christian missionaries only around AD 600. In more sophisticated regions, such as Italy, Spain, and Gaul, written documents were always important. For instance, the law code of the mid-seventh-century king of Lombard Italy, Rothari, recommended that the freeing of a slave be recorded in a charter, in order to avoid future problems, and also threatened anyone forging a charter 'or any other kind of document' with the amputation of a hand. If written documents were being forged, they were certainly important, and if former slaves were encouraged to use them to defend their freedom, they were also quite widely available.[32]

Almost all the references we have to writing in post-Roman times are to formal documents, intended to last (like laws, treaties, charters, and tax registers), or to letters exchanged between members of the very highest ranks of society. However, some remarkable texts from Visigothic Spain, of the sixth and seventh centuries, show that much more ephemeral written records were also once common. In the area south of Salamanca outcrops of good-quality slate are abundant, with the result that it was used in the early Middle Ages as a medium on which to write, the letters being scratched into the smooth surface. Because slate does not decay, a number of these scratched tablets have been recovered and published (153 complete or fragmentary texts are included in the most recent catalogue). A few of them carry religious texts, such as prayers, psalms, and an incantation against hail storms; others are formal documents, recording transfers of land. But many are estate documents of only temporary importance, listing animals (in one case carefully differentiated by age and sex), dues rendered, and distributions made; one slate carries an inventory of some clothing. For me the most evocative of all these texts is an 'Account of cheeses [*Notitia de casios*]', which lists some names, and, against each one, a number of cheeses. It is probably a record of payment of rent in kind. Hundreds of thousands of similar estate documents must once have existed in the post-Roman West; only the good fortune that the region of Salamanca is rich in slate has ensured these very few survivals.[33]

On the other hand, the evidence for the very widespread use of literacy, and, in particular, for its trivial use, which is such a striking feature of Roman times, is far less apparent in the centuries that followed the fall of the empire. The numerous stamps, seals, and painted or scratched inscriptions that had characterized the commercial and military life of the Roman world seem to disappear almost completely. The need to label and stamp large quantities of commercial goods appears to have evaporated, presumably because production and distribution were now much simpler and less extensive than they had been before. There are some rare stamped tiles known from the seventh and eighth centuries; but the wording of their inscriptions suggests that they were added to enhance their patrons' prestige, rather than as a means of keeping track of production.[34] Similarly, the disappearance of the professional army, maintained by a complex system of supply, brought to an end the thousands upon thousands of military inscriptions, and that very striking feature of Roman life, an army that was even more widely literate than the society that spawned it.

Most interesting of all is the almost complete disappearance of casual graffiti, of the kind so widely found in the Roman period. Graffiti are known from the fifth to ninth centuries, as the example carved by Turo shows. But these scratched inscriptions are primarily semi-formal and votive records of pilgrims' visits to shrines such as S. Michele sul Gargano and the catacombs around Rome. Some of the pilgrims undoubtedly wrote their own names (including a few visitors from the northern world to the Gargano, who wrote in runes), but others had their names carved by people practised in writing into stone or plaster.[35] Although rightly described as 'graffiti', in that they are lightly carved and unimpressive in appearance, these pilgrimage records had a much more formal intent than Phoebus' casual account of his visit to a Pompeian brothel.

Of course, we have no early medieval Pompeii that would allow us to make a true and fair comparison of levels of casual secular literacy between Roman and post-Roman times. But we do have plenty of domestic objects from both periods, and these are a rich source of scratched letters and names in the Roman period, as well as of occasional messages (like those we have seen on tiles from Britain). In the early Middle Ages, domestic objects are almost always mute.[36] They do very occasionally have names carved or scratched on them, but these are almost invariably very neat, suggesting that they have been applied with some care, perhaps even by a specialist writer, rather than roughly scratched by the owners themselves.[37] There is no group of finds from the post-Roman centuries that remotely compares with the 400 graffiti, mainly scratched initials, on the bottoms of pots from a Roman fort in Germany, which were almost certainly added by the soldiers themselves, in order to identify their individual vessels.[38]

In a much simpler world, the urgent need to read and write declined, and with it went the social pressure on the secular elite to be literate. Widespread literacy in the post-Roman West definitely became confined to the clergy. A detailed analysis of almost 1,000 subscribers to charters from eighth-century Italy has shown that just under a third of witnesses were able to sign their own names, the remainder making only a mark (identified as theirs by the charter's scribe). But the large majority of those who signed (71 per cent) were clergy. Amongst the 633 lay subscribers, only 93, or 14 per cent, wrote their own name. Since witnesses to charters were generally drawn from the ranks of the 'important' people of local society, and since the ability to write one's name does not require a profound grasp of literary skills, this figure suggests that even basic literacy was a very rare phenomenon amongst the laity as a whole.[39]

It is a striking fact, and a major contrast with Roman times, that even great rulers could be illiterate in the early Middle Ages. Many were not— the Frankish king Chilperic (561–84) and the Visigothic king Sisebut (612–21) both tried their hand at Latin poetry, and the latter also wrote a life of Saint Desiderius of Vienne.[40] But others are known to have lacked even the most basic facility with the written word. Einhard, the biographer of Charlemagne, tells us of the emperor's valiant efforts to master his letters in later life—his royal father had apparently not considered writing to be an essential part of a Frankish prince's education. According to Einhard, Charlemagne kept writing tablets under the pillows of his bed, so that he could practise writing during quiet moments; but even Einhard admits that this attempt at self-improvement was more of a pious hope than a great success.[41]

Was this the End of a Civilization?

The concept of the 'end of a civilization' has gone profoundly out of fashion, for reasons I shall examine in the final chapter. 'Civilization' is a word that people now prefer not to use. Certainly, if it is charged with any sense of moral superiority, the concept is best avoided. Twentieth-century experience has taught us that highly sophisticated and cultured people are capable of the most heartless and 'uncivilized' behaviour, often supported in this by a belief in their own superiority. The camp commandant, relaxing to the sound of Beethoven after a hard day's work slaughtering innocent people, has indeed entered the mythology of modern times. Even a cursory look at the Roman world provides plenty of evidence of similar attitudes. The Romans' certainty of their superiority over the barbarians justified merciless cruelty in defence of the 'civilized' world (Figs. 2.3 and 2.4, at pp. 26 and 27), and the cultivated aristocrat Symmachus saw the tragic and heroic suicide of his Saxon gladiators only as an irritant sent to try him (p. 24).

However, 'civilization' can also be used as a shorthand term for 'complex societies and what they produce' (as in the 'civilizations' of ancient Egypt or Mesopotamia). It is this sense that I have been exploring in this book, because it is my belief that modern scholars have thrown this particular baby out with the bath-water of moral judgement. In wanting to depict the post-Roman centuries as 'equal' to those of Roman times, they have ignored the extraordinary and fascinating decline in complexity that occurred at the end of the empire.

Although high culture was also affected, I have deliberately focused on people in the middle and lower ranks of society, and on the access that they had to sophisticated tools and products, such as writing and good-quality pottery. As we have seen, this access was widespread and impressive in the Roman period, and very restricted thereafter. In this sense, ancient 'civilization' came to an end in the West with the fall of the empire. Of course, what the ancients had done with their sophisticated 'civilization' was as varied, and often as questionable, as our own behaviour. It enabled a peasant near Luna to eat off a Campanian dinner plate, but it also built a mountain of rubbish at Monte Testaccio; it allowed a slave in Britain to express his wish for freedom, but it also enabled a Pompeian perfume-seller to record a particularly good fuck. Such things, as much as a multitude of books and impressive buildings, are the characteristics of a complex society, or, if one prefers, of a 'civilization'.

VIII

ALL FOR THE BEST IN
THE BEST OF ALL
POSSIBLE WORLDS?

I F THE WEST was overrun by violent invasion during the fifth century, and if the sophisticated civilization of the ancient world collapsed over the following centuries, how is it that such radically different, and rosier, views have recently been propounded? Why is this key period currently being interpreted in such a novel way?[1]

The Home of Late Antiquity

In part it is a question of perspective, and, as I have freely admitted, my own view has certainly been conditioned by a very 'Roman' upbringing and early experience. In Italy, the primacy of ancient civilization is seldom doubted, and a traditional view of the end of the Roman world is very much alive. Most Italians are with me in remaining highly sceptical about a peaceful 'accommodation' of the barbarians, and the 'transformation' of the Roman world into something new and equally sophisticated.[2] The idea that the Germanic incomers were peaceful immigrants, who did no harm, has not caught on.

In parts of Italy, indeed, some very simplistic and wholly negative views of the barbarian conquests are alive and well. *The Last Legion*, written by a professor of Classical Archaeology in Milan, is a best-selling popular novel set in the late fifth century. Its Romans are, almost to a man and woman, noble, brave, and pure—they fight, against impossible odds, to defend the last emperor and to uphold the values of Rome's glory days. At one point the band of heroes, Christians and pagans alike, lift their voices in the *Carmen Saeculare*, Horace's great hymn to the gods and to the glory of Rome. The barbarians, by contrast, are wreckers, taking on Roman ways

only if they think that this will help them in their mission to subdue the
Romans; they are brutal and cruel, consume untold quantities of bad meat
and beer, and have bits of food stuck in their beards.[3] I suspect that this
view, by an author who lives in Bologna, owes as much to his experience of
German and British tourists in the *pizzerie* of Rimini as it does to the fifth
century.

Unsurprisingly, it is in northern Europe and in North America that the
idea of the invaders as peaceable immigrants has its home. It is scholars
from Austria and Germany, from England, and from Scandinavia who
dominate the recent volumes, sponsored by the European Science Foundation, that examine the fifth-century settlements and depict them as essentially undisruptive. English and French were the official languages of this
project, but I am told that the discussions that produced these particular
volumes often veered into German, the obvious common language of the
participants.

ooo

The historians who have argued for a new and rosy Late Antiquity are
primarily North Americans, or Europeans based in the USA, and they
have shifted their focus right out of the western Roman empire. Much of
the evidence that sustains the new and upbeat Late Antiquity is rooted
firmly in the eastern Mediterranean, where, as we have seen, there is good
evidence for prosperity through the fifth and sixth centuries, and indeed
into the eighth in the Levant. I did a rough tally of the short entries in the
recent American *Guide* to Late Antiquity and found 183 entries concerned with people, places, and things that were specifically eastern, and
only 62, some 25 per cent, western. In the new Late Antiquity, parts of the
ancient world that were once considered marginal have become central,
and some western areas, which were once considered important, have
dropped out of sight. There are, for instance, in this *Guide*, no entries
for the Franks or Visigoths, the two peoples who dominated sixth- and
seventh-century continental Europe, and none for the Britons and
Anglo-Saxons.

There is a great deal that is positive in this approach. It is very healthy to
be reminded that the peoples of Britain might not merit an entry in a
handbook covering the third to eighth centuries, while the culture of the
East was flourishing into the later sixth century and beyond. The new
Late Antiquity is in part a deliberate corrective to a previous bias, which

assumed that the entire Roman world declined in the fifth century, because this is what happened in the West. Relocating the centre of the world in the fourth to eighth centuries to Egypt, the Levant, and Persia is a stimulating challenge to our mental framework and cultural expectations.

There is, however, an obvious problem in imposing, on the basis of eastern evidence, a flourishing Late Antiquity on the whole of the late Roman and post-Roman worlds. In the 'bad old days' western decline at the end of Antiquity was imposed on the eastern provinces. Now, instead of all the different regions of the empire being allowed to float free (some flourishing in the fifth to eighth centuries, others not), a new and equally distorting template is being imposed westwards. A long and rosy Late Antiquity, reaching even to AD 800, may well be an interesting and constructive way of examining the history of the Levant; but it seriously distorts the history of the West after about 400, and that of the Aegean region after around 600. For these areas, the imposition of a single and dynamic period, 'Late Antiquity', to cover the years between 250 and 800 has involved ignoring dramatic change and discontinuity in political, administrative, military, social, and economic life.[4]

The only way that 'Late Antiquity' can work as a unit for the whole Roman world, and a positive one at that, is by a concentration on the one 'positive' change that did impact on the entire post-Roman world and the whole period between 250 and 800: the spread, and momentous triumph, over the older religions of Rome and Persia, of two great monotheistic cults, Christianity and Islam. The new Late Antiquity has indeed been built around these developments and the remarkable changes that they brought about in attitudes towards many aspects of the human condition, such as sexuality, death, and identity. Modern Late Antiquity is primarily a spiritual and mental world, almost to the exclusion of the secular and material one. Until fairly recently it was institutional, military, and economic history that dominated historians' views of the fourth to seventh centuries.[5] Quite the reverse is now the case, at least in the USA. Of the thirty-six volumes so far published by the University of California Press in a series entitled 'The Transformation of the Classical Heritage', thirty discuss the world of the mind and spirit (primarily different aspects of Christian thought and practice); only five or six cover more secular topics (such as politics and administration); and none focuses on the details of material life.[6]

In some ways what we see in the new Late Antiquity is a return, in a much more sophisticated and less sectarian form, to an older interpretation of the post-Roman centuries as an age of the spirit, even an 'Age of Faith'. For instance, the opinion of the 'Dark Ages' expressed in 1932 by the English Catholic writer Christopher Dawson has close echoes in recent scholarship, although his religious enthusiasm and affiliation are much more transparent than those of most present-day historians:

> To the secular historian the early Middle Ages must inevitably still appear as the Dark Ages, as ages of barbarism, without secular culture or literature, given up to unintelligible disputes on incomprehensible dogmas . . . But to the Catholic they are not dark as much as ages of dawn, for they witnessed the conversion of the West, the foundation of Christian civilisation, and the creation of Christian art and Catholic liturgy. Above all, they were the Age of the Monks . . .[7]

A look at the short entries in the recent American *Guide* is again very instructive. If we seek the peoples of the late antique world, we have already found Visigoths, Franks, Britons, and Anglo-Saxons to be absent. But 'Demons' and 'Angels' both get entries; just as there is an entry for 'Hell', and separate ones for 'Heaven' and 'Paradise'. Secular officials get short shrift, whereas a host of different heretics and ascetics get individual entries. I looked in vain for one of the most powerful figures in late Roman politics and administration, the 'Praetorian Prefect', but found nothing between the entries for 'Pornography' and 'Prayer'. As with the geographical coverage, this new emphasis is a useful corrective to a previous interest in solidly administrative, political, and economic topics—but, again, perhaps it has got a little out of hand. The new Late Antiquity has opened up research into a mental and spiritual world that is fascinating and important; but most people in the past, like people today, spent the majority of their lives firmly in the material world, affected less by religious change than by their standard of living.

The Euro-Barbarian

The changing perspectives of scholarship are always shaped in part by wider developments in modern society. There is inevitably a close connection between the way we view our own world and the way we interpret the past. For instance, there is certainly a link between interpretations of the Germanic invaders as primarily peaceful, and the remarkable (and deserved) success that modern Germany has had at constructing a new and positive identity within Europe, after the disastrous Nazi years. Images of the fifth-century Germanic peoples and their settlement in the western empire have changed dramatically since the Second World War, as ideas about modern Germans and their role in the new Europe have altered.

At the time of the Nazi threat and in the immediate aftermath of the war, the fifth-century invaders were, not unnaturally, viewed by most Europeans in a very bleak light. In the 1930s, the English medievalist Eileen Power wrote an essay about the late Roman empire and its fall. It is full of foreboding, and presents a very straightforward contrast between Germanic barbarism, and the civilized Roman world, which it threatened and eventually overran:

> The battle sagas of the [Germanic] race, which have all but disappeared or have survived only as legends worked up in a later age; the few rude laws which were needed to regulate personal relationships, this was hardly civilization in the Roman sense. . . . Rome and the barbarians were . . . not only protagonists but two different attitudes to life, civilization and barbarism.[8]

In the immediate post-war period, two distinguished French scholars, André Piganiol and Pierre Courcelle, independently published books about the fall of the West, which were heavily influenced by the German invasion of France in 1940 and the occupation that followed. Piganiol laid responsibility for the destruction of a flourishing Christian empire at the door of Germanic tribes that, according to him, had achieved the remarkable feat of living for centuries on Rome's frontiers 'without becoming civilized'. He closed his book with two memorable sentences: 'Roman civilization did not pass peacefully away. It was assassinated.'[9] Courcelle meanwhile drew overt parallels between France's recent past and the fifth-century experience of barbarian invasion, and used arguments and language that are explicitly and richly anti-Germanic: the invaders were 'barbares', 'ennemies', 'envahisseurs', 'hordes', and 'pillards'; their passage through the empire was marked by 'incendies', 'ravages', 'sacs', 'prisonniers', and 'massacres'; they left behind them 'ruines désertes' and 'régions dévastées'.[10] Only the Franks, ancestors of the French, get a better write-up:

Courcelle's final chapter tells of how, eventually, they adopted Catholicism and other Roman ways, and thereby paved the way for the achievements of Charlemagne.[11]

Gradually, attitudes to twentieth-century Germans mellowed and softened, and with them the image of the fifth-century Germanic invaders. Already in the 1960s and 1970s the Germanic peoples had been rehabilitated from murderous and destructive thugs to become an essential element in the making of modern Europe, in book titles like 'The Formation of Europe and the Barbarian Invasions'.[12] When Goffart launched his theory of peaceful 'accommodation' in 1980 it therefore fell on fertile ground. Goffart himself seems to have intended his book to play down the role of the Germanic peoples in European history. He hoped to show that the settlements were in reality more 'Roman' than 'barbarian', since they had been decided by Roman policy and carried out within a Roman administrative structure: 'The more or less orderly garrisoning of Gaul, Spain, Africa, and Italy by alien troops gives us no compelling reason to speak of a "barbarian West".'[13] But ironically his theory has been used by scholars in a very different spirit: to elevate the Germanic peoples to the status of peaceful collaborators with the native Romans.

The European Union needs to forge a spirit of cooperation between the once warring nations of the Continent, and it is no coincidence that the European Science Foundation's research project into this period was entitled 'The Transformation of the Roman World'—implying a seamless and peaceful transition from Roman times to the 'Middle Ages' and beyond. In this new vision of the end of the ancient world, the Roman empire is not 'assassinated' by Germanic invaders; rather, Romans and Germans together carry forward much that was Roman, into a new Romano-Germanic world.[14] 'Latin' and 'Germanic' Europe is at peace.

Europeans have always had to work hard to find common roots and the origins of unity in their troubled past. A shared Christian heritage has good historical credentials as the basis for a common culture and identity, but is awkward for present-day reasons: Christianity, with its many sectarian squabbles, is now as divisive as it was once unifying; and adopting it as a badge of 'Europeanness' would, of course, definitely exclude all non-Christians from the club. Furthermore, linking Europe with Christianity might give the Pope ideas above his station, would be disturbingly 'American', and would certainly clash with liberal and left-wing European traditions of secularist politics.

The Roman empire on its own, although in some ways a wonderful precedent for much that modern Europe aspires to (with its free-trade zone, its common currency, and the undoubted loyalty that it inspired), has also never been entirely satisfactory as an ancestor for the European Union. Roman power was used too recently (by Mussolini) as part of a specifically Italian national and imperial agenda, and too much of northern and north-eastern Europe was never in Roman hands (whereas the southern and eastern shores of the Mediterranean were central to the Roman world). An entirely 'Roman' EU would marginalize northern Europe, and might be centred in Rome, Athens, and Istanbul, not in Strasbourg, Frankfurt, and Brussels. An interpretation of history that keeps the Roman past, but 'transforms' it into a post-Roman Europe dominated by the Franks, is therefore much more satisfactory. The centre of the present-day European Union, the Strasbourg–Frankfurt–Brussels triangle, and the centre of the eighth- and ninth-century Frankish empire coincide very closely: Brussels, for instance, is little more than 100 kilometres from Charlemagne's favoured residence and burial place at Aachen.

North of the Alps, the Franks have occasionally been wheeled out to support Europe in a more populist and explicit way, particularly because they are acknowledged as common ancestors by both the French and the Germans. Already in 1949 a 'Prix Charlemagne' was instituted, which is awarded annually to figures who have made a remarkable contribution towards European unity; and Charlemagne was also commemorated in an exhibition at Aachen in 1965, where he was presented as 'the first emperor who sought to unite Europe'.[15] Whether the Lombards who lost their Italian kingdom to him, or the Saxons who were massacred by him in their thousands, would have viewed this as a positive achievement is a moot point. In 1996 a second exhibition, the fruit of Franco-German collaboration, honoured the Franks of an earlier period, by commemorating the fifteen-hundredth anniversary of the baptism of Clovis (which supposedly took place in 496). The title chosen for the project was 'Les Francs, Précurseurs de l'Europe', 'Die Franken, Wegbereiter Europas'—'The Franks, Precursors (or Path-Finders) of Europe'.[16] Again it is doubtful whether the historical Franks can really live up to the projection upon them of such high ideals, though the baptism of Clovis, a powerful Germanic warrior accepted into the Catholic faith by the Gallo-Roman bishop of Reims, does fit rather well with a French vision of the respective roles of France and Germany within the European Union: German might, tamed and channelled to positive ends, by Gallic culture and civility (Fig. 8.1).

A 'Late Antiquity' for a New Age

The vision of Late Antiquity as full of positive cultural achievements also has obvious roots in modern attitudes to the world. It is, for instance, no great surprise that the Roman empire is not particularly in favour at the moment, and therefore that its demise is not deeply regretted. In Europe, empires and imperialism went firmly out of fashion in the decades follow- ing the Second World War, while in the United States, which traces its origins to a struggle for freedom from British imperial control, they have seldom enjoyed explicit favour. The 'Empire' in Hollywood's *Star Wars* is the force of evil, its storm troopers modelled partly on Roman praetorian guards.

I am no advocate of twenty-first-century imperialism—empires, it seems to me, have had their day—but it is a mistake to treat all empires of the past as universally bad in an undifferentiated way. The imposition of Roman power had certainly been brutal, and it was fiercely resisted by many. But in time the Roman empire evolved into something rather remarkable, very different from any modern empire. By the fourth century, the provincial aristocracies of the Roman world had largely forgotten their tribal ancestors and had settled down to be 'Roman'. Quite unlike any modern empire, Rome did not fall because its provincial subjects struggled to be 'free'. Amongst all the possible causes of Rome's fall canvassed by historians, popular uprisings to throw off the shackles of imperial rule come a very long way down any list. This is hardly surprising, since, as I have argued at length in this book, Roman rule, and above all Roman peace, brought levels of comfort and sophistication to the West that had not been seen before and that were not to be seen again for many centuries.

Connected with Rome's lessened prestige in the modern age, but extending beyond it, there has also been a marked decline over the last century in the status of 'Classics', the study of Graeco-Roman culture. In the nineteenth century all educated Europeans aspired to some knowledge of classical culture, because they viewed it as the product of a great civiliza- tion. I was very struck recently to see, in *Times* editorials of the 1880s,

8.1 Forging the Franco-German alliance—the baptism of Clovis by the Gallo-Roman bishop of Reims. As depicted in 1877 in the Panthéon of Paris.

short tags quoted in ancient Greek (without translation), while quotations in Latin are commonplace. For a *Times* reader of that period, it was self-evident that Homer and Virgil (despite their misfortune in not being born English) were superior even to outstanding representatives of Dark Age culture like the *Beowulf*-poet and Bede. A long Late Antiquity of equal status to classical times was quite simply unthinkable.

Much has changed since those days. The ancient Egyptians now feature in the British national curriculum for schoolchildren on an equal footing with the Romans, and, thanks to mummies and pyramids, are rather more popular. In northern Europe, at least, very few people now know any Latin or Greek: it is, for instance, rapidly becoming pedantic in Britain to insist that 'data', and even 'phenomena', are plural forms in modern English—new and highly unclassical phenomenas are entering our culture. When, recently, a possible tenth planet in the solar system was identified, it did not join the other planets in their Roman pantheon, but was named Sedna, after an Inuit goddess. Even in Oxford University, a bastion of traditional learning, the study of the classics has been steadily scaled down and is under threat of further restriction. Because Graeco-Roman culture has lost most of its privileged status, the post-Roman centuries are no longer automatically viewed as the 'Dark Age' that followed the demise of a great civilization.

Indeed, in the modern post-colonial world, the very concept of 'a civilization', be it ancient or modern, is now uncomfortable, because it is seen as demeaning to those societies that are excluded from the label. Nowadays, instead of 'civilizations', we apply universally the neutral word 'cultures'; all cultures are equal, and no cultures are more equal than others. This change has definitely been an important liberating force behind the rise of Late Antiquity. Authors of the post-Roman period no longer have to dwell in the long shadow cast by an earlier 'civilization'; and writers in local languages, such as Armenian, Syriac, and Coptic, can take their place in the sun alongside the established writers in Greek and Latin. In the new post-colonial world, local culture is indeed often felt to be more genuine and organic that the products of the dominant centre.

I have no objection to the main thrust of this change, and I am certainly delighted to see the demise of 'civilization' as a badge of moral superiority. But abandoning altogether the concept of 'a civilization' risks imposing too flat a view on the world's cultures. For better or worse (and often it is for the worse), some cultures are much more sophisticated than others. Societies with large cities, complex production- and distribution-networks, and the widespread use of writing, are markedly different from societies of villages, with essentially household production and an oral culture. The transition from Roman to post-Roman times was a dramatic move away from sophistication towards much greater simplicity.

ooo

My conception of Roman civilization, and its demise, is a very material one, which in itself probably renders it unfashionable. The capacity to mass-produce high-quality goods and spread comfort makes the Roman world rather too similar to our own society, with its rampant and rapacious materialism. Instead of studying the complex economic systems that sustained another sophisticated world, and their eventual demise, we seem to prefer to read about things that are wholly different from our own experience, like the ascetic saints of the late and post-Roman worlds, who are very fashionable in late-antique studies. In their lifetimes, the attraction of these saints was their rejection of the material values of their own societies, and our world, which is yet more materialistic and 'corrupt', seems to find them equally compelling. We have no wish to emulate the asceticism of a saint like Cuthbert of Lindisfarne, who spent solitary nights immersed in the North Sea praising God. But, viewed from a suitable distance, he is deeply attractive, in touch with both God and nature: after his vigils a pair of otters would come out of the sea to dry him with their fur and warm his feet with their breath.[17] This is a much more beguiling vision of the past than mine, with its distribution maps of peasant settlements, and its discussion of good- and bad-quality pottery.

A move away from economic history is not exclusive to Late Antiquity. Nowadays it is very difficult to persuade the average history student that it is worth spending even a few days researching an economic-history topic. In Oxford at least, the word 'economy' in its title is the kiss of death to an undergraduate history course, and I am also painfully aware that my repeated use of the word in this book may have prompted many a reader to set it down (so I am grateful if you have read this far). In the 1960s, economic history was highly fashionable, because it played an integral part in Marxist interpretations of the past. When the attraction of Marxist theory declined, as it did with the demise of Communism, most historians, and the reading public, seem to have withdrawn from economic history altogether, rather than seek out different ways of studying it and of understanding its importance.

∞

The new Late Antiquity is fascinated with the history of religion. As a secularist myself, I am bewildered by this development, and do not hold myself up as a confident commentator on the phenomenon. I have sometimes wondered whether it has found particular favour in the United States because religion plays a much more central role in modern life there than it does in most of Europe. It is certainly true that one has to look to Europe to find a community of historians like me, with an active interest in secular aspects of the end of the Roman world, such as its political, economic, and military history. On the other hand, the scholars who uphold the new Late Antiquity in the United States are from the west- and east-coast intelligentsia, so we are certainly not looking at a close link with the Bible Belt. Indeed, the emphasis in modern research is definitely not on the more intransigent and fundamentalist aspects of late-antique religion (of which there were many), but rather on its syncretism and flexibility.

It may be that our modern age has helped shape the particular way in which the religion of Late Antiquity is now studied, above all in the USA. The approach that is currently fashionable is not the traditional one, still practised, for instance, in parts of Catholic Europe, and characterized by the painstaking reconstruction of authoritative texts, and by the study of religious institutions (like the papacy) and of orthodox structures and beliefs. The religious figures who characterize the new Late Antiquity are not popes and bishops in council, determining doctrine or developing the liturgy, but charismatic ascetics and intellectuals, in isolation or in small communities, finding their path to God in a highly individualistic, rather than an institutional and formalized, way. Modern 'new-age' spirituality has perhaps had a profound impact on the way that late-antique religion is studied and presented.

Pluses . . .

Although I believe the new attitudes to the barbarian invasions, and to the 'transformation' of the ancient world, are flawed, there are undoubtedly positive aspects to them both. The theory that accommodates the

Germanic peoples peaceably into the empire does correct the myth that the fall of the West was a titanic and ideological struggle between two great united forces, Rome and 'the barbarians'. In truth, there was plenty of room for alliances and for a degree of accommodation between the Germanic tribes and the native Romans, and both were as often at war amongst themselves as they were between each other. But to stop at this point is like focusing on the degree of collaboration and accommodation that took place in occupied France or the Channel Islands during the Second World War, and arguing from this that the German presence was painless and uncontroversial. There is plenty of evidence from the fifth and sixth centuries that invasion was traumatic, and that living with the conquerors required very difficult adjustments.

The new conception of a long 'Late Antiquity' has, in my opinion, more in its favour than the theory of a peaceful barbarian takeover. There have definitely been gains from studying the fifth to eighth centuries as part of Antiquity rather than as part of the 'Middle Ages', even in the West, where I have argued that the model of a continuous and thriving period fits very badly. In particular, it is helpful that 'Late Antiquity' and 'late antique' are relatively new coinages, which have not yet entered into popular usage, and have therefore been spared the rich accretion of misleading connotations that the 'Middle Ages' and 'medieval' (not to mention the 'Dark Ages') carry with them. Popular images of the Middle Ages tend to be either highly romanticized (peopled by knights, ladies, and the odd unicorn) or exceptionally grim—there is little or no middle ground. Images of the kind are very much alive in the modern world—'to get medieval' has recently appeared in American English, meaning to get violent in an extremely unpleasant way. The new online edition of the *Oxford English Dictionary* illustrates its usage with a quotation from Tarantino's *Pulp Fiction*: 'I ain't through with you by a damn sight. I'm gonna git Medieval on your ass.'[18] 'Late Antiquity' and 'late antique' are a welcome relief, because they are terms that do not yet carry with them similar baggage.

'Late Antiquity' has other advantages too. The ancient world tends to be viewed as a whole, and historians who study it are often well informed about trends that affected the whole empire, and use comparisons and contrasts to point out what is specific about a particular region. However, this broad and inclusive vision narrows once we enter the 'Middle Ages'—I have several times been startled to realize quite how little some distinguished scholars of post-Roman Britain and Italy know about the neighbouring Frankish kingdom, despite the richness of its sources. 'Medieval' studies have tended to move backwards from the present, in search of the origins of the nation states of Europe, and, in doing this, they have frequently become rather parochial in focus.[19] 'Late Antiquity', which moves forward from the Roman world, offers a much broader and more cosmopolitan canvas.

... and Minuses

I have defended the right of historians to use difficult words like 'civiliza-tion' and 'crisis', though they have to be wielded with care and precision, because some of them are clearly contentious. I have indeed become increasingly puzzled that the word 'decline' should be so contested in historical writing, when 'rise' is used all the time, without anyone ever batting an eyelid.[20] Perhaps the difficulty lies in modern psychology. 'Decline', as well as its strongly negative connotations, perhaps also has moral ones. We tend to use it with a sense that somebody can and should be blamed for the change—as with a 'decline in educational standards'. I have used 'decline' in this book in its negative sense, very explicitly, because I believe a great deal was lost with the end of ancient sophistica-tion; but I hope that I am not blaming anyone for deliberately causing the decline that I have charted. I like the post-Roman period, and feel a deep sympathy for the people who coped with the headlong changes of the fifth and sixth centuries.

Present-day historians seem to feel more comfortable discussing the 'rise' of this or that, because there is absolutely no risk in this vocabulary of anyone being criticized or any negative value judgement being made; rather the reverse—everybody is being awarded a reassuring pat on the back. This is I think the main problem with the new way of looking at the end of the ancient world: all difficulty and awkwardness are smoothed out into a steady and essentially positive transformation of society. The Germanic invaders are peacefully accommodated into the Roman prov-inces, and the culture of Rome slowly evolves into new forms. Nothing ever goes badly wrong—in this vision of the past, there are no serious downward turns or abrupt changes, let alone complete ruptures; rather, everything moves forward along a level plain, or even on a slightly rising trajectory.[21]

I confess that I find this limiting; but, more importantly, I think it does not fit the evidence, and fails to reflect accurately what happened in the western half of the empire. In my opinion, the fifth century witnessed a profound military and political crisis, caused by the violent seizure of power and much wealth by the barbarian invaders. The native population was able, to some extent, to adapt to these new conditions, but what is interesting about this adjustment is that it was achieved in very difficult circumstances. I also believe that the post-Roman centuries saw a dramatic decline in economic sophistication and prosperity, with an impact on the whole of society, from agricultural production to high culture, and from peasants to kings. It is very likely that the population fell dramatically, and certain that the widespread diffusion of well-made goods ceased. Sophisticated cultural tools, like the use of writing, disappeared altogether in some regions, and became very restricted in all others.

My worries about the new Late Antiquity, however, go deeper than a concern that it is so restricted by its religious focus as to be deceptively wrong. I also think there is a real danger for the present day in a vision of the past that explicitly sets out to eliminate all crisis and all decline. The end of the Roman West witnessed horrors and dislocation of a kind I sincerely hope never to have to live through; and it destroyed a complex civilization, throwing the inhabitants of the West back to a standard of living typical of prehistoric times. Romans before the fall were as certain as we are today that their world would continue for ever substantially unchanged. They were wrong. We would be wise not to repeat their complacency.

APPENDIX
From Potsherds to People

Pottery plays a major part in my account of the Roman and post-Roman economies; and indeed in any scholarly discussion of early economic history that takes archaeological evidence seriously. In these few pages I explain how it is that we can deduce so much from mute potsherds about both the production and the diffusion of ceramics. As with most areas of the Roman and post-Roman economies, the available written evidence is negligible, so it is from the excavated objects themselves that we have to reconstruct the nature of production and distribution.

Pottery is an archaeologist's dream (or nightmare), because it survives in such large quantities. Pottery vessels are very easy to break, and so get made and discarded in quantity; but their individual broken sherds are highly durable, and usually emerge from the ground in perfect condition. Furthermore, the only common way of recycling pottery fragments is as hard core, and this does not destroy their original form (whereas the recycling of objects in metal, glass, or stone generally involved melting them down, or completely recarving them). Potsherds have been uncovered in their millions, and on almost all archaeological excavations are much the commonest artefact discovered. It is a reasonable sup-position that, somewhere in the soil, almost all the pottery vessels ever made survive in fragments, waiting to be excavated and studied.

Potsherds are not only common; they are also exceptionally rich in the information they contain. Because the precise make-up of clays varies, according to the geology of the extraction sites, and because the design of pots from one region to another also varies, individual potsherds can very often be accurately provenanced (in other words, attributed to a specific place of production). They can also be dated, because designs not only varied geographically, but also changed through time. Sometimes these changes were dramatic—as when, at the end of the first century BC, Roman potters moved from using a black gloss on their tablewares to a red one—but normally it was a much more subtle process, manifested in relatively minor alterations in shape and design. Much laborious and meticulous work by scholars, working from datable deposits, has established tight chronologies for some types of pottery. Tablewares of the Roman period, which were peculiarly susceptible to changes in fashion, can sometimes be dated to within a very few decades.

Because pottery can be provenanced and dated, and because it is such a common find, it is often possible to show changing patterns of importation to a specific site, as the proportion of vessels from particular regions swells or declines (Fig. A.1). Information from a single sample or site should always be questioned; but when, as increasingly happens, many excavations produce concordant patterns, these begin to look reliable. Painstaking work, charting the occurrence of particular types of pottery vessels on different sites, can even allow us to begin speculating intelligently about mechanisms of distribution. Fig. A.2, for instance,

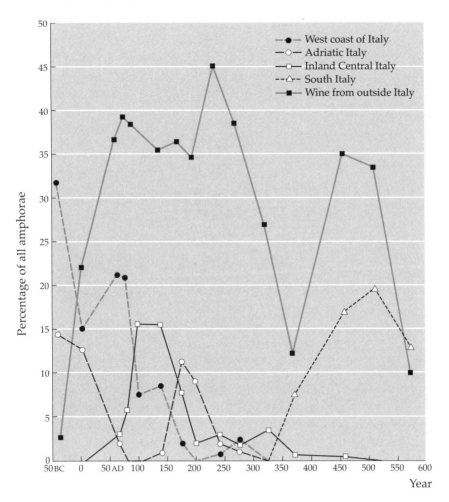

A.1 The changing origin of the wine-amphorae (and hence of the wine) that arrived at Rome's port, Ostia, between 50 BC and AD 600. Italian products fade out, except for a late surge of imports from southern Italy.

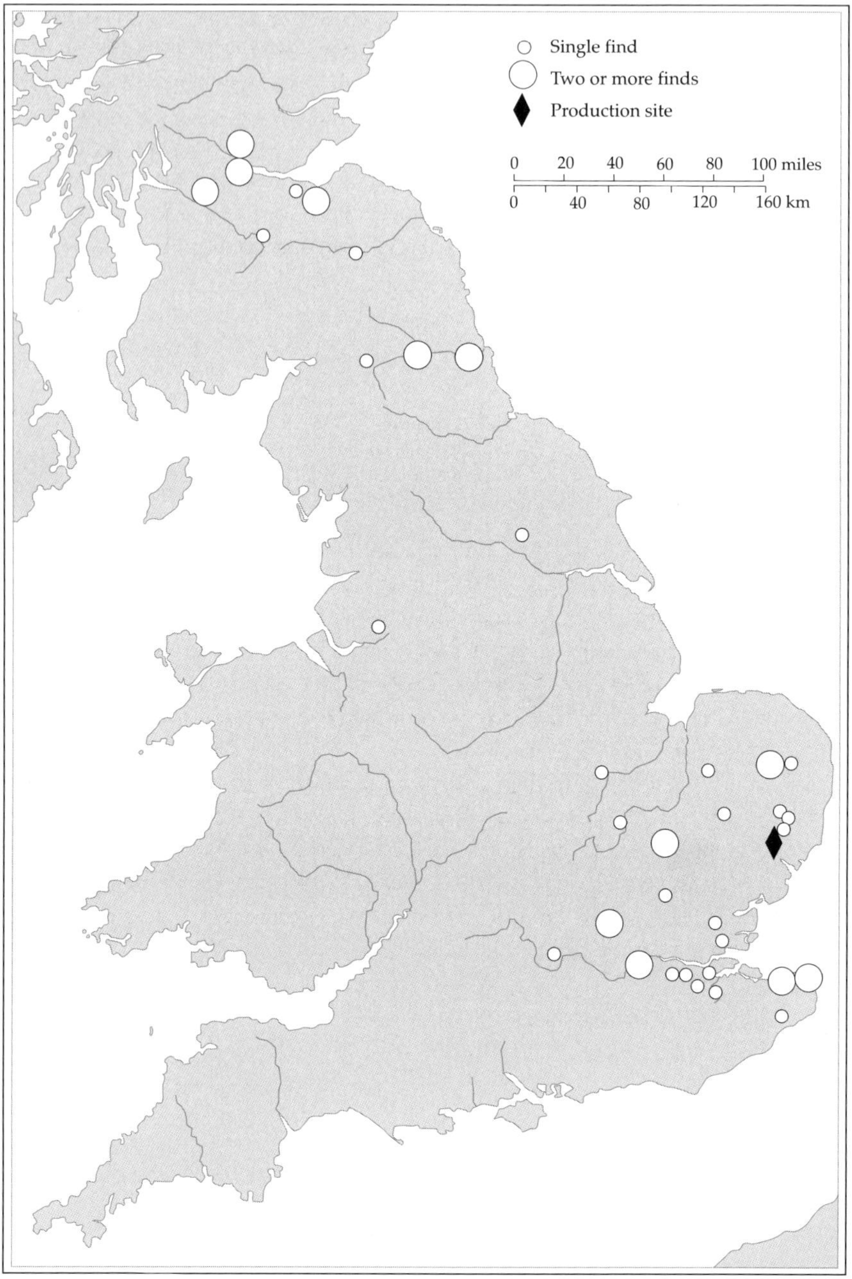

A.2 Two different markets: the diffusion of mixing-bowls made in Colchester in the second century AD. The lozenge is Colchester itself.

shows the known find spots of a type of *mortarium* (a grinding- and mixing-bowl, used in the preparation of food), made in Colchester within the period AD 140–200. There are two clearly distinct concentrations of these finds. The northern one consists of *mortaria* discovered along the Hadrianic and Antonine walls, and must represent vessels purchased or requisitioned by the army (and probably taken by sea up the east coast). By contrast, the pattern of distribution within an arc around Colchester looks commercial, falling off with growing distance, and hence transport costs, from the place of production—with the lesser cost of water-borne transport perhaps accounting for some of the outlying finds (for instance, in Kent and in the Thames Valley). The work of hundreds of archaeologists, excavating and publishing a large number of widely scattered sites, has slowly put together a complex and convincing economic picture.

Finally, like all artefacts, potsherds contain within themselves many indications of the level of skill and technology involved in their manufacture. In particular, the quality of a potsherd's clay (and of any decorative glazes or slips) tells us how carefully these primary materials were selected and prepared, while marks of wheel-turning and decoration tell us about the precise processes of building up the vessel (for instance, if it was hand-shaped, or made on a slow or fast wheel, and whether it was further worked when half-dry). Finally, much can be deduced about the firing of the pot from the appearance and consistency of its core and from the look and feel of its surface finish. A simple, if extreme, comparison—between Figs. 5.5 and 5.7, at pp. 99 and 105—makes this point more clearly than can any words.

All in all, pottery is probably as helpful and informative an artefact as any that exists (except objects that also carry inscriptions, such as coins); while its abundance renders it quite unique in the archaeological record. No other product is so readily available, nor so open to sophisticated comparative analysis. Pottery may be tedious to excavate and process, and it may not be thrilling to read about, but it is a gold mine of information.

CHRONOLOGY

376   Goths, fleeing the Huns, cross the Danube into the eastern empire.

378   The Goths crush the army of the eastern empire at the battle of Hadrianopolis, killing the eastern emperor, Valens.

391   The emperor Theodosius issues laws against anyone who performs pagan sacrifice.

401   Goths, led by Alaric, enter Italy from the Balkans.

402   Alaric and the Goths are driven out of Italy by the western commander, Stilicho.

405–6   A Germanic army, led by Radagaisus, invades Italy and is eventually defeated at Fiesole, near Florence.

406   On the last day of the year, Vandals, Sueves, and Alans cross the Rhine into the Roman empire. Much of Gaul is ravaged between 407 and 409.

407   The Roman armies of Britain and northern Gaul support an imperial usurper, Constantine III. Imperial control of Britain is thereafter very tenuous, and the island is increasingly subjected to raids and invasions by Irishmen, Picts, and Anglo-Saxons.

408   The Goths, under Alaric, re-enter Italy from the Balkans. The western imperial commander, Stilicho, is murdered with the connivance of his emperor, Honorius.

409   The Vandals and others cross the Pyrenees from Gaul into Spain.

410   The Goths, under Alaric, capture and sack the city of Rome.

411   The Iberian peninsula is partitioned between the Vandals, Alans, and Sueves.

412   The Goths, having failed in an attempt to reach Sicily and Africa by sea, leave Italy for Provence.

419   The western Goths (the 'Visigoths') are settled by treaty with the imperial government in south-western Gaul (Aquitaine).

429   The Vandals cross the Straits of Gibraltar into North Africa.

420s and 430s   Emergence of a Hunnic empire, north of the Danube.

439   The Vandals capture Carthage, establish a kingdom, and begin a period of sea-raiding across the Mediterranean.

441   The Huns capture the Balkan fortress town of Naissus.

447   The eastern emperor agrees to pay the Huns a yearly tribute of 2,100 pounds of gold.

around 443   The Burgundians are settled by treaty with the imperial government near Lake Geneva.

451   The Hunnic army, under Attila, is defeated in Gaul at the battle of the Catalaunian Fields by an army of Romans and Visigoths.

452   The Huns invade Italy and sack the great north-eastern city of Aquileia.

453   Death of Attila, leading to the slow dissolution of Hunnic power.

455   Second sack of Rome—by the Vandals, who arrive by sea from Carthage.

456 onwards   The Visigoths extend their power over Spain. By the end of the century, they control almost the whole Iberian peninsula.

468   Defeat of a combined attempt, by the eastern and western emperors, to recapture Africa from the Vandals.

476   Romulus Augustulus (the last emperor resident in Italy) is deposed by the Germanic general Odoacer, who sets himself up as king. Thereafter there is only one Roman emperor—that of the east, resident in Constantinople.

around 480   The Frankish king, Clovis, begins to extend his power in northern and central Gaul.

489–93   Theoderic the Ostrogoth captures Italy from Odoacer, and replaces him as king.

507   The Franks, under Clovis, defeat the Visigoths at the battle of Vouillé, and establish their control over most of Gaul. At around the same time, Clovis is converted from paganism to orthodox Catholic Christianity.

526   Death of Theoderic in Italy; his death begins a period of dynastic instability for the Ostrogoths.

533   An East Roman army, under orders from the emperor Justinian, defeats the Vandals and captures their African kingdom. This is incorporated into the eastern (or 'Byzantine') empire.

535   Byzantine armies invade Ostrogothic Italy, beginning a war that will last almost twenty years.

540   The Persians invade Syria and sack Antioch, reopening a period of intense warfare between the Byzantine and Persian empires.

541   Bubonic plague appears in Egypt and slowly spreads throughout the Roman world.

553   The Ostrogoths in Italy are decisively defeated, and Byzantine rule over the peninsula is established.

568–72 The Lombards invade Italy, and establish a kingdom centred on Pavia; but they fail to capture much of Italy, including Rome and Ravenna (which remain in Byzantine hands).

582   The Avars, with their Slav allies, capture the Byzantine city of Sirmium, near the Danube frontier. This event begins a long period of great insecurity in the Balkans and Greece. In 582 Athens is also captured and sacked.

587   The Visigoths, under their king Reccared, convert from Arian Christianity to the orthodox Catholicism of their Spanish subjects.

597   Gregory, bishop of Rome, sends a mission under Augustine to convert the pagan Anglo-Saxons of Britain.

603   A major war breaks out between the Persian and Byzantine empires.

611   The Persians capture Antioch, and, in the following year, push deep into Asia Minor, modern Turkey.

626   Constantinople is besieged by Avar and Persian armies.

629   The great war with Persia finally ends, in Persian defeat.

633   Arabs, newly united under the banner of Islam, begin the conquest of the Byzantine Levant.

636   Arab power over the Levant is confirmed by their victory over the Byzantines at the battle of the River Yarmuk. By 646 the Arabs also control all Egypt.

during the 640s   The Arabs begin raiding deep into Asia Minor, the Aegean region, and Africa.

674–8   The Arabs blockade Constantinople.

698   Carthage and the province of Africa fall to the Arabs.

711   An Arab army enters Spain, and begins the successful conquest of almost the whole peninsula.

716–18 Second Arab blockade of Constantinople.

732 A Muslim army, raiding into Francia from Spain, is defeated by the Frankish king, Charles Martel, near Poitiers.

768 Accession of the Frankish king Charles, known to posterity as 'Charlemagne'.

800 Charlemagne is crowned emperor in Rome, the first western emperor for over 300 years.

NOTES

Chapter 1. Did Rome Ever Fall?

1. Edward Gibbon, *Autobiography of Edward Gibbon as Originally Edited by Lord Sheffield* (Oxford, 1907), 160.

2. From the 'Introduction' to William Robertson, *The History of the Reign of the Emperor Charles V: With a View of the Progress of Society in Europe, from the Subversion of the Roman Empire, to the Beginning of the Sixteenth Century* (London, 1769).

3. I explore the rise of the new Late Antiquity in much greater depth in the forthcoming *Festschrift* for Wolf Liebeschuetz, edited by John Drinkwater and Benet Salway.

4. P. R. L. Brown, *The World of Late Antiquity: From Marcus Aurelius to Muhammad* (London, 1971).

5. P. R. L. Brown, 'The World of Late Antiquity Revisited', *Symbolae Osloenses*, 72 (1997), 5–30, at 14–15.

6. *Late Antiquity: A Guide to the Post-Classical World*, ed. G. W. Bowersock, Peter Brown, and Oleg Grabar (Cambridge, Mass., and London, 1999), ix.

7. Bernard Cornwall, *The Winter King* (Harmondsworth, 1996).

8. See, above all, Averil Cameron, 'The Perception of Crisis', in *Morfologie sociali e culturali in Europa fra Tarda Antichità e Alto Medioevo* (Settimane di studio del Centro italiano di studi sull' Alto Medioevo, 45; Spoleto, 1998), 9–31, at 10.

9. The papers that were given at the European conferences are gradually appearing in print, published by Brill.

10. The 'waves' (*vagues*) are from the title of L. Musset, *Les Invasions: Les Vagues germaniques* (Paris, 1965).

11. J. G. Herder, *Outlines of a Philosophy of History*, trans. T. Churchill (London, 1800), 421.

12. An interesting exception, anticipating recent thinking, was Alfons Dopsch, *The Economic and Social Foundations of European Civilization* (London, 1937).

13. E. A. Freeman, *Old English History for Children* (London, 1869), 28–9.

14. See pp. 173–4.

15. The title is from the English edition of Musset's *Les Invasions* (of 1965): L. Musset, *The Germanic Invasions: The Making of Europe AD 400–600*, trans. E. and C. James (London, 1975).

16. W. Goffart, *Barbarians and Romans AD 418–584: The Techniques of*

Accommodation (Princeton, 1980). Two important supplementary articles are: W. Goffart, 'Rome, Constantinople, and the Barbarians', *American Historical Review*, 86 (1981), 275–306; and Goffart 'The Theme of *"the* Barbarian Invasions" ', in E. Chrysos and A. Schwarcz (eds.), *Das Reich und die Barbaren* (Veröffentlichungen des Istituts für österreichische Geschichtsforschung, 29; Vienna, 1989), 87–107; both in Goffart, *Rome's Fall and After* (London and Ronceverte, 1989), 1–32, 111–32, the pagination cited in each case.

17. Goffart, 'The Theme', 132.
18. The quotations are from: Goffart, *Barbarians and Romans*, 230, 35 (see also Goffart, 'The Theme', 130).
19. W. Pohl (ed.), *Kingdoms of the Empire: The Integration of Barbarians in Late Antiquity* (Leiden, New York, and Cologne, 1997). Despite its title, the volume contains articles both for and against the Goffart line.
20. R. W. Mathisen and D. Shanzer (eds.), *Society and Culture in Late Antique Gaul: Revisiting the Sources* (Aldershot, 2001), 1–2. For similar views: P. Amory, 'The Meaning and Purpose of Ethnic Terminology in the Burgundian Laws', *Early Medieval Europe*, 2 (1993), 1–28, at 1–2; B. D. Shaw, 'War and Violence', in *Late Antiquity: A Guide*, 130–69, at 152–3, 163; G. W. Bowersock, 'The Vanishing Paradigm of the Fall of Rome', in G. W. Bowersock, *Selected Papers on Late Antiquity* (Bari, 2000), 187–97.

Chapter II. The Horrors of War

1. Leo, *Epistolae* XII.viii and xi (Migne, *Patrologia Latina* LIV, coll. 653–5).
2. P. Heather, *The Goths* (Oxford, 1996), 181–91; H. Wolfram, *History of the Goths*, trans. T. J. Dunlop (Berkeley and Los Angeles, and London, *c.* 1988), 172–89.
3. Sidonius Apollinaris, *Letters*, VII.7.3. For the defence of Clermont: J. Harries, *Sidonius Apollinaris and the Fall of Rome, AD 407–485* (Oxford, 1994), 224–9, 235–6.
4. Hydatius, *Chronicle*; entries 39 [47] for the scourges; 196 [201], 202 [207] for his capture and eventual release.
5. For events in 406–9: C. Courtois, *Les Vandales et l'Afrique* (Paris, 1955), 42–51; P. Courcelle, *Histoire littéraire des grandes invasions germaniques* (Paris, 1948), 58–79. For Visigothic devastation in 413: Wolfram, *History of the Goths*, 162.
6. Goths in Italy: J. Matthews, *Western Aristocracies and Imperial Court A.D. 364–425* (Oxford, 1975), 284–306; Wolfram, *History of the Goths*, 150–62. Tax remissions: *Theodosian Code* XI.28.7 (8 May 413), XI.28.12 (15 November 418).
7. Progressive starvation: Zosimus, *New History*, V.39 (trans. Ridley). The surrender of Rome: Olympiodorus, *History*, fragment xi.3 (trans. Blockley, pp. 168–9).

8. For the Vandals and the sack of 455: Courtois, *Les Vandales et L'Afrique*, 194–6; Victor of Vita, *Vandal Persecution*, I.25.

9. Eugippius, *Life of Severinus*. There is a useful discussion of the *Life*, on which I am in part dependent, in E. A. Thompson, *Romans and Barbarians: The Decline of the Western Empire* (Madison, 1982), 113–33.

10. Hydatius, *Chronicle*, entries 83 [93], 85 [95]; Sidonius Apollinaris, *Poem* VII, line 233.

11. Eugippius, *Life of Severinus*, ch. 20.

12. Rural insecurity: the soldiers in ibid., ch. 20; also ibid., chs. 4.1–5, 10.1 (the incident outside Favianis), 25.3.

13. Ibid., ch. 30 (defence of Lauriacum); chs. 5, 8, 19 (dealings with kings; 19 recounts the Alaman royal visit).

14. Ibid., chs. 17.4 (Tiburnia), 1.2–5 (Asturis); 24.1–3 (Ioviaco); 22.4–5, 27.3 (Batavis).

15. Ibid., chs. 27 (movement of the people of Quintanis), 31 (surrender of Lauriacum).

16. Ibid., ch. 31.6.

17. Ibid., chs. 1.4, 2.1–2. The troops are described as 'barbarians . . . who had entered a treaty with the Romans'. It is possible that the 'Romans' who made this treaty were not the townspeople themselves (as I have supposed), but the imperial government in Italy.

18. Hydatius, *Chronicle*, entries 188–91 [193–6].

19. Orosius, *History against the Pagans*, VII.39, II.19 (for more detail of the Gaulish sack).

20. Sack of Rome: Jordanes, *Gothic History*, 156 ('spoliant tantum, non autem, ut solent gentes, igne supponunt . . .'). Alliance of 451: ibid. 185–218.

21. Gildas, *The Ruin of Britain*, ch. 24.3–4 (quotation from Winterbottom's translation); Victor of Vita, *Vandal Persecution*, I.7.

22. Vandals: Possidius, *Life of Augustine*, 28.5, Gaul: Orientius of Auch, *Commonitorium*, in *Poetae Christiani Minores*, ed. R. Ellis (Corpus Scriptorum Ecclesiasticorum Latinorum, XVI; Vienna, 1888), lines 179–84 '– uno fumavit Gallia tota rogo'.

23. First, in the sixth century, by Jordanes, *Gothic History*, 219–22.

24. Leo, *Epistolae* CLIX (Migne, *Patrologia Latina* LIV, coll. 1136–7).

25. C. R. Whittaker, *Frontiers of the Roman Empire: A Social and Economic Study* (Baltimore and London, 1994), 194–200; A. Chauvot, *Opinions romaines face aux barbares au IVe siècle ap. J.-C.* (Paris, 1998).

26. Symmachus, *Letters*, II.46 (*Symmachi Opera*, ed. O. Seeck (Monumenta Germaniae Historica, Auctores Antiquissimi, VI.1; Berlin, 1885)).

27. Orosius, *History against the Pagans*, VII.35.19 (trans. Deferrari). Salvian, *The Governance of God*, IV.13.60, V.5.21. During the fifth century, attitudes to barbarians did slowly change: J. Moorhead, *The Roman Empire Divided*

400–700 (Harlow, 2001), 13–24; P. Heather, 'The Barbarian in Late Antiquity: Image, Reality and Transformation', in R. Miles (ed.), *Constructing Identities in Late Antiquity* (London, 1999), 234–58, at 242–55.

28. Priscus, *History*, fragment 22.3 (trans. Blockley, pp. 314–15). Who knows if Attila really had such a painting made? The iconography described is not implausible, since it can be found on late Roman consular diptychs.

29. Orosius, *History against the Pagans*, VII.37.

30. Stilicho: *Prosopography of the Later Roman Empire*, 3 vols. in 4 parts, ed. A. H. M. Jones, J. R. Martindale, and J. Morris (Cambridge, 1971–92), I, 'Stilicho'; *Corpus Inscriptionum Latinarum*, VI, 1731. Pogrom of 408: Zosimus, *New History*, V.35.5–6 (numbering the soldiers who deserted at 30,000). Slaves from Rome joining Alaric: ibid. V.42.3.

31. The classic work on this topic, on which I have depended heavily, is Courcelle, *Histoire littéraire*.

32. Jerome, *In Ezekiel*, I *Praef.* And III *Praef.* (Migne, *Patrologia Latina* XXV, coll. 15–16, 75D): 'in una Urbe totus orbis interiit.'

33. Augustine, *Concerning the City of God against the Pagans*, trans. H. Bettenson (Harmondsworth, 1972).

34. Orosius, *History against the Pagans*. His optimism was shared, in this same period, by the pagan aristocrat and poet Rutilius Namatianus: J. Matthews, *Western Aristocracies and Imperial Court A.D. 364–425* (Oxford, 1975), 325–8. Rutilius looked forward to the day when 'fearful Goths will bow their perfidious necks' before the renewed might of Rome: Rutilius Namatianus, *A Voyage Home*, I, line 142.

35. *The* Carmen de Providentia Dei, *attributed to Prosper of Aquitaine*, ed. and trans. M. P. McHugh (Washington, 1964), lines 903–9.

36. Orientius of Auch, *Commonitorium* (as cited in n. 22), lines 195–6.

37. Salvian, *The Governance of God*, IV.12.54, VII.6.24, and *passim* for similar passages.

38. Ibid. VI. 18. 98–9. *Chronicle of 452*, entry 138, p. 662.

39. A. Momigliano, 'La caduta senza rumore di un impero nel 476 d.C', *Annali della Scuola Normale Superiore di Pisa*, ser. III, vol. III.2 (1973), 397–418 (repr. in his collected essays *Sesto contributo alla storia degli studi classici e del mondo antico*, i (Rome, 1980), 159–79).

Chapter III. The Road to Defeat

1. A. Demandt, *Der Fall Roms: Die Auflösung der römischen Reiches im Urteil der Nachwelt* (Munich, 1984).

2. As rightly stressed by Goffart on several occasions: 'Rome, Constantinople'; 'The Theme' (especially at 7–17, 125–32); *Barbarians and Romans*, 3–35.

3. F. Millar, *The Roman Empire and its Neighbours* (London, 1981), 239–48. For

Valerian's skin: Lactantius, *De Mortibus Persecutorum*, ed. and trans. J. L. Creed (Oxford, 1984), 1.5.6 (pp. 10–11).

4. Vegetius, *Epitome* I.1.

5. Sea power: there was no repeat in our period of the daring seaborne raids, carried out across the Black Sea by Goths in the 250s and 260s, on the north coast of Asia Minor. Walls: Ammianus Marcellinus, *History*, XXXI.6.4: 'pacem sibi esse cum parietibus memorans.'

6. Ammianus Marcellinus, *History*, XXXI.15.

7. Ibid. XVI.12 for the whole battle (XVI.12.47 for the quoted passage).

8. Tacitus, *Annals* 1.61–2, in *Tacitus*, iii (Loeb Classical Library; Cambridge, Mass., and London, 1931), 346–9; W. Schlüter, 'The Battle of the Teutoburg Forest: Archaeological Research at Kalkreise near Osnabrück', in J. D. Creighton and R. J. A. Wilson (eds.), *Roman Germany: Studies in Cultural Interaction* (Portsmouth, RI, 1999), 125–59.

9. Ammianus Marcellinus, *History*, XXXI.13. There were, in the third century, other notable defeats, such as that which led to the death of the Emperor Decius (in 251) at the hands of the Goths. But the poor quality of our sources for the period makes it impossible to estimate the scale of the military losses.

10. See p. 24.

11. Regular use of Germanic and Hunnic mercenaries: J. H. W. G. Liebeschuetz, *Barbarians and Bishops* (Oxford, 1991), 33–6. Their loyalty to Rome: A. H. M. Jones, *The Later Roman Empire 284–602: A Social, Economic and Administrative Survey* (Oxford, 1964), 621–3.

12. Theodosius: *In Praise of Later Roman Emperors: The Panegyrici Latini*, ed. and trans. C. E. V. Nixon and B. S. Rodgers (Berkeley and Los Angeles, and London, 1994), panegyric II, chs. 32–3. 405–6 invasion: Zosimus, *New History*, V.26.4 (for the Huns and Alans); *Theodosian Code*, VII.13.16 of April 406 (for the recruiting of slaves).

13. Claudian, *Works*, trans. M. Platnauer, 2 vols. (Cambridge, Mass., and London, 1922), *De Bello Getico*, lines 423–9 (414–22 for the detail of where the troops were drawn from).

14. Edward Gibbon, *The History of the Decline and Fall of the Roman Empire*. The quotation is from the 'General Observations on the Fall of the Roman Empire in the West', which close volume iii (1781).

15. The classic discussion of army numbers remains Jones, *Later Roman Empire*, 679–86. R. MacMullen, *Corruption and the Decline of Rome* (New Haven and London, 1988) argues for growing corruption, and hence inefficiency, in the chain of supply between taxed citizen and paid soldier. He does show, very effectively, that the chain was inefficient; but I am not convinced that the problem was worsening (or worse than that found in all pre-modern states, and many modern ones).

16. For older views of economic decline, see the careful discussion in Jones, *Later*

Roman Empire, 812–23, 1039–45. More recent appraisals: R. Duncan-Jones, in S. Swain and M. Edwards (eds.), *Approaching Late Antiquity: The Transformation from Early to Late Empire* (Oxford, 2004), 20–52; B. Ward-Perkins, 'Specialized Production and Exchange', in *Cambridge Ancient History*, xiv. *Late Antiquity: Empire and Successors, A.D. 425–600*, ed. Averil Cameron, B. Ward-Perkins, and M. Whitby (Cambridge, 2000), 346–91, at 350–61. For more detail, see Ch. VI.

17. *Theodosian Code*, XI.28.7 (8 May 413). See p. 16.

18. *Theodosian Code*, VII.13.16 (slaves), 17 (those to be paid in full 'rebus patratis'), both of April 406.

19. 413 and 418 tax remissions: p. 16. Law of 444: *Nov. Val.* 15.1, in *Theodosian Code*. I cannot agree with H. Elton, *Warfare in Roman Europe AD 350–425* (Oxford, 1996), who argues for a decline of the western army only well into the fifth century (e.g. at pp. 265–8).

20. *Narratio de imperatoribus domus Valentinianae et Theodosianae, in Chronica Minora Saec. iv. v. vi. vii*, ed. T. Mommsen (Monumenta Germaniae Historica, Auctores Antiquissimi, IX; Berlin, 1891–2), 630. Orosius, *History against the Pagans*, VII.42, makes the same point from a more sympathetic angle. For the civil wars: J. B. Bury, *History of the Later Roman Empire* (2nd edn., London, 1923), i. 187–96; Goffart, 'Rome, Constantinople', 17–18; Goffart 'The Theme', 126–7; P. Heather, 'The Huns and the End of the Roman Empire in Western Europe', *English Historical Review*, 110 (1995), 4–41, at 23–5.

21. Zosimus, *New History*, VI.8.2 (eastern troops), V.50.1 (Huns), VI.1.2 (unavailability of the Gallic, Iberian, and British armies).

22. Thanks to the full account given by Zosimus (based on the lost *History* of Olympiodorus), we are comparatively well informed on all these events: Zosimus, *New History*, VI.1–6.

23. Eudoxius, 'arte medicus', a leader in 448: *Chronicle of 452*, p. 662, entry 133 (we do not know the status of Tibatto, the other named leader). The slaves of Gaul (in 435): *Chronicle of 452*, p. 660, entry 117 (for 435): 'omnia paene Galliarum servitia in Bacaudam conspiravere.' I. N. Wood, 'The North-Western Provinces', in *Cambridge Ancient History*, xiv. 497–524, at 502–4, provides a general discussion of the *Bacaudae*.

24. Rome: Zosimus, *New History*, V.42. Bazas: Paulinus of Pella, *Thanksgiving*, lines 333–6.

25. Goffart, 'Rome, Constantinople', 18–19.

26. The 399–400 revolt and the commemorative column are discussed, described, and illustrated in Liebeschuetz, *Barbarians and Bishops*, 100–3, 111–25, 273–8, and plates 1–7. Slaves and outcasts: Zosimus, *New History*, V.13 (trans. Ridley, lightly adapted).

27. Spain: Orosius, *History against the Pagans*, VII.40.6; *Prosopography of the Later Roman Empire*, II, 'Didymus 1' and 'Verenianus'. Italy: *Nov. Val.* 9, in

Theodosian Code. Clermont: Sidonius Apollinaris, *Letters*, III.3.3–8. Soissons: Gregory of Tours, *Histories*, II.27.

28. Tacitus, *Germania* 33, in *Tacitus*, i (Loeb Classical Library; Cambridge, Mass., and London, 1914), 182–3; Seneca, *De Ira* I.xi.3–4, in *Seneca*, i (The Loeb Classical Library; Cambridge, Mass., and London, 1928), 132–5.

29. Increasing Germanic unity: Heather, *Goths*, 51–65. Recruits to the Gothic force in 376–8: Ammianus Marcellinus, *History*, XXXI.6.5–6. W. Pohl, 'Conceptions of Ethnicity in Early Medieval Studies', in L. K. Little and B. H. Rosenwein (eds.), *Debating the Middle Ages: Issues and Readings* (Oxford, 1998), 15–24, is a useful introduction in English to the recent debate on 'ethnogenesis' (the process whereby disparate groups slowly formed into single 'peoples').

30. Goffart, 'The Theme', 112–13. See, for instance, the Visigoths' campaigns against the Siling Vandals and Alans in Spain 'on behalf of the Roman name' (Hydatius, *Chronicle*, entries 55 [63], 59 [67], 60 [68]).

31. Paulinus of Pella, *Thanksgiving*, lines 383–5.

32. Hydatius, *Chronicle*, entry 60 [68]: 'oblito regni nomine Gunderici regis Vandalorum . . . se patrocinio subiugarent.'

33. 'Rex Vandalorum et Alanorum': A. Gillett (ed.), *On Barbarian Identity: Critical Approaches to Ethnicity in the Early Middle Ages* (Turnhout, 2002), 109 n. 30. The Latin poet Dracontius, at the court of the Vandal king Gunthamund (484–96), included the Alans in a disparaging list of barbarian peoples (while, of course, omitting the Vandals), which suggests a degree of Vandal disdain for their Alan partners: Dracontius, *Romulea* V, lines 34–5 (Monumenta Germaniae Historica, Auctores Antiquissimi, XIV, ed. F. Vollmer, Berlin, 1905, p. 141).

34. Possidius, *Life of Augustine*, 28.4.

35. Goffart, 'The Theme'; Goffart, 'Rome, Constantinople'.

36. Matthews, *Western Aristocracies*, 284–306; Wolfram, *History of the Goths*, 117–81; Heather, *Goths*, 130–51, 181–7.

37. For the treaties of 435 and 442: Courtois, *Les Vandales et L'Afrique*, 169–75.

38. Visigoths: Hydatius, *Chronicle*, entry 61 [69]; Prosper, *Epitoma Chronicon*, in *Chronica Minora Saec. iv. v. vi. vii*, ed. T. Mommsen (Monumenta Germaniae Historica, Auctores Antiquissimi, ix; Berlin, 1891–2), p. 469, entry 1271. Burgundian and Alan grants: *Chronicle of 452*, entries 124, 127, 128 (p. 660). Location of Burgundian settlement: P. Duparc, 'La Sapaudia', *Comptes rendus de l'Académie des Inscriptions et Belles-Lettres* (1958), 371–83.

39. For the distinction between imperial and local interests: M. Kulikowski, 'The Visigothic Settlement in Aquitaine: The Imperial Perspective', in Mathisen and Shanzer (eds.), *Society and Culture*, 26–38. For possible reasons behind the 419 settlement: I. N. Wood, 'The Barbarian Invasions and First Settlements', in *Cambridge Ancient History*, xiii. *The Late Empire, A.D. 334–425*, ed. Averil Cameron and P. Garnsey (Cambridge, 1998), 516–37, at 531–2.

40. 442 settlement: *Chronicle of 452*, entry 127 (p. 660); Wood, in *Cambridge Ancient History*, xiv. 534.

41. Sidonius Apollinaris, *Letters*, VII.7.2: 'Facta est servitus nostra pretium securitatis alienae.'

42. A. Loyen, 'Les Débuts du royaume wisigoth de Toulouse', *Revue des études latines*, 12 (1934), 406–15.

43. Paulinus of Pella, *Thanksgiving*, lines 498–515 (the 420s is a probable, but uncertain, date: *Prosopography of the Later Roman Empire*, I, 'Paulinus 10'). Visigothic expansion: Heather, *Goths*, 185–6; Wolfram, *History of the Goths*, 175–6.

44. The most impressive case for the fall of the West as a 'consequence of *a series of contingent events*', remains Bury, *Later Roman Empire*, 308–13 (the quotation, with Bury's own italics, is from p. 311). Whether Stilicho could have destroyed Alaric (and, if so, why he didn't) has been hotly debated: S. Mazzarino, *Stilicone: La crisi imperiale dopo Teodosio* (Rome, 1942), 272–5, 310–18.

45. Courtois, *Les Vandales et L'Afrique*, 173, 199, 201.

46. Heather, *Goths*, 230–5.

47. For the possibility that the eastern government might have faced lesser problems in raising its taxes than the West: Jones, *Later Roman Empire*, 1066–7; B. Ward-Perkins, 'Land, Labour and Settlement', in *Cambridge Ancient History*, xiv. 342–3; and, specifically for western problems, Matthews, *Western Aristocracies*, 268–9, 277–8, 285.

48. Events immediately following Hadrianopolis: Ammianus Marcellinus, *History*, XXXI.15–16. The rebuilding of the eastern army: Liebeschuetz, *Barbarians and Bishops*, 23–31. Western help to the East in 395 and 397: Jones, *Later Roman Empire*, 183. Imperial policy towards the Goths: P. Heather and D. Moncur, *Politics, Philosophy, and Empire in the Fourth Century: Select Orations of Themistius* (Translated Texts for Historians, 36; Liverpool, 36), 199–207, 211–13.

49. Campaigns against the Huns: S. Williams and G. Friell, *The Rome that Did Not Fall: The Survival of the East in the Fifth Century* (London and New York, 1999), 63–93. Naissus: Priscus, *History*, fragments 6.2, 11.2.51–5 (Blockley, ii. 230–3, 248–9). 447 tribute: Priscus, *History*, fragment 9.3.1–35 (Blockley, ii. 236–9). The peoples present in Aetius' army: Jordanes, *Gothic History*, 191.

50. Long Walls: J. G. Crowe, 'The Long Walls in Thrace', in C. Mango and G. Dagron (eds.), *Constantinople and its Hinterland* (Aldershot, 1995), 109–24. City wall: F. Krischen, B. Meyer-Plath, and A. M. Schneider, *Die Landmauern von Konstantinopel*, 2 vols. (Berlin, 1938–43). Law of 418: *Theodosian Code*, IX.40.24.

51. Hunnic raid of 395: E.A. Thompson, *A History of Attila and the Huns*, (Oxford, 1948), 26–8. Value of different parts of the empire: M. F. Hendy, *Studies in the Byzantine Monetary Economy c.300–1450* (Cambridge, 1985), 616–18. Policy debates: Goffart, 'Rome, Constantinople', 16–17.

52. Roman–Persian relations: R. C. Blockley, *East Roman Foreign Policy: Formation and Conduct from Diocletian to Arcadius* (Leeds, 1992), 30–96, 123–7. Effects on Balkan security of a major campaign elsewhere: ibid. 57, 59–62, 76–7.

53. Goths in 410 and 415: Wolfram, *History of the Goths*, 159, 170. Vandal sea-power after 439: Courtois, *Les Vandales et L'Afrique*, 185–96.

Chapter IV. Living under the New Masters

1. Hydatius, *Chronicle*, entry 41 [49].

2. Africa: *Nov. Val.* 34.1–2, in *Theodosian Code*. Other African evidence of dispossession and exile: Courtois, *Les Vandales et L'Afrique*, 279–82. Britain: Gildas, *The Ruin of Britain*, 25.1 (as translated by Winterbottom). Migration to Brittany: L. Fleuriot, *Les Origines de la Bretagne* (Paris, 1980), esp. 110–18.

3. See, in particular, Goffart, *Barbarians and Romans*, H. Wolfram, *Das Reich und die Barbaren zwischen Antike und Mittelalter* (Berlin, 1990), 173–7, and Wolfram, *History of the Goths*, 295–7 (arguing for tax grants); versus S. J. B Barnish, 'Taxation, Land and Barbarian Settlement in the Western Empire', *Papers of the British School at Rome*, 54 (1986), 170–95, and J. H. W. G. Liebeschuetz, 'Cities, Taxes and the Accommodation of the Barbarians: The Theories of Durliat and Goffart', in W. Pohl (ed.), *Kingdoms of the Empire: The Integration of Barbarians in Late Antiquity* (Leiden, New York, and Cologne, 1997), 135–51 (arguing for land grants).

4. Cassiodorus, *Variae* II.16 (as translated by Barnish, 29–30; the emphases are, of course, my own).

5. Jones, *Later Roman Empire*, 257; Cassiodorus, *Variae* VII.3 (for the *comes Gothorum*).

6. Barbarians acquiring land by fair means or foul: Goffart, *Barbarians and Romans*, 93–7. Example of an earlier, Roman abuser of power: Sidonius Apollinaris, *Letters*, II.1.1–3. Theodahad: Procopius, *Wars*, V.3.2 (supported by Cassiodorus, *Variae* IV. 39, V.12). Tanca: Cassiodorus, *Variae* VIII.28 (as translated by Barnish). Cunigast: Boethius, *Philosophiae Consolatio*, ed. L. Bieler (Corpus Christianorum, Series Latina, XCIV, Turnholt, 1984), I.4 (English translation: Boethius, *The Consolation of Philosophy*, trans. V. E. Watts (Harmondsworth, 1969), 41).

7. Cassiodorus, *Variae* XII.5.4.

8. *Sermo* 24 ('In litanis'), in *Patrologiae Latinae Supplementum*, III, ed. A. Hamman (Paris, 1963), cols. 605–8, at col. 606: 'et tamen Romano ad te animo venit, qui barbarus putabatur' (translation, slightly adapted, from R. W. Mathisen, *Roman Aristocrats in Barbarian Gaul: Strategies for Survival in an Age of Transition* (Austin, Tex., 1993), 120).

9. Survival of Roman families in Gaul: K. F. Stroheker, *Der senatorische Adel im*

spätantiken Gallien (Darmstadt, 1970); Mathisen, *Roman Aristocrats*, 60–4. From Spain we have, unfortunately, no detailed evidence. Victorianus of Hadrumentum: Victor of Vita, *Vandal Persecution*, III.27; Courtois, *Les Vandales et L'Afrique*, 276–9 (for other examples). Ine's laws: F. Liebermann (ed.), *Die Gesetze der Angelsachsen*, i. (Halle, 1903), clause 24.2 (translation from D. Whitelock, *English Historical Documents*, i. *c.500–1042* (London, 1955), 367).

10. Victor of Vita, *Vandal Persecution*, I.2 (as translated by Moorhead); discussed by Goffart, *Barbarians and Romans*, 231–4.

11. C. Courtois et al., *Tablettes Albertini: Actes privés de l'époque vandale* (Paris, 1952).

12. Ostrogothic Italy: Cassiodorus, *Variae* IX.14.8: 'Gothorum laus est civilitas custodita' (for the meaning of 'civilitas': J. Moorhead, *Theoderic in Italy* (Oxford, 1992), 79–80).

13. Victor of Vita, *Vandal Persecution*, III.3 (decree of 484), II.8 (Catholic North Africans in the Vandal household).

14. Liebermann (as cited in n. 9), clause 33, 'the king's horse-Welshman (*cyninges horswealh*)'. See p. 71 for Romans in Frankish royal service in around AD 500.

15. Gallic aristocrats in barbarian service: Mathisen, *Roman Aristocrats*, 125–9. Cassiodones, *Variae* I.4.17 and IX.25.9, testify to Cassiodorus' wealth, but not to its origins. Paulinus of Pella, *Thanksgiving*, lines 293–303 (service to Attalus); lines 498–515 (sons at Visigothic court); lines 306–7 (those flourishing under Gothic rule).

16. Syagrius: Sidonius Apollinaris, *Letters*, V.5.3. Romans in Visigothic military service: Mathisen, *Roman Aristocrats*, 126–7. Cyprianus: P. Amory, *People and Identity in Ostrogothic Italy 489–554* (Cambridge, 1997), 154–5, 369–71 (390–1, for the similar career of Liberius).

17. *Salic Law*, 41.1. 5, 8, and 9. A Roman in the king's retinue was worth 300 *solidi*, a Frank 600.

18. In my discussion of Italy I am disagreeing with Amory, *People and Identity*— an intelligent and useful book, but, in my opinion, a wrong-headed one. Amory sees the ethnic labels of early sixth-century Gothic Italy as artificial— used to distinguish soldiers (termed 'Goths') from civilians (termed 'Romans'). He is right to stress that the Goth/Roman distinction was not black and white, that some people had moved towards delicate shades of grey, and that people had other preoccupations and loyalties, which sometimes overrode ethnic identity. But this does not prove that Roman and Gothic identities had disappeared. Modern experience shows that all ethnic groups have fuzzy edges and potentially divided loyalties.

19. 537–8 story: Procopius, *Wars*, VI.1.11–19 (*tē patriō glōssē*)—this Goth was also able to communicate with an enemy soldier (presumably in Latin). Bessas: Procopius, *Wars*, V.10.10 (*tē Gotthōn phōnē*), with V.16.2. Amory, *People and Identity*, discusses language at pp. 102–8 (arguing, very implausibly, that

the 'Gothic' learned by Cyprianus and spoken by these soldiers was just the universal argot of the late Roman army).

20. Senigallia medallion: W. Wroth, *Catalogue of the Coins of the Vandals, Ostrogoths and Lombards . . . in the British Museum* (London, 1911), 54. Amory, *People and Identity*, 338–46 is wrong to assume that a moustache alone (as worn by Theoderic and Theodahad) is the same as a beard-with-moustache (which some Romans did wear). Theodahad's coins: Wroth, *Catalogue*, 75–6. Theodahad's learned nature: Procopius, *Wars*, V.3.1.

21. Letter to Clovis: Cassiodorus, *Variae* II.40 (the quotation, as translated by Barnish, is from II.40.17). Letter to Gallic subjects: Cassiodorus, *Variae* III.17 (trans. by Barnish).

22. Lampridius: *Prosopography of the Later Roman Empire*, II, 'Lampridius'; Sidonius Apollinaris, *Letters*, VIII 9.1. Bridge at Mérida: J. Vives, *Inscriptiones cristianas de la Espāna romana y visigoda* (2nd edn., Barcelona, 1969), 126–7, no. 363. Epiphanius: Ennodius, *Vita Epifani*, in Ennodius, *Works*, 84–109, at 95 (paras. 89–90): 'gentile nescio quod murmur infringens'.

23. Limited Visigothic persecution: Heather, *Goths*, 212–15; Wolfram, *History of the Goths*, 197–202. Romans in Visigothic service: Mathisen, *Roman Aristocrats*, 126–8; *Prosopography of the Later Roman Empire*, II, 'Leo 4'. Freda: Ruricius, *Letters*, I.11; *Prosopography of the Later Roman Empire*, II, 'Freda'. Romans at the battle of Vouillé in 507: Gregory of Tours, *Histories*, II.37; *Prosopography of the Later Roman Empire*, II, 'Apollinaris 3'.

24. Events in 506–7: Wolfram, *History of the Goths*, 193–202; W. E. Klingshirn, *Caesarius of Arles: The Making of a Christian Community in Late Antique Gaul* (Cambridge, 1994), 94–7. Preface and Subscription to the *Breviarium*, describing its making and diffusion: *Theodosian Code*, Vol. I/1, pp. xxxii–xxxv of the Mommsen and Meyer edition (they are not translated by Pharr). Council of Agde: *Concilia Galliae A.314–A.506*, ed. C. Munier (Corpus Christianorum, Series Latina, 148, Turnholt, 1963), 192–213 (quotation is from p. 192). Projected council of 507: *Sancti Caesarii Episcopi Arelatensis, Opera Omnia*, ed. G. Morin, ii (Maredsous, 1942), Ep.3 (translation in Caesarius of Arles, *Life, Testament, Letters*, trans. W. E. Klingshirn (Translated Texts for Historians, 19, Liverpool, 1994), Letter 3).

25. Procopius, *Wars*, VIII.xxxiv.1–8.

26. Examples of changes of identity that have occurred: B. Ward-Perkins, 'Why did the Anglo-Saxons not Become More British?', *English Historical Review*, 115 (2000), 513–33, at 525–7.

27. Droctulft: Paul the Deacon, *History of the Lombards*, III.19. For an introduction to the debate over Germanic identities and 'ethnogenesis': Pohl, 'Conceptions of Ethnicity', 15–24; and the early and influential article by Patrick Geary, 'Ethnic Identity as a Situational Construct', *Mitteilungen der Anthropologischen Gesellschaft in Wien*, 113 (1983), 15–26. It is unsurprising that the two Europeans most centrally involved in this debate, Wolfram and Pohl,

are both from Austria, a nation that had to rethink its position within the Germanic world three times in the twentieth century (in 1918, 1938, and 1945).

28. *Salic Law*, 41.1. The phrase 'If any kills a free Frank *or barbarian who lives by the Salic law . . .*' (my emphasis) shows that individuals from other tribes were already choosing to live by Salic law in around AD 500 (and were therefore halfway to becoming 'Franks'). Romans apparently did not yet have the choice (or were not making it), unless this is reading too much into a single phrase. Gregory of Tours: E. James, 'Gregory of Tours and the Franks', in A. C. Murray (ed.), *After Rome's Fall: Narrators and Sources of Early Medieval History: Essays Presented to Walter Goffart* (Toronto, 1998), 51–66. However, a contemporary of Gregory, Venantius Fortunatus, who had come to Gaul from Italy, remained very aware of a distinction between those of Roman and those of 'barbarian' blood.

29. Cyprianus and his sons: Cassiodorus, *Variae* V.40.5, VIII.21.6–7 (from which the quotation is taken), VIII.22.5; Amory, *People and Identity*, 444, 'Anonymi 20–20a+'. For a good general discussion of cultural mixing: Moorhead, *The Roman Empire Divided*, 21–4.

30. Jovinianus: Ennodius, *Works*, 157, *Poems* 2.57, 58, 59. Syagrius: Sidonius Apollinaris, *Letters*, V.5 (the quotation is from V.5.3).

31. Gregory of Tours, *Histories*, V.17. Gregory, certainly, was unimpressed.

32. Romanization of the Franks: P. J. Geary, *The Myth of Nations: The Medieval Origins of Europe* (Princeton, 2002), 135–41. Visigothic Spain: Heather, *Goths*, 287–97; D. Claude, 'Remarks about Relations between Visigoths and Hispano-Romans in the Seventh Century', in W. Pohl and H. Reimitz (eds.), *Strategies of Distinction: The Construction of Ethnic Communities, 300–800* (Leiden, Boston, and Cologne, 1998), 117–30.

33. Sidonius Apolliniaris, *Letters*, IV.17 (quotation from IV.17.1). For Arbogastes, who also received a verse letter from Auspicius bishop of Toul: *Prosopography of the Later Roman Empire*, II, 'Arbogastes'.

34. Remigius's letter: *Epistolae Austrasicae*, ed. W. Gundlach, in *Epistolae Merowingici et Karolini Aevi*, i, (Monumenta Germaniae Historica, Epistolae, III; Berlin, 1892), 113, no. 2.

Chapter V. The Disappearance of Comfort

1. I have rehearsed some of the arguments of the following two chapters in Ward-Perkins, 'Specialized Production and Exchange'.

2. The classic expositions of this view are M. I. Finley, *The Ancient Economy* (London, 1973), 17–34, and Jones, *Later Roman Empire*, 465, 824–58. Changing views of the ancient economy are fully discussed (with further bibliography) in P. Horden and N. Purcell, *The Corrupting Sea: A Study of Mediterranean History* (Oxford, 2000), 146–50, 566–7.

3. A good brief overview of much of the evidence is K. Greene, *The Archaeology of the Roman Economy* (London, 1986). Many aspects of the later Roman economy are covered by C. Panella, 'Merci e scambi nel Mediterraneo tardoantico', in A. Carandini, L. Cracco Ruggini, and A. Giardina (eds.), *Storia di Roma*, III. ii. *L'età tardoantica: I luoghi, le culture* (Turin, 1993); and by the papers in *Hommes et richesses dans l'Empire byzantin*, i. *IVe–VIIe siècle* (Paris, 1989), and *Economy and Exchange in the East Mediterranean during Late Antiquity*, ed. S. Kingsley and M. Decker (Oxford, 2001).

4. D. P. S. Peacock, *Pottery in the Roman World: An Ethnoarchaeological Approach* (London and New York, 1982), is an excellent and thoughtful introduction to Roman pottery. D. P. S. Peacock and D. F. Williams, *Amphorae, and the Roman Economy: An Introductory Guide* (London and New York, 1986), however, is disappointing, being little more than a typology. The groundbreaking work on late antique tablewares was J. W. Hayes, *Late Roman Pottery: A Catalogue of Roman Fine-Wares* (London, 1972).

5. For a fuller discussion of the evidence potsherds can provide, see 'From Potsherds to People', at pp. 184–7.

6. Hayes, *Late Roman Pottery*, 422.

7. If I remember rightly, all decorated and fine-ware sherds, and all fragments of rims, bases, and handles, were spared this cull.

8. For a recent attempt to circumvent these problems: *Economy and Exchange*, 55.

9. E. Rodriguez Almeida, *Il Monte Testaccio: Ambiente, storia, materiali* (Rome, 1984).

10. However, it must also be said that we are in a league all our own—the Romans normally reused their amphorae, while I have just learned on the radio that the Naples area has such a serious refuse-disposal problem that it sends up to twenty trainloads of garbage a week to Germany for disposal. The report did not say why it had to travel quite so far.

11. See the distribution maps in Hayes, *Late Roman Pottery*, and *Atlante delle forme ceramiche*, i. *Ceramica fine romana nel bacino mediterraneo, medio e tardo impero* (supplement to *Enciclopedia dell' Arte Antica*; Rome, 1981).

12. For the details, unfortunately not quantified: C. Delano Smith et al. 'Luni and the *Ager Lunensis*', *Papers of the British School at Rome*, 54 (1986) 117.

13. This evidence is usefully summarized (with the relevant bibliography) in A. Wilson, 'Machines, Power and the Ancient Economy', *Journal of Roman Studies*, 92 (2002), 1–32, at 25–7.

14. C. Malone and S. Stoddart (eds.), *Territory, Time and State: The Archaeological Development of the Gubbio Basin* (Cambridge, 1994), 184; J. Carter, 'Rural Architecture and Ceramic Industry at Metaponto, Italy, 350–50 B.C.', in A. McWhirr (ed.), *Roman Brick and Tile* (Oxford, 1979), 45–64, at 47.

15. Malone and Stoddart (eds.), (as cited in n. 14), 192–6.

16. My Mum lives under one, so I know.

17. Peacock, *Pottery in the Roman World*. I am simplifying somewhat Peacock's full categorization.

18. R. Marichal, *Les Graffites de la Graufesenque* (XLVIIe supplément à *Gallia*, Paris, 1988). For the excavated remains of one of these kilns: A. Vernhet, 'Un Four de la Graufesenque (Aveyron): La Cuisson des vases sigillées', *Gallia*, 39 (1981), 25–43. These graffiti are discussed further by me at pp. 159–60.

19. This refuse pit is not yet published—my information derives from a serious (but ephemeral) booklet, produced with some slides of the site and formerly on sale in Millau: L. Balsan and A. Vernhet, *Une Industrie gallo-romaine: La Céramique sigillée de la Graufesenque* (Rodez, n.d.), 16. For the deliberate breaking of seconds, see also G. B. Dannell, 'Law and Practice: Further Thoughts on the Organization of the Potteries at la Graufesenque', in M. Genin and A. Vernhet (eds.), *Céramiques de la Graufesenque et autres productions d'époque romaine: Nouvelles recherches* (Montagnac, 2002), 218.

20. Peacock, *Pottery in the Roman World*, 103–13.

21. Horden and Purcell, *The Corrupting Sea*, 372; using the pioneering work of synthesis of A. J. Parker, *Ancient Shipwrecks of the Mediterranean and the Roman Provinces* (BAR International Series; Oxford, 1992).

22. *Life of John the Almsgiver*, ch. 10, as translated by E. Dawes and N. H. Baynes, *Three Byzantine Saints* (Oxford, 1948).

23. See Peacock, *Pottery in the Roman World*, 167–9, for the impact (detectable in the archaeological record) of the different transport costs by water and by land, and of competition from a contemporary rival (the 'New Forest ware' potteries). On this general issue, see also Ward-Perkins, 'Specialized Production and Exchange', 377–9.

24. For the *fabricae*: O. Seeck (ed.), *Notitia Dignitatum* (Berlin, 1876), 145, 'Occidentis IX'; summarized by K. Randsborg, *The First Millennium A.D. in Europe and the Mediterranean: An Archaeological Essay* (Cambridge, 1991), 94–102. See Fig. 3.3 at p. 36, for some of their products.

25. For an excellent general discussion of the role of the state in late Roman trade: M. McCormick, 'Bateaux de vie, bateaux de mort: Maladie, commerce, transports annonaires et le passage économique du bas-empire au moyen âge', *Settimane di studio del Centro italiano di studi sull'alto medioevo*, 45 (1998) 35–122. For the bricks: R. Tomber, 'Evidence for Long-Distance Commerce: Imported Bricks and Tiles at Carthage', *Rei Cretariae Romanae Fautorum Acta*, 25/26 (1987), 161–74.

26. A. K. Bowman, *Life and Letters on the Roman Frontier: Vindolanda and its People* (London, 1994), 68–72, and, for the two letters cited, 131–2, 139–40.

27. I am heavily dependent in this section on the excellent recent synthesis by Chris Wickham, *Framing the Early Middle Ages* (Oxford, 2005), ch. xi. The following are particularly useful regional surveys. For Britain: M. Fulford, 'Pottery Production and Trade at the End of Roman Britain: The Case against Continuity', in P. J. Casey (ed.), *The End of Roman Britain,*

(BAR British Series, 71; Oxford, 1979), 120–32; and K. R. Dark, 'Pottery and Local Production at the End of Roman Britain', in Dark (ed.), *External Contacts and the Economy of Late Roman and Post-Roman Britain* (Woodbridge, 1996), 53–65. For Spain and northern Gaul: the papers by Gutiérrez Lloret and by Lebecq in *The Sixth Century: Production, Distribution and Demand*, ed. R. Hodges and W. Bowden (Leiden, Boston, and Cologne, 1998). For Italy: several of the papers in *Ceramica in Italia VI–VII secolo*, ed. L. Saguì, 2 vols. (Florence, 1998); and P. Arthur and H. Patterson, 'Ceramics and Early Medieval Central and Southern Italy: "A Potted History" ', in *La Storia dell'Alto Medioevo italiano (VI–X secolo) alla luce dell'archaeologia*, ed. R. Francovich and G. Noyé (Florence, 1994), 409–41.

28. For declining quantities in Italy: E. Fentress and P. Perkins, 'Counting African Red Slip Ware', in A. Mastino (ed.), *L'Africa romana: Atti del V convegno di studi, Sassari 11–13 dicembre 1987* (Sassari, 1988), 205–14.

29. This find is discussed by L. Saguì, in *Ceramica in Italia*, at 305–33; and by the same author in 'Indagini archeologiche a Roma: Nuovi dati sul VII secolo', in P. Delogu (ed.), *Roma medievale: Aggiornamenti* (Florence, 1998), 63–78.

30. For the capacity of a ship of the period: *Economy and Exchange*, 55.

31. T. W. Potter, *The Changing Landscape of South Etruria* (London, 1979), 143, fig. 41.

32. Bede, *Lives of the Abbots*, ch. 5, in Venerabilis Beda, *Opera Historica*, ed. C. Plummer (Oxford, 1896) (translation in J. F. Webb and D. H. Farmer, *The Age of Bede* (2nd edn., Harmondsworth, 1983), 185–208.

33. See the papers in *Edilizia residenziale tra V e VIII Secolo*, ed. G. P. Brogiolo (Mantova, 1994); and the discussion of towns in B. Ward-Perkins, 'Continuitists, Catastrophists and the Towns of Northern Italy', *Papers of the British School at Rome*, 65 (1997), 157–76.

34. There is, admittedly, a massive debate about the precise significance of the use of marble *spolia*, which I cannot go into here. For the (limited) new carving of the period, see the various volumes of the *Corpus della Scultura Altomedievale* (Spoleto 1961–).

35. *Edilizia residenziale*, 8, 30–2.

36. Bradley Hill coins: R. Leech, 'The Excavation of the Romano-British Farmstead and Cemetery on Bradley Hill, Somerton, Somerset', *Britannia*, 12 (1981), 205–10. Roman coins in general, and evidence for their use: C. Howgego, 'The Supply and Use of Money in the Roman World', *Journal of Roman Studies*, 82 (1992), 16–22; F. Millar, 'The World of the Golden Ass', *Journal of Roman Studies*, 71 (1981), 72–3; L. de Ligt, 'Demand, Supply, Distribution: The Roman Peasantry between Town and Countryside: Rural Monetization and Peasant Demand', *Münstersche Beiträge zur antiken Handelsgeschichte*, IX.1 (1990), 33–43; R. Reece, *Roman Coins from 140 Sites in Britain* (Dorchester, 1991).

37. Tintagel has produced one small hoard of late fourth-century coins—but this

may have been deposited in the fourth century, and hoards are anyway much less revealing of regular coin use than scattered finds. The coin evidence for post-Roman Britain is collected and discussed (though with a different conclusion) in K. R. Dark, *Britain and the End of the Roman Empire* (Stroud, 2000), 143–4 and K. R. Dark, *Civitas to Kingdom: British Political Continuity 300–800* (Leicester, 1994), 200–6.

38. For the coinages of the various Germanic kingdoms: P. Grierson and M. Blackburn, *Medieval European Coinage*, i. *The Early Middle Ages (5th–10th Centuries)* (Cambridge, 1986) 17–54, 74–80 (for the copper coinage of Italy: 31–3). For broad surveys of coin use in Italy: A. Rovelli, 'Some Considerations on the Coinage of Lombard and Carolingian Italy', in *The Long Eighth Century: Production, Distribution and Demand*, ed. I. L. Hansen and C. Wickham (Leiden, Boston, and Cologue, 2000), 194–223; E. A. Arslan, 'La circolazione monetaria (secoli V–VIII)', in *La Storia dell'Alto Medioevo italiano alla luce dell'archeologia*, 497–519. For the Visigothic copper coins: M. Crusafont i Sabater, *El sistema monetario visigodo: Cobre y oro* (Barcelona and Madrid, 1994); D. M. Metcalf, 'Visigothic Monetary History: The Facts, What Facts?', in A. Ferreiro (ed.), *The Visigoths: Studies in Culture and Society* (Leiden, 1999), 201–17, at 202–4. For the copper coins of Marseille: C. Brenot, 'Monnaies en cuivre du VIe siècle frappées à Marseille', in P. Bastien et al. (eds.), *Mélanges de numismatique, d'archéologie et d'histoire offerts à Jean Lafaurie* (Paris, 1980), 181–8.

39. For the seventh-century Byzantine coinage of Italy and Sicily: P. Grierson, *Byzantine Coins* (London, 1982), 129–44; C. Morrisson, 'La Sicile byzantine: Une lueur dans les siècles obscurs', *Numismatica e antichità classiche*, 27 (1998), 307–34. For the large number of seventh- and eighth-century coins found at Rome's Crypta Balbi: A. Rovelli, 'La circolazione monetaria a Roma nei secoli VII e VIII. Nuovi dati per la storia economica di Roma nell'alto medioevo', in P. Delogu (ed.), *Roma medievale. Aggiornamenti* (Florence, 1998), 79–91.

40. For coins in the sixth- and seventh-century Byzantine East: C. Morrisson, 'Byzance au VIIe siècle: Le Témoignage de la numismatique', in *Byzantium: Tribute to Andreas Stratos* (Athens, 1986), i. 149–63. For the Arab Levant: C. Foss, 'The Coinage of Syria in the Seventh Century: The Evidence of Excavations', *Israel Numismatic Journal*, 13 (1994–9), 119–32.

41. Grierson and Blackburn, *Medieval European Coinage*, i. 65.

42. There are good introductory pages on barter in C. Humphrey and S. Hugh-Jones, *Barter, Exchange and Value: An Anthropological Approach* (Cambridge, 1992), 1–20.

43. For periods of 'abatement' and 'intensification': Horden and Purcell, *The Corrupting Sea, passim* (for their discussion of the post-Roman period specifically: 153–72).

44. R. Bruce-Mitford, *The Sutton Hoo Ship-Burial*, 3 vols. (London, 1975–83) (for the pottery bottle, vol. 3.2. 597–610). For some of the remarkable

expertise behind the native jewellery: E. Coatsworth and M. Pinder, *The Art of the Anglo-Saxon Goldsmith* (Woodbridge, 2002) (e.g. at 132, 141–2, 147, 151–2); and N. D. Meeks and R. Holmes, 'The Sutton Hoo Garnet Jewellery: An Examination of Some Gold Backing Foils and a Study of their Possible Manufacturing Techniques', *Anglo-Saxon Studies in Archaeology and History*, 4 (1985), 143–57.

45. For an impression of the iron-age economy: B. Cunliffe, *Iron Age Communities in Britain* (2nd edn., London, 1978), 157–9, 299–300, 337–42.

46. R. Hodges, *The Anglo-Saxon Achievement* (London, 1989), 69–114.

Chapter VI. Why the Demise of Comfort?

1. I would certainly not want to go to the stake over the precise positioning at a particular moment of any of the regions. For example, my placing of Britain in around AD 300 is not a confident statement that it was exactly half as complex as contemporary North Africa (whatever that might mean!); and setting Africa over central and northern Italy at the same date is nothing more than a guess, which also ignores local differences within both regions.

2. For Britain, with differences of interpretation: Esmonde Cleary, *The Ending of Roman Britain*; Dark, *Civitas to Kingdom*; Faulkner, *The Decline and Fall of Roman Britain*; N. Faulkner 'The Debate about the End: A Review of Evidence and Methods', *Archaeological Journal*, 159 (2002), 59–76.

3. There are no general surveys of conditions in Italy and Africa. I present some of the evidence in Ward-Perkins, 'Specialized Production and Exchange', 354–8.

4. For the wealth and complexity of the late antique East: M. Whittow, *The Making of Orthodox Byzantium 600–1025*, (Basingstoke, 1996) 59–68 (with further references); C. Foss, 'The Near Eastern Countryside in Late Antiquity: A Review Article', *The Roman and Byzantine Near East: Some Recent Archaeological Research* (*Journal of Roman Archaeology*, Supplementary Series, 14; Ann Arbor, 1995), 213–34; and the papers in *Hommes et richesses*, and in *Economy and Exchange*.

5. It is possible, but disputed, that eastern prosperity dipped in the second half of the sixth century—contrast H. Kennedy, 'The Last Century of Byzantine Syria', *Byzantinische Forschungen*, 10 (1985), 141–83, with M. Whittow, 'Ruling the Late Roman and Early Byzantine City', *Past and Present*, 129 (1990), 3–29, and M. Whittow, 'Recent Research on the Late–Antique City in Asia Minor; The Second Half of the Sixth Century Revisited', in L. Lavan (ed.), Recent Research in Late Antique Urbanism (Portsmouth, RI: 2001), 137–53.

6. C. Foss, *Ephesus after Antiquity: A Late Antique, Byzantine and Turkish City* (Cambridge, 1979), 103–15; R. R. R. Smith, 'Late Antique Portraits in a Public Context: Honorific Statuary at Aphrodisias in Caria, A.D. 300–600',

Journal of Roman Studies, 89 (1999), 155–89 (for the statues of Aphrodisias, abandoned *in situ*, until they fell from their pedestals).

7. Whittow, *The Making of Orthodox Byzantium*, 89–95; C. Morrisson, 'Byzance au VIIe siècle: Le Témoignage de la numismatique', in *Byzantium: Tribute to Andreas Stratos* (Athens, 1986), i. 149–63; J. W. Hayes, 'Pottery of the 6th and 7th Centuries', in N. Cambi and E. Marin (eds.), *L'Époque de Justinien et les problèmes des VI et VIIe siècles* (Vatican City, 1998), 541–50; Foss, *Ephesus after Antiquity*, 103–15. Pottery in Greece: J. Vroom, *After Antiquity: Ceramics and Society in the Aegean from the 7th to the 20th Century A.C.* (Leiden, 2003), 49–58.

8. General on Constantinople: C. Mango, *Le Développement urbain de Constantinople (IVe–VIIe siècles)* (Paris, 1985), 51–62. For coins and pottery in the seventh-century city: M. F. Hendy, 'The Coins', in R. M. Harrison, *Excavations at Saraçhane in Istanbul 1* (Princeton, 1986), 278–373; J. W. Hayes, *Excavations at Saraçhane in Istanbul, 2 The Pottery* (Princeton, 1992); J. W. Hayes, 'A Seventh-Century Pottery Group', *Dumbarton Oaks Papers*, 21 (1968), 203–16.

9. For a general account of the Arab Levant (with full further references): A. Walmsley, 'Production, Exchange and Regional Trade in the Islamic East Mediterranean: Old Structures, New Systems?', in *The Long Eighth Century*, 265–343. For the finds at Déhès, and at Baysān: J.-P. Sodini et al., 'Déhès (Syrie du Nord): Campagnes I–III (1976–1978). Recherches sur l'habitat rural', *Syria*, 57 (1980), 1–304; E. Khamis, 'Two Wall Mosaic Inscriptions from the Umayyad Market Place in Bet Shean/Baysān', *Bulletin of the School of Oriental and African Studies*, 64 (2001), 159–76. It is beyond the scope of this book, and of my knowledge, to consider the important question of when Levantine sophistication disappeared.

10. For the argument that radical change began in the fourth century: N. Faulkner, *The Decline and Fall of Roman Britain* (Stroud, 2000), 121–80.

11. Dramatic economic decline and military failure were first clearly linked by Clive Foss, 'The Persians in Asia Minor and the End of Antiquity', *English Historical Review*, 90 (1975), 721–47. He may have been mistaken in attributing change to a single period of destruction (that by the Persians between 615 and 626), but his general conclusions about the seventh century have not been seriously challenged.

12. P. Lemerle, *Les Plus Anciens Recueils des miracles de Saint Démétrius*, 2 vols. (Paris, 1979–81).

13. The prolonged Gothic War (535–54) and Lombard wars (from 568) are often (and perhaps rightly) seen as very damaging to Italy—the archaeological evidence does not contradict a link; but it is not yet precisely datable enough to prove it. For the Berbers in Africa: Y. Modéran, *Les Maures et et l'Afrique romaine (IVe–VIIe siècle)* (Rome, 2003).

14. Procopius, *Wars*, V.9.3–6.

15. Matthews, *Western Aristocracies*, 25–30.
16. P. Laurence, *Gérontius: La Vie latine de Sainte Mélanie* (Jerusalem, 2002), XXI.4, XXII.1.
17. Panella, 'Merci e scambi'. For the seventh-century trade, see Ch. V n. 29.
18. For tax as a potentially positive force economically: K. Hopkins, 'Taxes and Trade in the Roman Empire (200 B.C.–A.D. 400)', *Journal of Roman Studies*, 70 (1980), 101–25.
19. The negative evidence is admittedly problematic, because the entire habit of erecting secular inscriptions ended during the fifth and sixth centuries.
20. Evagrius, IV.29 (M. Whitby (trans.), *The Ecclesiastical History of Evagrius Scholasticus* (Translated Texts for Historians, 33; Liverpool, 2000), 231).
21. See the papers by Farquharson and Koder, in P. Allen and E. Jeffreys (eds.), *The Sixth Century: End or Beginning?* (Brisbane, 1996).
22. For a useful and full discussion of this issue: Horden and Purcell, *The Corrupting Sea*, 298–328, 338–41.
23. Eugippius, *Life of Severinus*, ch. 22 (local market), and ch. 28 (distribution of oil): 'quam speciem in illis locis difficillima negotiatorum tantum deferebat evectio.'
24. Ibid., ch. 20.
25. A connection between complexity and collapse is a well-known argument in discussion of the disappearance of early 'civilizations': the classic article is C. Renfrew, 'Systems Collapse as Social Transformation: Catastrophe and Anastrophe in Early State Societies', in C. Renfrew and K. L. Cooke (eds.), *Transformations: Mathematical Approaches to Culture Change* (New York, San Francisco, and London, 1979), 481–506. Renfrew depicts collapse as an inevitable result of complexity—the Roman case, as set out above, however, suggests a particular crisis was also needed before a complex system would disintegrate. K. R. Dark, 'Proto-Industrialisation and the End of the Roman Economy', in Dark (ed.), *External Contacts*, 1–21, argues (in the case of Roman Britain) along very similar lines to me.

Chapter VII. The Death of a Civilization?

1. Some surveys in the area of the lower Rhône have discovered more sites of the fifth and sixth centuries than of the third and fourth, but these are very unusual results: F. Trémont, 'Habitat et peuplement en Provence à la fin de l'Antiquité', in P. Ouzoulias et al. (eds.), *Les Campagnes de la Gaule à la fin de l'Antiquité* (Antibes, 2001), 275–301.
2. R. Leech, 'The Excavation of the Romano-British Farmstead and Cemetery on Bradley Hill, Somerton, Somerset', *Britannia*, 12 (1981), 177–252; B. Hope-Taylor, *Yeavering, an Anglo-British Centre of Early Northumbria* (London, 1977).
3. See the overview article: Foss, 'The Near Eastern Countryside'.

4. C. Delano Smith et al., 'Luni and the *Ager Lunensis*', *Papers of the British School at Rome*, 54 (1986), 142–3.

5. M. Decker, *'Tilling the Hateful Earth': Agrarian Life and Economy in the Late Antique Levant* (Oxford, forthcoming).

6. There is an excellent recent summary, with a good bibliography, of the animal-bone evidence and its implications: G. Kron, 'Archaeozoological Evidence for the Productivity of Roman Livestock Farming', *Münstersche Beiträge zur antiken Handelsgeschichte*, 21.2 (2002), 53–73. I must emphasize that the sizes given in Fig. 7.3 are *very* approximate. I achieved them by averaging the average sizes on different sites presented by Kron, which is not a statistically accurate procedure.

7. Faulkner, *The Decline and Fall of Roman Britain*, 11–12, 54, 70, 180 (the 'Golden Age' sentence closes his book). Chris Wickham, from a similar (but now far less extreme) Marxist background, sometimes makes similar points: e.g. in Wickham, *Framing the Early Middle Ages*, ch. xi, where Roman economic sophistication is described as more a sign of 'exploitation' and 'resultant hierarchies of wealth' than of 'development'. Marxists are by nature suspicious of commerce, and of empires.

8. Diodorus of Sicily V.38 (trans. C. H. Oldfather, in the Loeb Classical Library edition, slightly adapted).

9. Dung-foundlings: M. Manca Masciadri and O. Montevecchi, *I Contratti di baliatico* (Milan, 1984), 11–12.

10. F. R. Trombley and J. W. Watt (trans. from the Syriac), *The Chronicle of Pseudo-Joshua the Stylite* (Liverpool, 2000), 37–46.

11. L. Duchesne (ed.), *Le Liber Pontificalis*, i (Paris, 1886), 385 (R. Davis (trans.), *The Book of the Pontiffs* (Liber Pontificalis) (Liverpool, 1989), 88); S. Waetzoldt, *Die Kopien des 17. Jahrhunderts nach Mosaiken und Wandmalereien in Rom* (Vienna and Munich, 1964), figs. 477–83, 489.

12. A good impression of these seventh-century churches can be formed from X. Barral I Altet, *The Early Middle Ages: From Late Antiquity to A.D. 1000*, (Cologne, 2002), 98–117.

13. C. Wickham, 'L'Italia e l'alto Medioevo', *Archeologia Medievale*, 15 (1988), 105–24, at 110. For similar sentiments: M. Carver, *Arguments in Stone: Archaeological Research and the European Town in the first Millennium* (Oxford, 1993), 50; T. Lewit, 'Vanishing Villas: What Happened to Elite Rural Habitation in the West in the 5th and 6th Centuries A.D.?', *Journal of Roman Archaeology*, 16 (2003), 260–74.

14. For two particularly splendid examples: M. M. Mango, *The Sevso Treasure. Part 1* (Ann Arbor, 1994); K. J. Shelton, *The Esquiline Treasure* (London, 1981).

15. *Corpus Inscriptionum Latinarum*, IV, no. 2184 (and Tab. XXXVI.22): 'Hic Phoebus unguentarius optime futuet'.

16. For general discussions of Roman literacy: W. V. Harris, *Ancient Literacy* (Cambridge, Mass., 1989); J. H. Humphrey (ed.), *Literacy in the Roman World* (*Journal of Roman Archaeology*, supplementary series, no. 3; Ann Arbor, 1991) (in which the article by Keith Hopkins is particularly useful); G. Woolf, 'Literacy', in A. K. Bowman, P. Garnsey, and D. Rathbone (eds.), *The Cambridge Ancient History. Second Edition*, xi. *The High Empire, A.D. 70–192* (Cambridge, 2000), 875–97.

17. *Corpus Inscriptionum Latinarum* IV, nos. 575 (*universi dormientes*), 576 (*furunculi*), 581 (*seri bibi*). See also A. E. Cooley and M. G. L. Cooley, *Pompeii: A Sourcebook* (London and New York, 2004), 115.

18. *Corpus Inscriptionum Latinarum* IV, no. 1245.

19. Discussed by J. L. Franklin, 'Literacy and the Parietal Inscriptions of Pompeii', in Humphrey (ed.), *Literacy in the Roman World*, 82–3. See also Cooley and Cooley (as cited in n. 17), 79.

20. S. S. Frere, R. S. O. Tomlin et al. (eds.), *The Roman Inscriptions of Britain*, vol. II (in 9 fascicles) (Gloucester, 1990–5).

21. W. S. Hanson and R. Conolly, 'Language and Literacy in Roman Britain: Some Archaeological Considerations', in A. E. Cooley (ed.), *Becoming Roman, Writing Latin? Literacy and Epigraphy in the Roman West* (Portsmouth, RI, 2002), 151–64 (see also the paper by Tomlin in the same volume).

22. *The Roman Inscriptions of Britain*, II.5, p. 138 (no. 2491.147), p. 142 (no. 2491.159), p. 140 (no. 2491.153).

23. A. K. Bowman, *Life and Letters on the Roman Frontier: Vindolanda and its People* (London, 1994), 82–99, esp. p. 88.

24. *Corpus Inscriptionum Latinarum* I, n. 684; C. Zangemeister, *Glandes plumbeae Latine inscriptae* (*Ephemeris Epigraphica, Corporis Inscriptionum Latinarum Supplementum*, vol. VI; Rome and Berlin, 1885), 59–60 n. 65.

25. B. P. Grenfell and A. S. Hunt, *New Classical Fragments and Other Greek and Latin Papyri* (Oxford, 1897); the papyrus illustrated in Fig. 7.8 is published on p. 82, as no. 50f2.

26. R. Marichal, *Les Graffites de la Graufesenque* (XLVIIe supplément à *Gallia*; Paris, 1988).

27. A. Grenier, *Manuel d'archéologie gallo-romaine*, pt 2 (J. Déchelette (ed.), *Manuel d'archéologie préhistorique et gallo-romaine*, Vol. VI.2; Paris, 1934), 643–63.

28. The best collection is that from Monte Testaccio: *Corpus Inscriptionum Latinarum* XV.2.1, nos. 3636–4528; J. M. Blázquez Martinez, *Excavaciones arqueológicas en el Monte Testaccio (Roma): Memoria campaña 1989* (Madrid, 1992), 39–178. These particular amphorae were for the state-run distribution of oil in Rome; but other similar painted inscriptions have been recovered from all over the empire.

29. R. Egger, *Die Stadt auf dem Magdalensberg, ein Grosshandelsplatz, die ältesten*

Aufzeichnungen des Metallwarenhandels auf den Boden Österreichs (Vienna, 1961).

30. Justin: Procopius, *Secret History*, 6.11–16 (Procopius, *Works*, vol. VI, 70–3). Maximinus: *Scriptores Historiae Augustae*, trans. D. Magie (Loeb Classical Library; London and Cambridge, Mass., 1924), ii. 316–17, 331–3 ('Maximini Duo', II.5 and IX.3–5). See B. Baldwin, 'Illiterate Rulers', *Historia: Zeitschrift für alte Geschichte*, 38 (1989), 124–6.

31. C. Carletti, 'Iscrizioni murali', in C. Carletti and G. Otranto (eds.), *Il santuario di S. Michele sul Gargano dal VI al IX secolo: Atti del convegno tenuto a Monte Sant'Angelo il 9–10 dicembre 1978* (Bari, 1980), 7–180 (Turo is p. 86, no. 79.)

32. Code of Rothari, 224 and 243, in G. H. Pertz (ed.), *Legum*, iv, (Monumenta Germaniae Historica; Hanover, 1868), 55, 60; *The Lombard Laws*, trans. K. Fischer Drew (Philadelphia, 1973), 93, 100. N. Everett, *Literacy in Lombard Italy c. 568–774* (Cambridge, 2003), is an excellent survey of the uses of writing in one post-Roman society.

33. I. Velásquez Soriano, *Documentos de época visigoda escritos en pízarra (siglos VI–VIII)*, 2 vols. (Turnhout, 2000) (the 'Notitia de casios' is vol. i, no. 11).

34. For instance, the tiles of two proud builders, the Lombard king Agilulf (591–616) and the Roman pope John VII (705–7): G. P. Bognetti, *Santa Maria di Castelseprio* (Milan, 1948), tav. VIIa; A. Augenti, *Il Palatino nel medioevo: Archeologia e topografia (secoli VI–XIII)*, (Rome, 1996), 56, fig. 29.

35. Other groups of similar graffiti exist, but Rome's catacombs and the Gargano have produced much the largest and finest collections (327 and 159 graffiti respectively, for the most part shorter than Turo's—often just a name). For the catacombs: C. Carletti, '*Viatores ad martyres*: Testimonianze scritte altomedievali nelle catacombe romane', in G. Cavallo and C. Mango (eds.), *Epigrafia medievale greca e latina: Ideologia e funzione* (Spoleto, 1995), 197–226. For the Gargano, see n. 31.

36. A post-Roman tile found near Crema, in northern Italy, with a Germanic name and part of the alphabet written with a finger into the clay while wet, is, to the best of my knowledge, quite exceptional: A. Caretta, 'Note sulle epigrafi longobarde di Laus Pompeia e di Cremasco', *Archivio storico lombardo*, ser. 9, vol. 3 (1963), 193–5.

37. K. Düwel, 'Epigraphische Zeugnisse für die Macht der Schrift im östlichen Frankenreich', in *Die Franken, Wegbereiter Europas* (Mainz, 1996), i. 540–52; É. Louis, 'Aux débuts du monachisme en Gaule du Nord: Les Fouilles de l'abbaye mérovingienne et carolingienne de Hamage (Nord)', in M. Rouche (ed.), *Clovis, histoire et mémoire*, ii (Paris, 1997), 843–68.

38. B. Galsterer, *Die Graffiti auf der römischen Gefäßkeramik aus Haltern* (Münster, 1983).

39. A. Petrucci, *Writers and Readers in Medieval Italy: Studies in the History of*

Written Culture, trans. C. M. Radding, (New Haven and London, 1995), 67–72: of 988 subscribers, 326 wrote their own name.

40. P. Riché, *Éducation et culture dans l'occident barbare VIe–VIIe siècles* (Paris, 1962), 268–9, 304–5.

41. Einhard, *Vita Karoli* 25 (Éginhard, *Vie de Charlemagne*, ed. L. Halphen (Paris, 1947), 76).

Chapter VIII. All for the Best in the Best of All Possible Worlds?

1. For much of what follows, see also a number of interesting articles that have discussed the new Late Antiquity: Cameron 'The Perception of Crisis'; G. Fowden, 'Elefantiasi del tardoantico', *Journal of Roman Archaeology*, 15 (2002), 681–6 (which is in English, despite its title); A. Giardina, 'Esplosione di tardoantico', *Studi Storici*, 40.1 (1999), 157–80; J. H. W. G. Liebeschuetz, 'Late Antiquity and the Concept of Decline', *Nottingham Medieval Studies*, 45 (2001), 1–11.

2. A. Carandini, 'L'ultima civiltà sepolta o del massimo desueto, secondo un archeologo', in A. Carandini, L. Cracco Ruggini, and A. Giardina (eds.), *Storia di Roma*, III.2. *L'età tardoantica. I luoghi e le culture* (Rome, 1994), 11–38. Giardina, 'Esplosione di tardoantico'; A. Schiavone, *La storia spezzata: Roma antica e Occidente moderno* (Rome and Bari, 1996). English edition, *The End of the Past: Ancient Rome and the Modern West*, trans. M. J. Schneider, (Cambridge, Mass., 2000). P. Delogu, 'Transformation of the Roman World: Reflections on Current Research', in E. Chrysos and I. Wood (eds.), *East and West: Modes of Communication* (Leiden, Boston, and Cologne, 1999), 243–57.

3. Valerio Massimo Manfredi, *The Last Legion: A Novel*, English edn. (London, 2003).

4. In practice, the new Late Antiquity acknowledges this by abandoning most aspects of western history after about 500, and of the Byzantine world after the early seventh century.

5. Exemplified by Jones' magisterial *The Later Roman Empire*.

6. For a strong statement of the new, above all American, position: Fowden, 'Elefantiasi del tardoantico'.

7. C. Dawson, *The Making of Europe: An Introduction to the History of European Unity* (London, 1932), pp. xvii–xviii.

8. E. Power, *Medieval People* (10th edn., London and New York, 1963), 1–17 (this particular essay was included in *Medieval People* only after her death, by her husband Michael Postan). Power is somewhat reticent about the Anglo-Saxons.

9. A. Piganiol, *L'Empire chrétien (325–395)* (Paris, 1947), 422: 'La civilisation romaine n'est pas morte de sa belle morte. Elle a été assassinée.' Ungendered English, unfortunately, cannot quite capture the full horror of a feminine 'Civilisation' murdered by barbarians.

10. Courcelle, *Histoire littéraire*. His book is divided into three parts, 'L'invasion', 'L'occupation', and 'La libération'—the latter referring rather implausibly (as he himself admitted) to Justinian's conquests.

11. Ibid. 197–205, 59–60 (for a case of Frankish fidelity to Rome), 197–205. See Demougeot, *La Formation de l'Europe*, Vol. 2.2, 873–6, for almost the same sentiments, thirty years later.

12. E. Demougeot, *La Formation de l'Europe et les invasions barbares*, 2 vols. in 3 parts (Paris, 1969–79).

13. Goffart, 'Rome, Constantinople', 21.

14. The project, of course, pre-dated the 2004 enlargement of the EU: it is not clear where the Slavs fit into this history. The Celts have already been honoured with an exhibition at Palazzo Grassi in Venice in 1991: 'The Celts. The First Europe'.

15. *Karl der Grosse: Werk und Wirkung* (Aachen, 1965), p. ix.

16. *Die Franken, Les Francs. Wegbereiter Europas, Précurseurs de L'Europe, 5. bis 8. Jahrhundert* (Mainz, 1996).

17. Bede, *Vita Sancti Cuthberti*, X, ed. and trans. B. Colgrave, *Two Lives of Saint Cuthbert* (Cambridge, 1940), 188–91.

18. Quentin Tarantino, *Pulp Fiction* (1994), 131, as cited in *Oxford English Dictionary*, 3rd. edn. *OED Online*, 'medieval' (draft of June 2001).

19. See, above all, C. J. Wickham, *Framing the Early Middle Ages*, (Oxford, forthcoming), ch.1.

20. e.g. Brown, *The Rise of Western Christendom*.

21. For other recent critiques of 'smooth historiography' and 'unruptured' History: Schiavone, *La storia spezzata*; P. Horden 'The Christian Hospital in Late Antiquity: Break or Bridge?', in F. Steger and K. P. Jankrift (eds.), *Gesundheit-Krankheit* (Cologne and Weimar, forthcoming).

BIBLIOGRAPHY

Contemporary Sources

Wherever possible, I have cited texts that include an English translation; or I have also cited a separate translation. The translations of passages used in this book are my own, unless specifically attributed to a particular translation.

Ammianus Marcellinus, *History* — Ammianus Marcellinus, *Rerum Gestarum Libri qui Supersunt*, parallel Latin and English text, trans. J. C. Rolfe, 3 vols. (Loeb Classical Library; Cambridge, Mass., and London, 1935–9).

Cassiodorus, *Variae* — *Magni Aurelii Cassiodori Variarum Libri XII*, ed. Å. J. Fridh (Corpus Christianorum, Series Latina, XCVI; Turnholt, 1973). There is a translation of a selection of the *Variae* in S. J. Barnish, *The Variae of Magnus Aurelius Cassiodorus Senator* (Translated Texts for Historians, 12; Liverpool, 1992). All the letters (but only in abbreviated translations) are available in English in T. Hodgkin, *The Letters of Cassiodorus, being a Condensed Translation of the Variae Epistolae of Magnus Aurelius Cassiodorus Senator* (London, 1886).

Chronicle of 452 — *Chronica Gallica a. CCCCLII*, in *Chronica Minora saec. IV. V. VI. VII*, ed. T. Mommsen (Monumenta Germaniae Historica, Auctores Antiquissimi, IX; Berlin, 1891–2), 646–62.

Ennodius, *Works* — *Magni Felicis Ennodi Opera*, ed. F. Vogel (Monumenta Germaniae Historica, Auctores Antiquissimi, VII; Berlin, 1885). For an English translation of the *Life* of Epiphanius: G. M. Cook, *The Life of Saint Epiphanius by Ennodius* (Washington, 1942).

Eugippius, *Life of Severinus* — Eugippius, *Das Leben des heiligen Severin*, ed. and German trans. R. Noll (Schriften und Quellen der alten Welt, 11; Berlin, 1963). English translation: Eugippius, *The Life of Saint Severin*, trans. L. Bieler with L. Krestan (The Fathers of the Church, 55; Washington, 1965).

Gildas, *The Ruin of Britain* — Gildas, *The Ruin of Britain* (*De Excidio Britanniae*), ed. and trans. M. Winterbottom (London, 1978).

Gregory of Tours, *Histories*

Gregori Episcopi Turonensis Historiarum Libri X, ed. B. Krusch (Monumenta Germaniae Historica, Scriptores Rerum Merovingicarum, I.1; Hanover, 1937–42). English translation: Gregory of Tours, *History of the Franks*, trans. L. Thorpe (Harmondsworth, 1974).

Hydatius, *Chronicle*

R. W. Burgess (ed. and trans.), *The* Chronicle *of Hydatius and the* Consularia Constantinopolitana: *Two Contemporary Accounts of the Final Years of the Roman Empire* (Oxford, 1993).

Jordanes, *Gothic History*

Iordanis Romana et Getica, ed. T. Mommsen (Monumenta Germaniae Historica, Auctores Antiquissimi, V.1; Berlin, 1882). English translation: *The Gothic History of Jordanes*, trans. C. C. Mierow (2nd edn., Princeton, 1915).

Olympiodorus, *History*

Olympiodorus' fragmentary history, parallel Greek and English text, ed. and trans. R. C. Blockley, *The Fragmentary Classicising Historians of the Later Roman Empire: Eunapius, Olympiodorus, Priscus and Malchus*, 2 vols. (Liverpool, 1981–3), ii. 151–210.

Orosius, *History against the Pagans*

Pauli Orosii Historiarum adversum Paganos, ed. C. Zangemeister (Corpus Scriptorum Ecclesiasticorum Latinorum, V; Vienna, 1882). English translation: Orosius, *The Seven Books of History against the Pagans*, trans. R. J. Deferrari (Washington, 1964).

Paul the Deacon, *History of the Lombards*

Pauli historia langobardorum, ed. L. Bethmann and G. Waitz (Monumenta Germaniae Historica, Scriptores rerum Langobardicarum et Italicarum saec. VI–IX; Hanover, 1878). English translation: Paul the Deacon, *History of the Lombards*, trans. W. D. Foulke (Philadelphia, 1907).

Paulinus of Pella, *Thanksgiving*

Paulin de Pella, *Poème d'action de grâces et prière*, Latin and French text, ed. C. Moussy (Sources Chrétiennes, 209; Paris, 1974). Parallel Latin and English text in Ausonius, *Works*, trans. H. G. Evelyn White (Loeb Classical Library; Cambridge, Mass., and London, 1921), ii. 304–51.

Possidius, *Life of Augustine*

Possidius, *Life of Augustine*, in A. A. R Bastiaensen (ed.), *Vita di Cipriano, Vita di Ambrogio, Vita di Agostino* (Verona, 1975). English translation: in *Early Christian Biographies*, trans. R. J. Deferrari et al. (Fathers of the Church, 15; Washington, 1952).

Priscus, *History*   Priscus' fragmentary history, in ed. and trans. R. C.
                              Blockley, *The Fragmentary Classicising Historians of the
                              Later Roman Empire: Eunapius, Olympiodorus, Priscus
                              and Malchus*, 2 vols. (Liverpool, 1981–3), ii. 222–377.

Procopius, *Secret History*   in Procopius, *Works*, parallel Greek and English text,
and *Wars*   trans. H. B. Dewing, 7 vols. (Loeb Classical Library;
                              Cambridge, Mass., and London, 1914–40).

Ruricius, *Letters*   *Ruricii Lemovicensis epistularum libri duo*, in *Foebadius,
                              Victricius, Leporius, Vincentius Lerinensis, Evagrius,
                              Ruricius*, ed. R. Demeulenaere (Corpus Christian-
                              orum, Series Latina, 64; Turnholt, 1985), 313–94.
                              English translation: *Ruricius of Limoges and Friends:
                              A Collection of Letters from Visigothic Gaul*, trans.
                              R. W. Mathisen (Translated Texts for Historians, 30;
                              Liverpool, 1999).

Rutilius Namatianus, *A*   Rutilius Namatianus, *De reditu suo*, parallel Latin
Voyage Home   and English text, in *Minor Latin Poets*, trans. A. M.
                              Duff (Cambridge, Mass., and London, 1934),
                              764–829.

Salic Law   *Lex Salica*, ed. K. A. Eckhardt (Monumenta Germa-
                              niae Historica, Leges Nationum Germanicarum, IV.2;
                              Hanover, 1969). English translation: *Laws of the Sal-
                              ian and Ripuarian Franks*, trans. T. J. Rivers (New
                              York, 1986). [I have used the older numbering of the
                              laws, used by Rivers.]

Salvian, *The Governance*   Salvien de Marseille, *Œuvres*, ii. *Du Gouvernement de
of God*   Dieu*, ed. and French trans. G. Lagarrigue (Sources
                              Chrétiennes, 220; Paris, 1975). English translation:
                              Salvian, *On the Government of God*, trans. E. M. San-
                              ford (New York, 1930).

Sidonius Apollinaris,   Sidonius Apollinaris, *Poems and Letters*, parallel Latin
Poems and *Letters*   and English text, trans. W. B. Anderson, 2 vols. (Loeb
                              Classical Library; Cambridge, Mass., and London,
                              1936–65).

Theodosian Code   *Theodosiani Libri XVI cum Constitutionibus
                              Sirmondianis, et Leges Novellae ad Theodosianum per-
                              tinenetes*, ed. T. Mommsen and P. M. Mayer, 2 vols.
                              in 3 parts (2nd printing; Dublin and Zurich, 1971).
                              English translation: *The Theodosian Code and Novels
                              and the Sirmondian Constitutions*, trans. C. Pharr
                              (Princeton, 1952).

Vegetius, *Epitome*	*P. Flavii Vegeti Renati Epitoma Rei Militaris*, ed. A. Önnerfors (Stuttgart and Leipzig, 1995). English translation: Vegetius, *Epitome of Military Sciences*, trans. N. P. Milner (Translated Texts for Historians, 16; Liverpool, 1993).
Victor of Vita, *Vandal Persecution*	*Victoris Vitensis Historia Persecutionis Africanae Provinciae sub Geiserico et Hunirico Regibus Wandalorum*, ed. C. Halm (Monumenta Germaniae Historica, Auctores Antiquissimi, III; Berlin 1879). English translation: Victor of Vita, *History of the Vandal Persecution*, trans. J. Moorhead (Translated Texts for Historians, 10; Liverpool, 1992).
Zosimus, *New History*	Zosime, *Histoire Nouvelle*, ed. and French trans. F. Paschoud, 3 vols. in 5 parts (Paris, 1971–89). English translation: Zosimus, *New History*, trans. R. T. Ridley (Sydney, 1982).

Modern Scholarship

Works listed here are either particularly useful, or have been cited by me on several occasions.

AMORY, P., *People and Identity in Ostrogothic Italy 489–554* (Cambridge, 1997).

Atlante delle forme ceramiche, i. *Ceramica fine romana nel bacino mediterraneo, medio e tardo impero* (supplement to *Enciclopedia dell'Arte Antica*; Rome, 1981).

BARNISH, S. J. B., 'Taxation, Land and Barbarian Settlement in the Western Empire', *Papers of the British School at Rome*, 54 (1986), 170–95.

BROWN, P. R. L., *The Rise of Western Christendom: Triumph and Diversity, AD 200–1000* (2nd edn., Oxford, 2003).

—— *The World of Late Antiquity: From Marcus Aurelius to Muhammad* (London, 1971).

BURY, J. B., *History of the Later Roman Empire* (2nd edn., London, 1923).

Cambridge Ancient History, xiii. *The Late Empire, A.D. 334–425*, ed. Averil Cameron and P. Garnsey (Cambridge, 1998).

Cambridge Ancient History, xiv. *Late Antiquity: Empire and Successors, A.D. 425–600*), ed. Averil Cameron, B. Ward-Perkins, and M. Whitby (Cambridge, 2000).

CAMERON, AVERIL, *The Mediterranean World in Late Antiquity AD 395–600* (London and New York, 1993).

——'The Perception of Crisis', in *Morfologie sociali e culturali in Europa fra Tarda*

Antichità e Alto Medioevo (Settimane di studio del Centro italiano di studi sull'Alto Medioevo, 45; Spoleto, 1998), 9–31.

CARANDINI, A., 'L'ultima civiltà sepolta o del massimo desueto, secondo un archeologo', in A. Carandini, L. Cracco Ruggini, and A. Giardina (eds.), *Storia di Roma*, III.2. *L'età tardoantica. I luoghi e le culture* (Rome, 1994), 11–38.

CARVER, M., *Arguments in Stone: Archaeological Research and the European Town in the First Millennium* (Oxford, 1993).

Ceramica in Italia VI–VII secolo, ed. L. Saguì, 2 vols. (Florence, 1998).

COURCELLE, P., *Histoire littéraire des grands invasions germaniques* (Paris, 1948).

COURTOIS, C., *Les Vandales et l'Afrique* (Paris, 1955).

DARK, K. R., *Civitas to Kingdom: British Political Continuity 300–800* (Leicester, 1994).

——(ed.), *External Contacts and the Economy of Late Roman and Post-Roman Britain* (Woodbridge, 1996).

DELOGU, P., 'Transformation of the Roman World: Reflections on Current Research', in E. Chrysos and I. Wood (eds.), *East and West: Modes of Communication*, (Leiden, Boston, and Cologne, 1999), 243–57.

DEMANDT, A., *Der Fall Roms: Die Auflösung des römischen Reiches im Urteil der Nachwelt* (Munich, 1984).

——*Die Spätantike: Römische Geschichte von Diocletian bis Justinian 284–565 n. Chr.* (Munich, 1989).

DEMOUGEOT, E., *La Formation de l'Europe et les invasions barbares*, 2 vols. in 3 parts (Paris, 1969–79).

Economy and Exchange in the East Mediterranean during Late Antiquity, ed. S. Kingsley and M. Decker (Oxford, 2001).

Edilizia residenziale tra V e VIII secolo, ed. G. P. Brogiolo (Mantova, 1994).

ESMONDE CLEARY, A. S., *The Ending of Roman Britain* (London, 1989).

EVERETT, N., *Literacy in Lombard Italy c.568–774* (Cambridge, 2003).

FAULKNER, N., *The Decline and Fall of Roman Britain* (Stroud, 2000).

FOSS, C., 'The Near Eastern Countryside in Late Antiquity: A Review Article', *The Roman and Byzantine Near East: Some Recent Archaeological Research* (*Journal of Roman Archaeology*, supplementary series, 14; Ann Arbor, 1995), 213–34.

FOWDEN, G., 'Elefantiasi del tardoantico', *Journal of Roman Archaeology*, 15 (2002), 681–6.

GEARY, P. J., *The Myth of Nations: The Medieval Origins of Europe* (Princeton, 2002).

GIARDINA, A., 'Esplosione di tardoantico', *Studi Storici*, 40.1 (1999), 157–80.

GOFFART, W., *Barbarians and Romans AD 418–584: The Techniques of Accommodation* (Princeton, 1980).

——'Rome, Constantinople, and the Barbarians', *American Historical Review*, 86 (1981), 275–306; also in Goffart, *Rome's Fall and After*, 1–32 (the pagination I have cited).

——*Rome's Fall and After* (London and Ronceverte, 1989). [Collected articles.]

——'The Theme of "*the* Barbarian Invasions" ', in E. Chrysos and A. Schwarcz (eds.), *Das Reich und die Barbaren* (Veröffentlichungen des Istituts für österreichische Geschichtsforschung, 29; Vienna, 1989), 87–107; also in Goffart, *Rome's Fall and After*, 111–32 (the pagination I have cited).

GREENE, K., *The Archaeology of the Roman Economy* (London, 1986).

GRIERSON, P., *Byzantine Coins* (London, 1982).

——and BLACKBURN, M., *Medieval European Coinage*, i. *The Early Middle Ages (5th–10th Centuries)* (Cambridge, 1986).

HARRIS, W. V., *Ancient Literacy* (Cambridge, Mass., 1989).

HAYES, J. W., *Late Roman Pottery: A Catalogue of Roman Fine-Wares* (London, 1972). [Hayes also published a brief *Supplement to Late Roman Pottery* in 1980, with some additional information, most notably the identification of 'Late Roman C Ware' as from Phocaea.]

——*Excavations at Saraçhane in Istanbul, 2 The Pottery* (Princeton, 1992).

HEATHER, P., 'The Huns and the End of the Roman Empire in Western Europe', *English Historical Review*, 110 (1995), 4–41.

——*The Goths* (Oxford, 1996).

Hommes et richesses dans l'Empire byzantin, i. *IVe–VIIe siècle* (Paris, 1989).

HORDEN, P., and PURCELL, N., *The Corrupting Sea: A Study of Mediterranean History* (Oxford, 2000).

HUMPHREY, J. H. (ed.), *Literacy in the Ancient World* (*Journal of Roman Archaeology*, supplementary series, no. 3; Ann Arbor, 1991).

JONES, A. H. M., *The Later Roman Empire 284–602: A Social, Economic and Administrative Survey* (Oxford, 1964).

Late Antiquity: A Guide to the Post-Classical World, ed. G. W. Bowersock, Peter Brown, and Oleg Grabar (Cambridge, Mass., and London, 1999).

LIEBESCHUETZ, J. H. W. G., *Barbarians and Bishops* (Oxford, 1991).

——'Cities, Taxes and the Accommodation of the Barbarians: The Theories of Durliat and Goffart', in W. Pohl (ed.), *Kingdoms of the Empire: The Integration of Barbarians in Late Antiquity* (Leiden, New York, and Cologne, 1997), 135–51.

——'Late Antiquity and the Concept of Decline', *Nottingham Medieval Studies*, 45 (2001), 1–11.

The Long Eighth Century: Production, Distribution and Demand, ed. I. L. Hansen and C. Wickham (Leiden, Boston, and Cologne, 2000).

McCORMICK, M., 'Bateaux de vie, bateaux de mort: Maladie, commerce, transports annonaires et le passage économique du bas-empire au moyen âge', *Settimane di studio del Centro italiano di studi sull'alto medioevo*, 45 (1998), 35–122.

MATHISEN, R. W., *Roman Aristocrats in Barbarian Gaul: Strategies for Survival in an Age of Transition* (Austin, Tex., 1993).

——and SHANZER, D. (eds.), *Society and Culture in Late Antique Gaul: Revisiting the Sources* (Aldershot, 2001).

MATTHEWS, J., *Western Aristocracies and Imperial Court A.D. 364–425* (Oxford, 1975).

MOORHEAD, J., *The Roman Empire Divided 400–700* (Harlow, 2001).

MUSSET, L., *Les Invasions: Les Vagues germaniques* (Paris, 1965).

PANELLA, C., 'Merci e scambi nel Mediterraneo tardoantico', in A. Carandini, L. Cracco Ruggini, and A. Giardina (eds.), *Storia di Roma*, III.ii. *L'età tardoantica: I luoghi, le culture* (Turin, 1993).

PEACOCK, D. P. S., *Pottery in the Roman World: An Ethnoarchaeological Approach* (London and New York, 1982).

POHL, W., (ed.), *Kingdoms of the Empire: The Integration of Barbarians in Late Antiquity* (Leiden, New York, and Cologne, 1997).

——'Conceptions of Ethnicity in Early Medieval Studies', in L. K. Little and B. H. Rosenwein (eds.), *Debating the Middle Ages: Issues and Readings* (Oxford, 1998), 15–24.

——and REIMITZ, H. (eds.), *Strategies of Distinction: The Construction of Ethnic Communities, 300–800* (Leiden, Boston, and Cologne, 1998).

POTTER, T. W., *The Changing Landscape of South Etruria* (London, 1979).

Prosopography of the Later Roman Empire, A. H. M. Jones, J. R. Martindale, and J. Morris, 3 vols. in 4 parts (Cambridge, 1971–92).

RANDSBORG, K., *The First Millennium A.D. in Europe and the Mediterranean: An Archaeological Essay* (Cambridge, 1991).

RENFREW, C., 'Systems Collapse as Social Transformation: Catastrophe and Anastrophe in Early State Societies', in C. Renfrew and K. L. Cooke (eds.), *Transformations: Mathematical Approaches to Culture Change* (New York, San Francisco, and London, 1979), 481–506.

SCHIAVONE, A., *La storia spezzata: Roma antica e Occidente moderno* (Rome and Bari, 1996). English edition, *The End of the Past: Ancient Rome and the Modern West*, trans. M. J. Schneider (Cambridge, Mass., 2000).

The Sixth Century: Production, Distribution and Demand, ed. R. Hodges and W. Bowden (Leiden, Boston, and Cologne, 1998).

La Storia dell'Alto Medioevo italiano (VI–X secolo) alla luce dell'archeologia, ed. R. Francovich and G. Noyé (Florence, 1994).

SWAIN, S., and EDWARDS, M. (eds.), *Approaching Late Antiquity: The Transformation from Early to Late Empire* (Oxford, 2004).

WALMSLEY, A., 'Production, Exchange and Regional Trade in the Islamic East Mediterranean: Old Structures, New Systems?', in *The Long Eighth Century: Production, Distribution and Demand*, ed. I. L. Hansen and C. Wickham (Leiden, Boston, and Cologne, 2000), 265–343.

WARD-PERKINS, B., 'Specialized Production and Exchange', in *Cambridge Ancient History*, xiv. *Late Antiquity: Empire and Successors, A.D. 425–600*, ed. Averil Cameron, B. Ward-Perkins, and M. Whitby (Cambridge, 2000), 346–91.

——'Why did the Anglo-Saxons not Become More British?', *English Historical Review*, 115 (2000), 513–33.

WHITTOW, M., *The Making of Orthodox Byzantium 600–1025* (Basingstoke, 1996).

WICKHAM, C. J., *Framing the Early Middle Ages* (Oxford, forthcoming).

WILLIAMS, S., and FRIELL, G., *The Rome that Did Not Fall: The Survival of the East in the Fifth Century* (London and New York, 1999).

WILSON, A., 'Machines, Power and the Ancient Economy', *Journal of Roman Studies*, 92 (2002), 1–32.

WOLFRAM, H., *Das Reich und die Barbaren zwischen Antike und Mittelalter* (Berlin, 1990).

——*History of the Goths*, trans. T. J. Dunlop (Berkeley and Los Angeles, and London, *c.*1988). [A revised text, and authorized translation of a German-language first edition.]

——and SCHWARCZ, A., *Anerkennung und Integration: Zu den wirtschaftlichen Grundlagen der Völkerwanderungenzeit 400–600* (Vienna, 1988).

PICTURE LIST
INCLUDING CREDITS

Maps and Figures that have been prepared specifically for this book are the work of Paul Simmons

Front and Back Endpapers

Front endpaper The Roman World in about AD 400.

Back endpaper The New World Order, in about AD 500.

Chapter I

Fig. 1.1   London in ruins, as imagined by Gustave Doré in 1873. Mary Evans Picture Library

Fig. 1.2   The Germanic invasions, as shown in an historical atlas. From F.W. Putzger, *Historischer Weltatlas*, 1970 edition (© Velhagen & Klasing, Berlin and Bielefeld), 38.

Fig. 1.3   Attila trampling Italy and the Arts, as painted by Delacroix. Assemblée Nationale Palais-Bourbon, Paris, France; Giraudon/www.bridgeman.co.uk

Fig. 1.4   Two recent images of Germanic settlers: the king buried at Sutton Hoo, and a seventh-century Frankish couple. Fig. 1.4a from M. O. H. Carver, *Arguments in Stone* (Oxbow Monograph 29; Oxford, 1993), fig. 15; 1.4b from L.-C. Feffer and P. Périn, *Les Francs: À l'origine de la France* (Armand Colin, Paris, 1987), ii.177.

Fig. 1.5   Romans and barbarians fighting it out in a recent illustration. From Warrior 17, S. MacDowall and A. McBride, *Germanic Warrior 236–568 AD* illustrated by Angus McBride (© Osprey Publishing Ltd, 1996), plate D.

Chapter II

Fig. 2.1   Map showing the 419 settlement, and subsequent conquests, of the Visigoths.

Chapter IV

Fig. 4.1   Gold coin issued in the name of the emperor Anastasius by
the Ostrogothic king of Italy Theoderic.
© British Museum.

Fig. 4.2   Gold medallion of Theoderic.
Su concessione del Ministero per i Beni e le Attività Culturali—
Soprintendenza Archeologica di Roma.

Fig. 4.3   Copper coin of the Ostrogothic king Theodahad.
© British Museum.

Chapter V

Fig. 5.1   Roman pottery being excavated at Caesarea (Israel).

Fig. 5.2   Monte Testaccio in Rome, in an engraved view of the city of
1625.
Map by Giovanni Maggi, Biblioteca Nazionale di Roma.

Fig. 5.3   Map showing the diffusion of pottery manufactured in the
third and fourth centuries near modern Oxford.
Based on D. P. S. Peacock, *Pottery in the Roman World* (Longman,
London and New York, 1982), fig. 56. After C. J. Young, *The Roman
Pottery Industry of the Oxford Region* (British Archaeological
Reports 43; Oxford, 1977), fig. 45.

Fig. 5.4   Map showing the diffusion of the Roman fine-ware manu-
factured at la Graufesenque (southern France).
Based on C. Bémont and J.-P. Jacob, *La Terre sigillée gallo-romaine:
Lieux de production du Haut-Empire: implantations, produits, relations*
(Documents d'archéologie française 6; Paris, 1986), 102. © Éditions
de la Maison des sciences de l'homme, Paris.

Fig. 5.5   A refuse pit during excavation at the pottery-production site
of la Graufesenque.
From a set of slides illustrating the la Graufesenque potteries;
CDDP, Aveyron.

Fig. 5.6   A Roman shipwreck, loaded with amphorae, off Giens on
the south coast of France.
CNRS-CCJ, photo by G. Réveillac.

Fig. 5.7   Sixth- and seventh-century pottery from the Anglo-Saxon
site of Yeavering (Northumberland).
From B. Hope-Taylor, *Yeavering, an Anglo-British Centre of Early
Northumbria* (HMSO, London, 1977), fig. 81; © Crown Copyright.

Fig. 5.8   Alternative reconstructions of a seventh-century house excavated at Cowdery's Down (Hampshire).
From M. Millett and S. James, 'Excavations at Cowdery's Down', *The Archaeological Journal*, 140, 1983, 246, fig. 71.

Fig. 5.9   Numbers of newly minted copper coins from five different sites in the Mediterranean.
The information is from the following sources: A. Bertino, 'Monete', in A. Frova (ed.), *Scavi di Luni* (Rome, 1973), 837–82, and in A. Frova (ed.), *Scavi di Luni II* (Rome, 1977), 679–707; M. Thompson, *The Athenian Agora: Volume II, the Coins* (Princeton, 1954); C. Foss, *Ephesus after Antiquity: A Late Antique, Byzantine and Turkish City* (Cambridge, 1979), 197, and interim reports on subsequent coin-finds by H. Vetters, published in *Österreichische Akademie der Wissenschaften, philosophische-historische Klasse*, Vols. 116–23 (1979–86); M. F. Hendy, 'The Coins', in R. M. Harrison, *Excavations at Saraçhane in Istanbul*, I (Princeton, 1986), 278–373; G. C. Miles, 'Islamic Coins', in F. O. Waagé (ed.), *Antioch on the Orontes: Volume IV, Part 1, Ceramics and Islamic Coins* (Princeton, 1948), and D. B. Waagé, *Antioch on the Orontes: Volume IV, Part 2, Greek, Roman, Byzantine and Crusaders' Coins* (Princeton, 1952).

Fig. 5.10   Shoulder-clasp and bottle from the Sutton Hoo ship-burial of around AD 625.
British Museum, London; UK/www.bridgeman.co.uk (shoulder clasp); © British Museum (bottle).

Chapter VI

Fig. 6.1   Graphs to show changing levels of economic complexity, between AD 300 and 700, in five regions of the Roman world.

Fig. 6.2   Reconstruction drawing of houses of the fourth to sixth centuries, in the Syrian village of Déhès.
From J.-P. Sodini and others, 'Déhès (Syrie du Nord): Campagnes I–III (1976–1978)', *Syria*, LVII, 1980, fig. 243 (Librairie Orientaliste Paul Geuthner).

Fig. 6.3   Reconstruction drawing of the porticoed shops in Baysān (Israel), and drawing of the mosaic inscription recording their construction in 737/8.
Drawing of the shops (by M. Drewes) from Y. Tsafrir and G. Foerster, 'From Scythopolis to Baysān', in G. R. D. King and Averil Cameron (ed.), *The Byzantine and Early Islamic Near East II, Land*

Use and Settlement Patterns (Princeton, 1994), fig. 16. Drawing of the inscription from E. Khamis, 'Two Wall Inscriptions from the Umayyad Market Place in Bet Shean/Baysān', *Bulletin of the School of Oriental and African Studies*, 64.2, 2001, fig. 5.
By kind permission of Yoram Tsafrir, Gideon Foerster, and Elias Khamis.

Chapter VII

Fig. 7.1   Two maps showing rural settlements north of Rome, in around AD 100, and in the fifth to eighth centuries.
Based on T. W. Potter, *The Changing Landscape of South Etruria* (Paul Elek, London, 1979), figs. 35 and 41.

Fig. 7.2   The ancient village of Bamuqqa in Syria, and the cultivable land around it.
From G. Tchalenko, *Villages antiques de la Syrie du Nord* (Paris, 1953), ii, fig. xcii. (Librairie Orientaliste Paul Geuthner, Paris).

Fig. 7.3   Diagram showing the changing size of cattle from iron-age to early medieval times.

Fig. 7.4   The ground-plans, drawn to the same scale, of some fourth- to ninth-century churches in Italy.

Fig. 7.5   The Sevso (or Seuso) silver treasure, hidden probably in the fifth century AD
By courtesy of The Trustee of the Marquess of Northampton 1987 Settlement.

Fig. 7.6   Drawing of some of the brothel-graffiti from Pompeii.
From *Corpus Inscriptionum Latinarum*, vol. 4, fig. xxxvi.

Fig. 7.7   Drawing of a Roman tile from Calleva (Silchester, in Hampshire), with the word 'SATIS (enough)' written on it.
From R. G. Collingwood and R. P. Wright, *The Roman Inscriptions of Britain*, vol. II fascicule 5 (Sutton Publishing Ltd, Stroud, 1993), no. 2491.159.

Fig. 7.8   A papyrus tax receipt from Roman Egypt.
Bodleian Library, University of Oxford (Ms Gr. Class. G.27 (P)).

Fig. 7.9   Graffito from la Graufesenque recording a kiln-load of pottery, and a reconstruction drawing of one of the site's kilns during firing.
Reconstruction drawing from A. Vernhet, 'Un four de la Graufesenque (Aveyron)', *Gallia*, 39, 1981, fig. 10; (CNRS Editions).

Fig. 7.10 Fresco of a Pompeian couple, with stylus, wax tablets, and papyrus roll.
Museo Archeologico Nazionale, Naples, Italy; www.bridgeman.co.uk.

Fig. 7.11 Graffito of the pilgrim Turo at the shrine of S. Michele sul Gargano (southern Italy).
From C. Carletti and G. Otranto (eds.), *Il Santuario di S. Michele sul Gargano dal VI al IX secolo* (Edipuglia, Bari, 1980), 86, no. 79.

Chapter VIII

Fig. 8.1 The baptism of Clovis, as painted in 1877 by Joseph Paul Blanc (1846–1904) in the Panthéon of Paris.
Lauros / Giraudon/www.bridgeman.co.uk.

Appendix

Fig. A.1 Graph showing the origin of the different wines that reached Ostia, Rome's port-city.
Based on C. Panella and A. Tchernia, 'Produits agricoles transportés en amphores. L'huile et surtout le vin', in *L'Italie d'Auguste à Dioclétien* (Collection de l'École française de Rome 198; Rome, 1994), 156, graphique 3.

Fig. A.2 Map showing the diffusion of mixing-bowls made in Colchester in the second century AD
Based on D. P. S. Peacock, *Pottery in the Roman World* (Longman, London and New York, 1982), fig. 51. After K. F. Hartley, 'The Marketing and Distribution of Mortaria', in A. Detsicas (ed.), *Current Research in Romano-British Coarse Pottery* (Council for British Archaeology, London, 1973), 50, fig. 7.

INDEX

(Numbers in italics refer, by page-number, to illustrations, maps, and diagrams.)

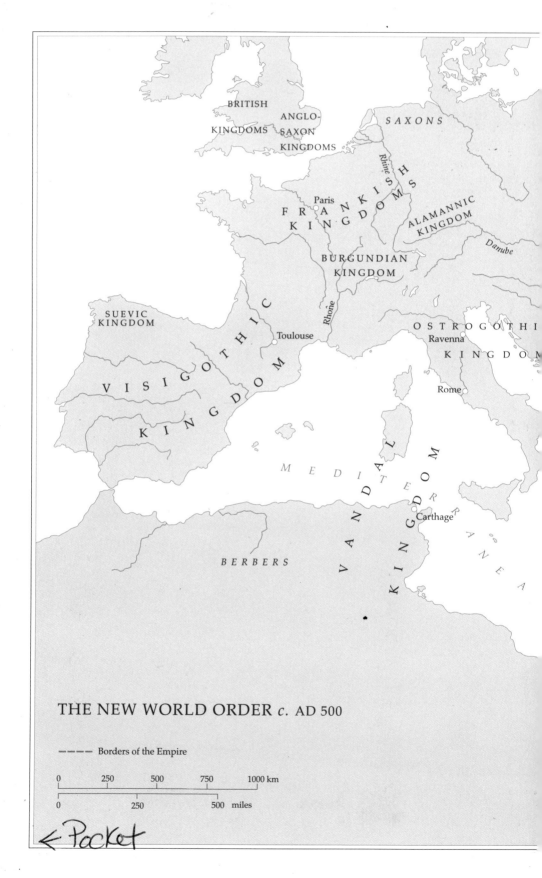

BRITISH
KINGDOMS

ANGLO-
SAXON
KINGDOMS

SAXONS

Rhine

FRANKISH

Paris

FRA
KINGDOMS

ALAMANNIC
KINGDOM

Danube

BURGUNDIAN
KINGDOM

Rhône

SUEVIC
KINGDOM

VISIGOTHIC

Toulouse

OSTROGOTHI
Ravenna

KINGDOM

KINGDOM

Rome

MEDITE

R
R
A
N
E
A

BERBERS

VANDAL
KINGDOM

Carthage

THE NEW WORLD ORDER *c.* AD 500

---- Borders of the Empire

0	250	500	750	1000 km

0	250	500 miles

← Pocket